THE DAY

❧ I ❧

BECAME
AN
AUTODIDACT

AND THE ADVICE,
ADVENTURES, AND ACRIMONIES
THAT BEFELL
ME THEREAFTER

THE DAY

I

BECAME
AN
AUTODIDACT

AND THE ADVICE,
ADVENTURES, AND ACRIMONIES
THAT BEFELL
ME THEREAFTER

Kendall Hailey

DELACORTE PRESS/ NEW YORK

Published by
Delacorte Press
a division of
The Bantam Doubleday Dell Publishing Group, Inc.
1 Dag Hammarskjold Plaza
New York, New York 10017

Library of Congress Cataloging in Publication Data

Hailey, Kendall, 1966-
    The day I became an autodidact and the advice,
adventures, and acrimonies that befell me thereafter.

    1. Hailey, Kendall, 1966-   . 2. High school
dropouts--United States--Biography.   3. Self-culture.
I. Title.
LC146.5.H345   1988   373.12'913'0924   87-30459
ISBN 0-385-29636-3

Manufactured in the United States of America

March 1988

10 9 8 7 6 5 4 3 2 1

BG

*for my family
who forgave me for
writing nonfiction*

Staring at the list today's mail brought, I made a solemn vow (my very first solemn vow, I believe—I'm only fifteen). I am going to become an autodidact. I am never going back to school.

Of course, as bad luck would have it, I have only just finished the tenth grade. But as soon as I can extricate myself from high school, it's over between me and formal education. And all because of that list.

As I opened the envelope from my school, I was already suspicious of what school would have to say to me during the summer. And what I saw made me shudder. A mandatory (my least favorite word) summer reading list.

I read (rarely skimming) everything school tells me to from the middle of September to the middle of June, but the summer is mine. And being told what to read during the summer suddenly made me realize that I don't really like being told what to read during the fall, winter, and spring either.

I cannot wait to tell Mom and Dad what I am becoming. Though I wonder if they'll know what an autodidact is. I discovered the word thanks to the writer Jessica Mitford. Once asked on a forbidding form to list her degrees and not having any, she wrote "autodidact"—a swell word for one who is self-taught. It is nice indeed to have parents who, though they might not know what an autodidact is until I explain, will still welcome one into the family.

Just to be on the safe side (there's always the possibility they could turn on a word they don't know), I took the most erudite approach I could manage. I said Milton's family had supported him for five years while he educated himself (I did not mention this was after his graduation from Cambridge—though perhaps I should have. Go to Cambridge and you still have to educate yourself). I was asking for only one year.

They said to take ten. But as it only took five to send Milton on the road to blindness, I said I'd stick to one for now. Of course I can't really become a full-time autodidact until I finish high school, but I can start practicing this summer. And make sure I like this word I've taken for my life. Though I know I will.

Thinking of Milton sitting in his family's country home reading everything ever published, I know that's what I want to do. And if I need glasses later on, then that's not too much of a price to pay.

FIFTY-SEVEN
DAYS TILL SCHOOL

WHAT I HOPE TO DO:

*Get a Head Start on Reading Everything Ever
Published.*

It's the beginning of summer and the morning of the first day of my self-education. Actually, it's the middle of July and a little past noon, but it feels like the beginning and the morning.

I've said something pleasant to every member of my family, almost, so now I can ignore them for a while in favor of literature. And it is Leo Tolstoy who is giving me the eye. No, not *War and Peace*. I'm not that brave this early. But I do think I have enough courage for *Anna Karenina*.

Great books rarely make their way into daily conversation (or at least my daily conversation), but I remember my father saying once that he disagreed with the first sentence of *Anna Karenina*. Unlike Tolstoy, Dad thinks all unhappy families are alike, and every happy family is happy in its own way. I hate to disagree with Tolstoy so early in our relationship, and yet I do trust Dad. But to put them both in their place, I can't imagine finding a family that could manage to be always happy or always unhappy, hard though they might try.

I have begun *Anna*, and this is my favorite sentence yet about families:

> Every person in the house felt that there was no sense in their living together, and that the stray people brought together by chance in any inn had more in common with one another than they . . .

It would be hard to find an honest family member who would not admit to that thought crossing his mind several times a day. I love my family, but I do sometimes wonder what I would think of them had I not started out loving them and then gotten to know them.

We are an odd bunch. A father, a mother (not too odd yet), a younger sister (getting odder), a grandmother (approaching the bend), and an uncle (and round it).

It was my uncle who sparked my first battle with formal education. He had infantile paralysis when he was ten years old, and one day when I was in kindergarten I decided to paint a picture of his wheelchair. My teacher looked at it and said it was the most depressing picture she'd ever seen because it was all gray. And wouldn't it be nice to put some yellow in it? At the age of five, I did my best to explain that the painting was a true rendering of my uncle's wheelchair, not a comment on my life.

And that was the only trouble my uncle Thomas's being in a wheelchair ever caused me. When we went to Europe as a break from kindergarten, I rode in his lap across the continent. There is little better in life than a moveable lap. In Paris, I had a nightmare —Thomas had learned to walk. And there had gone my lap.

And so if sometimes I wonder how I ever got to know my family, I am almost always glad I did. The great gift of family life is to be intimately acquainted with people you might never even introduce yourself to, had life not done it for you.

I have great autodidact news.

At sixteen, Tolstoy entered the University of Kazan but was hopelessly disappointed (I confess the encyclopedia did not actually say "hopelessly") and returned to his estate to conduct his own education. (Little did I know what a big role country homes and estates played in literary life. I've got to get one.)

I shared this information with all available family members, and when I returned to the encyclopedia was very glad I had not read them the next phrase, which said that he did not achieve much success.

Of course, now that I think about it, that's wonderful. It turns out that to be a great literary genius, not only do you not have to go to college, you don't even have to be very good at educating yourself.

I always like to begin a new phase of life on a comforting note.

I've finished *Anna Karenina.* My favorite characters were Levin and Kitty, though I loved Anna too. I never cared much for Vronsky.

As it turns out, Levin and Kitty are based on Tolstoy and his wife. Which just confirms my suspicion that the best writing is about what you know. However, the happiness Levin finds at the end of the book was soon lost by Tolstoy, who spent much of his life in confusion and agony.

His novel has aroused in me many doubts about how we can hope to do good things. I dreamed last night that the only way I wouldn't feel guilty spending my life being a writer would be to cure cancer first—and even then I would still feel a little guilty.

A little exhausted from having read every one of *Anna's* nine hundred fifty pages, I have started the four-hundred-page and larger print *Madame Bovary* (I wonder if Flaubert ever thought his book would be described like that). Despite the print size, I like *Anna Karenina* better, and I was very disappointed to hear from Mom that the distinguishing characteristic of Flaubert's work is his desire to choose exactly the right word. A gift I wonder if I'll ever be able to appreciate because when it comes to French, my gift is choosing exactly the wrong one.

Discovery: After failing his law examinations, Flaubert was allowed to remain at home devoting himself to literature.

I have new respect for the man and his parents.

Tonight at dinner with friends, conversation, as usual, centered on Dad. He swears half his body does not work as well as the other half. However, no one has been able to diagnose what he has (Dad always questions friends before resorting to doctors), and we all think it is just the psychosomatic result of his highly nervous nature. At the beginning of dinner, someone made a very brief statement about how people spend all their time getting tense and worrying about themselves. Yet everyone spent the rest of the evening talking about nothing but themselves and their tensions. It made me very tense.

Despite the fact that Flaubert endeared himself to me by failing his law examinations, I still cannot get involved in *Madame Bovary*.

So as a Flaubert break, I read three Katherine Mansfield short stories, and I am going to name my first daughter or my first heroine—whichever comes first—Katherine.

"The Daughters of the Late Colonel" was especially sublime. I had put off reading it because it was longer than her other stories in *The Garden Party* (when will length stop playing a major part in my literary choices?), but I think it may be my favorite. She has such a wondrous way of letting the details of life slip into her stories.

Speaking of slipping in the details of life, I must slip in my retainer, as I go to the orthodontist tomorrow. If only I could learn to straighten my own teeth.

My orthodontist told me I never had to see him again, but I am supposed to keep wearing my retainer every night anyway. Since I only wore it once a week before, now I'm only going to wear it once a month and stop when I get married.

I am not speaking to my sister Brooke after a weekend in the mountains (the Tehachapi mountains, famous for their women's prison. Humphrey Bogart says to Mary Astor at the end of *The Maltese Falcon,* "Well, if you get a good break, you'll be out of Tehachapi in twenty years!" The prison has since gone coed, robbing Tehachapi of a lot of charm).

Brooke and I have fought about everything. I suppose high altitude does that. We began with croquet (she is an extremely bad sport—though there's always the possibility I am) and ended with England's Royal Family (a fight I feel must go unexplained).

Mom and Dad came home from a party tonight furious with each other. Of course, since Dad was the one doing the yelling, it would seem to the outside observer that he was the furious one, but I knew Mom was furious in her own quiet way. I wanted to know immediately what had gone on. Mom promised to fill me in later.

Always good to her word (you can get anything out of that woman while she's undressing), she told me that at the dinner party, Dad got up and demonstrated the difference in the performance of the halves of his body. He showed everybody that his left arm no longer swings when he walks, and his right leg is weakened. Everybody thought he was being funny, but he was being serious. He was trying to find someone who recognized his symptoms.

Hypochondria has always been a hobby with him, but tonight he is so angry. Is this old age encroaching?

I have had enough neuroticism. From Anna Karenina to Madame Bovary to my father. I need someone who has the proper slant on life.

I think I'm ready for *Vile Bodies* by Evelyn Waugh.

I've wanted to read it since I read Jessica Mitford's *Daughters and Rebels*. Along with my mother and Helene Hanff, Jessica Mitford makes up the triumvirate of writers nearest and dearest to my soul—I have read all their books twice, and I never read anything twice. But back to Evelyn Waugh.

The story goes that when visiting Nancy Mitford on the family estate (I have just got to get an estate if I am to become a great writer!), he was so taken by her little sister Jessica's pet lamb that he promised to substitute the word "sheepish" for "divine" in his new book.

The new book was *Vile Bodies*, the frankness of which caused such a stir with the Mitford parents, Lord and Lady Redesdale, that Nancy was forbidden to associate with Evelyn Waugh.

The Mitfords are, without a doubt, my favorite literary family. Certainly, when it comes to fun, they've got the Brontës beat hands down. Before last Christmas when we went to London and saw a musical called *The Mitford Girls*, I had never heard of any of them. As we walked along Shaftesbury Avenue to the theatre, my mother tried to give me a brief history, but I paid no attention. I entered under the vague impression we were going to see the story of a singing group. Instead, it was the history of a remarkable British family, so wonderfully done it sowed the seeds of my self-education. The Mitfords were the first subject I had to know more about.

The six famous sisters came into the world between 1904 and 1920. It takes books—which have and are being written—to describe in full the rest of the story. To put it the way I see it, Nancy Mitford, the firstborn, became one of my favorite novelists. Pamela, the second, seemed to be the sister most contented with life as it was first presented to her and still lives in the small Cotswold village where they all grew up. A son, Tom, born next, was killed in World War Two. The fact that the next four daughters all came from the same family requires quite an explanation from biologists. The first two, Diana and Unity, were fervent Nazis, the next Jessica, a Communist (and, later, a famous muckraker) and the last, Deborah, totally apolitical and now Duchess of Devonshire.

Nancy, Diana, Jessica, and Deborah have all published books, and any family that can produce four writers out of seven children must be doing something right, if not politically, then at least literarily.

I am reading *Vile Bodies* and Dad is reading about his. He stays up late into the night with his dog-eared medical books, trying to find a disease to fit his symptoms. Since his friends failed him, he was finally forced to go to his doctor. However, the doctor could find nothing wrong with him either. He wrote out a prescription for Valium and told him to calm down. Dad has been fond of Valium ever since Mom's obstetrician introduced him to it to ease his tension while Mom was giving birth to me. But he has never yet shown any interest in calming down.

I live in a world of people I will never meet. I am a trifle depressed, having just looked at a lot of Mitford pictures and wishing I'd known the non-Nazis all my life.

I finished *Vile Bodies* today. I love how it begins so frivolously, then slowly traces the destruction of the Bright Young People.

And though Evelyn Waugh did go to Oxford, he never studied (I may exaggerate, but only slightly).

In contrast to all my reading of late, Brooke said to me today, on again pushing back her self-imposed deadline for finishing her one read of the summer, *The Secret Garden,* "Kendall, I love reading, but, oh, what the world is without it."

Brooke's speech is so full of extractable quotes that I usually dash from kissing her good night to the nearest notepad to get down for future works whatever she has said.

She is so original I sometimes wonder if we didn't get her through more extraordinary means than just the mixing of this family's genes. However, my first memory is of riding to the hospital early one morning, wrapped in my blue blanket, to bring Brooke home. So she must be ours.

Brooke did not really make much of an impression on me, though, until the night when, at three months old, she discovered her toes. That was a fascinating process. But I soon tired of it and spent the rest of the evening pretending to smoke my miniature pipe, which matched Uncle Thomas's real one.

Whenever I try to picture Brooke as a very young child, the pose that always comes to mind is of her midscream. Her face would turn so red her blond hair seemed very pale by comparison, tears would gather in her eyes, and her mouth would open to let out a sound I can still hear even while looking at a photograph.

Volume has always been a strong point with Brooke. She has talked louder than anyone else in the family ever since she learned how (Mom was usually the only tolerant listener, explaining, while the rest of us were plugging our ears, that second children not only have to try harder, they have to speak louder—and this from a first child. Mom is all compassion).

Brooke and I spent a lot of our early lives at war with each other. And had she been taken from me in childhood (a fear which cropped up after reading *Little Women),* I would have been filled with guilt for the rest of my life at how I had treated her. But we have outlived and outgrown the days when "I hate you" was heard hourly.

And now, when a sticky situation occurs, Brooke and I find that the love and respect of a sister is almost more wonderful than getting her into trouble.

George Orwell's *Keep the Aspidistra Flying* has upset me. It is about the hardships of a young and struggling author, material that I think tends to upset any soon-to-be young and struggling author.

Yet he writes so well that he makes the pain into art, which explains the greatness of his art and the use of his pain.

I stayed up all night reading. This is the first time I've ever stayed up all night, and it is as strange an experience as I've always thought it would be.

I hate sleep and I hate how much time I spend doing it, but, quite frankly, I think it is the only thing that keeps human beings from going mad: the illusion that life is not one continuous stream, but the more manageable concept of days. A day, contemplated in its entirety, is hard enough to deal with. A life, contemplated in its entirety, is an impossible concept.

The only two times I am absolutely terrified of life are when I think how short it is and when I think how long it is. In retrospect, it all goes by so fast and yet when I really contemplate the length of it, day after day after day, I am sometimes scared to death.

I do love life, but to live a life as absolutely void of schedule as mine is this summer—well, perhaps I should be more appreciative of the slight, but useful, structure of night and day.

Intrigued by the fact that Evelyn Waugh converted to Catholicism late in life, I decided to investigate early and began *Frost in May* by Antonia White. I am finding it a tragic book about the Catholic Church and, in one case, the Church's destructive influence. Although I will never believe in hell and damnation, it did set me wondering. And I was awfully sweet all day long.

Stayed up so late with the Catholic Church that I heard the morning footsteps of Nanny (who is my grandmother, not an English nanny, though I suppose life would be more literary if she were).

I kissed her and she went on with her day and I with my night. And just as she is shocked that I am still up, I am equally proud of her for getting up. How she finds the strength is a beautiful wonder to me. She has never had or wanted a career (except perhaps deep down to be an actress), and the only things she really likes are her family, chocolate, movie stars, books, and Merv Griffin. I worry too much about life. She has lived seventy-seven years and gets up early for her family, chocolate, movie stars, books, and Merv Griffin.

Dreadful school bulletin came today telling how excited the whole faculty is about next year. They must lead very dull lives.

The young are apt to be arrogant with those older because of an assurance that they have their whole lives in front of them and an idea that they will do things differently. I am this way too.

A masseur came to work on Dad today. But a massage—instead of helping—only left Dad red, tired, and quite nasty.

I have no idea what's wrong with him and he has no idea and it's beginning to make him crazy, I know, but how long is he going to stay crazy?

I know he thinks none of us is concerned enough. Or maybe I just think that. Days go by and I don't ask how he is or what we're going to do about how he is.

I never think about the real dilemmas of life. Mainly because I don't have to. I don't have to earn a living yet. I'm free to think only about what I'm reading and what one day I will write (a writer being my chosen profession before and after I knew there were other choices). And it's too easy to go a whole day and not think about anything but myself.

I have thought of nothing else today except Ingrid Bergman. She died last night.

Somehow her death makes me believe more in an afterlife. I might be able to get through this life without ever meeting her and telling her how much I loved her, but I'm not going through eternity that way.

Today is the first time I have cried because of the death of someone I didn't know. But she had that extraordinary gift of letting us all feel we knew her. And yet today it almost doesn't seem like a gift. It is a gift that today broke our hearts.

Valium is not calming Dad down, so he went back to his doctor who sent him to a psychiatrist, though I can't imagine how he got him there.

Dad hates the idea of psychiatry. He feels he works out his problems in his plays and has always said that once Tennessee Williams was psychoanalyzed, he never wrote as well again.

When he came home, Dad told us the psychiatrist had tried to connect Dad's losing his ability to walk with Thomas's being in a

wheelchair all his life. After Dad got through with him, I wonder
if that psychiatrist could still walk.

At five this morning I finished *Great Expectations*. I
just love the way Pip has so many faults and yet is always seeing
them and being troubled by them. He is so human. It's one thing
to be able to create characters, but Dickens and God know how to
create humans.

I read that a publisher made Dickens add the happy ending. Of
course, I love a happy ending wherever I can find one, but why do
Victorians always want to span a decade in the last chapter? By
that time everyone is so old. However, I don't want to criticize
Dickens even if he does have a penchant for discovering parents.

Puli, my dog (he is a puli and his name is Puli and it
wasn't my idea), is so wonderful. In the eleven years we have had
him we have always called him to dinner in the same way (briefly
—"Dinner, Puli") and yet every day he turns his head in sheer
wonderment and happiness for a few moments before dashing to
it, not quite believing that he is really getting dinner again tonight.
He may be a dog, but don't tell me he doesn't have a real grip on
life.

Of course schools are made for the average. The
holes are all round, and whatever shape the pegs are they must
wedge in somehow.

Nice to have an ally in Somerset Maugham. I can just squeeze
in *Of Human Bondage* before returning to mine.

As part of my education, I've been asking people
what their favorite book is. Today I got a letter from my stepgrandmother Georgia (Georgia married Nanny's husband, Jack,
after Nanny got through with him) in which she said that she

used to read when she was young but didn't now, and proceeded to recommend her favorite soap operas.

Dad told me that the first time I met Georgia I took hold of her hand and wouldn't let go of it the whole day. And so, as I read book after book, trying to become what I think I want to be, I should remember Georgia, who has given up books, but whose kindness of soul has always been seen by those who are the best judge of character, all of us under five.

A little time left for education before school starts, and I just read the sentence "I am writing for myself and strangers" from *The Making of Americans* by Gertrude Stein.

That is the way I have always felt, but I never knew how to say it. Little did I know Gertrude Stein had said it for me.

I can't wait to say to any teacher who makes a snide remark about one of my papers, "Well, I only wrote it for myself and *strangers.*"

However, I have still not got the courage to write on a quiz, as Gertrude Stein once did, "I do not feel like taking a quiz today."

I wonder if Miss Stein would have had the courage had she not had a great teacher. He wrote on her empty quiz paper: "I know just how you feel—A+."

Just found out Katherine Mansfield was ugly. I know that's a stupid thing to say—especially after admiring Gertrude Stein—but the way Katherine Mansfield writes . . . I had always thought of her as a beautiful young girl with pen in hand. Perhaps, while writing, she was.

I bought some wonderful books today. *David Copperfield.* More lost and found parents, I'm sure, but I adore Dickens.

Also *Scoop* by Evelyn Waugh, as well as his letters. So far I have read only the ones to Mitfords. Listen to this from a letter to Nancy Mitford:

All my children are here for the holidays—merry, affectionate, and madly boring—except Harriet who has such an aversion to me that she screams when she catches sight of me a hundred yards away.

Life is so confusing in a world of so many opinions. Here I am reading about Gertrude Stein and her circle, and yet in every other letter Evelyn Waugh writes he says, "Death to Picasso." My head hurts—I'm going to bed.

I feel mundanity creeping over me—I went to bed and forgot about Waugh and Picasso and thought about what I would wear the first day of school, the day after tomorrow. At least I can look forward to tomorrow.

I think the family must have noticed how badly I was taking my last night of freedom. So they suggested a visit with the Van Scoyks, our favorite family, if you don't count ourselves.

The main purpose of the visit was to cheer up Leona, who is worried about a spot on her lung. I would be more worried if this were not the time for Dad's and Leona's summer sicknesses. Matthew (who, as a faithful son, shares my level of faithful-daughter-type compassion) referred to Leo's latest worry as her "illness du jour."

While Mom and Bob (docile marriage partners that they have to be, just for contrast's sake) listened, Dad and Leona compared symptoms and competed for who now had the most fatal diseases.

Matthew decided to provide the entertainment for Brooke and me by broadcasting the news (an aspiring journalist, that is his idea of entertainment).

He dressed up as Lloyd Dobyns and Brooke dressed up as Linda Ellerbee, and they broadcast *Overnight* a few hours earlier than its regular starting time of 1:30 A.M. There was trouble on the set, however, due to Brooke mispronouncing every other word, so at the commercial break she was let go, and I took over. Matthew and I worked very well together, despite the fact I invented all my news stories.

Once the news was over, Matthew announced it was time to search the house for either *The Last of the Wine* or *I, Claudius*—one of which he has to read for school Monday. I told him it was against my principles to read anything for school over the summer, and I was impressed to see those were his principles too, but why was he going back on them now? He said those weren't his principles. He just hadn't thought school started till Tuesday.

When we couldn't find either of the books, I told him about my decision to become an autodidact. He liked learning the word, but didn't show much interest in living it. However, time is on my side. He is two years younger than I, and open-minded.

Why do I see myself being a rather lonely autodidact unless Matthew is one too? I don't quite know. I met Matthew when I was five and he was three, and I spent the first nine years of the acquaintanceship loathing him. I stopped loathing him one evening when we were sitting together at a dinner party, and I was very impressed by how much he could eat.

I just remembered my favorite Matthew memory—when he went with us to see a production of *Hamlet*. And afterwards we went backstage to see Hamlet himself, who did not realize that we were not brother and sisters. And I remember being overwhelmed by the sweetest feeling that we could have been. That we could have spent all our lives together, and forever be tied to each other. And I thought how nice that would have been. And how nice that for a moment at least, through Hamlet's eyes, we were.

The sun is rising. Though I have not gone to bed yet, I have to get up in a few hours to go to school, but I have no intention of missing my last dawn. Besides, I think a little unconsciousness always helps the first day of school.

It was my parents who set my inner clock so askew. As a baby, I would take my afternoon nap in the early evening as the curtain rose on a production of one of my father's plays. And be wide awake to go out with the cast after the show. I remember my mother having to dress my limp-with-sleep body for the afternoon session of kindergarten. So tomorrow will be quite traditional. But traditional or not, it is arriving too quickly—as is the dawn.

I am told we must live for the days, and I did this summer, but they went so quickly. I always felt I had a lot of "live for" left over. The nights seemed to end before I did. And I fell asleep hoping tomorrow would have more than those paltry twenty-four hours that were all we got out of today.

===

WHAT I DID:

Fell in love with a University of Kazan dropout, a fellow who couldn't pass his law examinations, and a lad who spent more time in debtors' prison visiting Dad than in school. Not to mention a few less famous, if better educated, authors than Leo, Gustave, and Charles.

===

SCHOOL
(Decline, Fall, and
Graduation)

The dreary rigors of formal education are in full swing.

Mine is a progressive school. The faculty allows the students to call them by their first names, all except Madame Tokar, who refuses to be called anything but Madame Tokar, and frankly I cannot ever imagine wanting to call her anything else.

The highlight of the first day was learning how little schooling Benjamin Franklin had. Inspired by my commitment to being an autodidact, I felt compelled to ask: If Benjamin Franklin had done all he had done without ever going to high school, why are we all here?

I could not have expected my teacher to have an answer for that one. Except perhaps to answer me with a question: If I had to be in high school, why did I have to be in her class? Luckily, that was a question she was too gracious to pose.

Dad is going to see a diagnostician tomorrow. As a friend said, "You're the only person I know who wants a second opinion when a doctor tells you nothing's wrong."

As soon as Dad walked into his office, the diagnostician said, "You have . . ." and Dad formed a "P" on his lips. The doctor said, "Say it" and Dad said, "I've got Parkinson's." And the doctor smiled and said, "How would you like to join me in this business? You're remarkable at self-diagnosis." (Little did he know the practice Dad's had.)

The next question out of Dad's mouth was, "What do I do about my doctor who is an idiot?" to which the diagnostician replied, "Your doctor's not an idiot. Parkinson's is very hard to diagnose. Go back to see him and let him discover it with your help."

Dad raced to his doctor's office, stormed in demanding to see the doctor immediately . . . just the kind of behavior that gets results.

He told his doctor he was going to walk across his office and to pay attention. The doctor watched him walk, then said, "Oliver, it's stress. Have you run out of Valium?" To which Dad replied with a scream, "Does the word 'Parkinson's' mean nothing to you?"

The now badly shaken doctor replied, "I know you're frightened and if you think you have Parkinson's, I'll send you to a neurologist. But you don't have Parkinson's! You need a good dose of Valium! Now relax!"

Today Dad went to the neurologist. He does have Parkinson's and he's set for a brain scan next week—to make sure it's nothing more serious than Parkinson's. Though Parkinson's sounds serious enough to me.

It's a neurological disorder. Nonfatal, but progressive. Not affecting the mind, but doing its damnedest in time to mess up life for the body.

Dad has waited two weeks for the results of his brain scan. His doctor says he hasn't gotten them yet. But Dad is, of course, convinced his doctor's lying and that he's got a brain tumor. He goes around saying he probably has a brain tumor as large as a basketball.

There are times I wish I had an emotionally locked-up father. But having one who constantly reveals his worst fears and anxieties, I want to break down in tears of sympathy and shared fear at first, and then, since he never stops revealing his worst fears and anxieties, I am finally driven to callousness. Today I told him his head isn't as large as a basketball.

Dad got the results of his brain scan. The doctor said it was clearly Parkinson's, but he did have an anomaly in his brain.

"What the hell is an anomaly?" Dad shouted. We looked it up in the medical books, but we still don't quite know what it is. It is defined as a deviation from the usual. Since my father is a walking anomaly, I am not too surprised to learn his brain has one of its own.

The neurologist said that had Dad been diagnosed ten years earlier, he couldn't have done anything for him, but now they have this new drug called Sinemet. His leg will regain its strength and his arm will begin to swing again. The doctor also said a cure for Parkinson's is imminent. If only imminent were tomorrow.

What do you think of these two words: "Graduating Early"? At the end of this year.

A friend, who wants to be a ballerina, told me she was going to graduate early so she could devote herself to ballet a year earlier, and it occurred to me that I could devote myself to what I want to devote myself to (namely myself) a year earlier too.

And I cannot help but feel that I am ready to go. For example, this morning, we were in the mountains and I was dreaming that all these people were applauding me and the applause got louder and louder until it finally woke me up, and I realized it was hailing. Now don't you think a person who dreams that is just about bursting to take control of her own life?

With the cost of tuition, I couldn't have two better allies than Mom and Dad. But I have not yet told the school of my decision. I'll need an extra credit, so it will mean taking up French again (I do hope Madame Tokar will be pleasant about my forced return to the flock). Plus, I will have to somehow manage to take Beginning Painting and Advanced Painting simultaneously. Though I suppose that will be a more lifelike way of doing things since no one ever stops being a beginner, and it is hard to be advanced all the time.

I don't think I'll mind taking six classes and an extra art. Last year I felt very loaded down, but the load seems to lighten as you get ready to leave—I think to fool you into college.

There is just one thing that worries me about graduating early. I would like, if possible, to make sure I love life as much as I think I do. I would just hate to leave school for life and then find out I am not all that fond of it.

Our plane has just taken off for New York-Boston-Chicago-Cleveland-Minneapolis-Nashville-Atlanta-Houston-Dallas. My beloved parents have saved me yet again.

Each minute in the air takes me further away from authority and boredom and doing my French homework in English class because if I listen to another inane comment about *The Scarlet Letter,* I'll lose my mind. And all thanks to Mom and Dad.

Mom's second novel has just hit the bookstores and so, of course, Dad, Brooke, and I are accompanying her to do all we can to make sure *Life Sentences* gets prime shelf space. I say "of course" when really I should say "very unusually," but my parents are so exemplary in their behavior that they have made the very unusual a matter of course.

Mom and Dad never leave home without Brooke and me. It began with Dad. Whenever he had an important production of one of his plays, we all went. He feels our presence—to say nothing of our production notes—much too valuable to be left at home.

In fact, when we were very young, in those grades where homework played a very small part, we were not only plucked from school in the cause of careers, but Mom and Dad also planned most of their pleasure traveling during the school year. I remember extensive sightseeing during my mostly absentee year in the second grade.

Luckily, that was also my winning year in the teacher's pet competition, so my teacher gave me a camera for a going-away present and told me not to bother with assignments. The class spent the time I was away studying nutrition, and I arrived back on the day of their grand finale. The room was scattered with pictures of food cut out from magazines, and the test was to see if they could pick out one thing from each of the four food groups. The teacher asked if I wanted to try, just for fun. I could see she didn't expect much though, since I had missed all those weeks of study. But I played it safe, staying away from pictures of oatmeal (I'd always had a suspicion it might be a vegetable), and came up with four winners—so I felt that the guardian angel who, with divine skill, had guided me toward a vegetable, grain, meat, and dairy product had given me the go-ahead for not going to school.

However, my guardian angel almost deserted me in the seventh grade when I began going to the school I will soon be leaving. Mom and Dad—in an unusual lapse of character—weren't sure if we could get away with the long absences I had taken so casually in grammar school, and they were days from leaving on a trip without me when suddenly it hit me, sitting in a class, listening to material I already understood explained once again for those who didn't, that I had to go.

So, preparing myself for failure of all classes and complete ruination of my life, I took my books and hit the road. I came back weeks ahead of my class (thanks to optimistic teachers who assigned me much more than my classmates let them cover) and haven't given up traveling yet.

Even, occasionally, under false pretenses. My school has an irritating habit of organizing mandatory wilderness trips once a year for all the students. When I heard about the first one, I had a similar reaction to opening the mandatory summer reading list. School is always making me shudder. And so I've never gone on a single school trip, mandatory or not. But I had heard about another person who didn't go and had to sit in the library all week. So I always told the school that, by unhappy accident, our family would be out of town during the wilderness expedition.

One year the school trip was moved back two weeks due to weather conditions (they hated to take the students out unless there was a good chance they could lose a few) and the principal came up and patted me on the back and said, with a sadistic gleam in her eye, wasn't it lucky because I could go now. Somehow I kept a straight face when I walked into her office the next day and said that by strange coincidence our family trip had just been moved back two weeks.

But enough happy memories of an education filled with absence and deceit. I am about to open my English book and begin educating myself, though I still have to use the tools school has assigned me.

And how well I use these tools will decide whether or not I will graduate early. If I come back hopelessly behind and not understanding a thing I was supposed to have learned about Physics, English, Classics, History, Painting, and Math, then adding French and Advanced Painting will be out of the question. However, I'm not really worried about the school angle of the book tour. Homework and hotel rooms go wonderfully together—the combination creates a very illicit feeling.

What the book tour is giving me is what I have been looking for —a test of life. I predict this trip is going to be the best of life. If I can take the best of life, then I can take the rest of life. And if I can't take the best, then I should quit now. And make plans for graduate school.

New York. After spending the morning visiting bookstores and moving *Life Sentences* to more prominent shelf space when necessary, tonight we saw Beth Henley's play, *The Wake of Jamie Foster.*

After it was over, we went backstage and found Beth in tears. She had just found out the play would close Saturday because of the reviews. It's only been running twelve nights. Dad was wonderful. He said, "Listen, you've already had twelve times the run of one of my plays on Broadway."

Belita Moreno is giving the performance of a lifetime and yet she said she's thrilled she can play it for the rest of the week. Why must actresses always be forced to ask so little from life?

The play is such a perfect mix of comedy and tragedy. There was a man sitting in front of us who after each line would laugh and then give a little moan at the truth behind it.

I am so glad I saw that play and the pain of its early closing. It has forced me to confess the most awful secret of my existence.

My father hates it when anyone has a failure, but whenever one of our friends has had a failure on Broadway, I felt it was fair that they were having some of the bad luck my father has had.

And though I, unlike my father, have been bitter that of all his Broadway plays, none has ever turned into the great success he deserved, it is equally awful, I now realize, to see Beth Henley, who won the Pulitzer with her first play last year, be so cruelly treated her second time out. Bad luck spread around is not made any better.

I saw Harvard today. Very beautiful, but I'm afraid I was without envy for the backpack-laden students. I long only for the day when my shoulder will not have a permanent backpack dent.

And let us not forget that Harvard was the place Henry David Thoreau said bored him. And since he and I were born on the same day, I'm pretty sure I would have a similar reaction.

I have just completed my final school assignment (an essay on *The Scarlet Letter*—you would not believe the lengths to which I have had to go to find symbolism), in our final book-tour city, Dallas. This trip has confirmed all my suspicions about life.

I have loved every minute of it, so I'm heading back to school to ask them very politely if they will please open the door and let me out.

Home. Quite thematically on the subject of being let out from where you don't want to be, *The Nun's Story* with Audrey Hepburn was on television tonight, the night before I return to school. I adored it, but Brooke (whom I am never allowing to watch a movie with me again) made rude comments throughout about a nun's life. I assume you can guess her basic objection.

My graduating early news went over surprisingly well. Turns out my principal, whom, despite my lack of love for formal education, I have always adored, also graduated from high school a year early.

One of the English teachers was very disappointed I was leaving early and would not get a chance to take her Great Novels course.

I asked what the great novels were going to be.

"Anna Karenina."

"Oh, well, I've read that."

"Great Expectations."

"Oh, well, I've read that."

"Vanity Fair."

"Oh, well, I've read that."

"Well, maybe you won't be missing much by missing my Great Novels course."

Today is the first day of midyear finals, so I have time to talk. If you study all year, it is surprising the free time you can find during finals. So I can tell you about the most extraordinary scene which occurred tonight.

The family was returning from an excellent play. Dad said to Mom, "Betsy, go in and unlock the door." Problem: Dad always unlocks the door. It's not that my mother can't use a key, but we recently had installed a complicated burglar, or rather preventive burglar, system. Mom asked for detailed instructions, which were given intermittently with phrases like "Betsy, I'm gonna be dead soon and you can't get in the house."

Mom walked bravely to the door, opened it with confidence, and set off the alarm. We all called her an idiot, and then Dad decided to show her how to do it and, of course, set off the alarm himself.

Once the alarm was turned off for a second time, Dad went to get his nightly chocolate milk and bran. He opens the icebox to find that the usually squeezable chocolate syrup has been replaced by nonsqueezable chocolate syrup. This discovery is followed by accusations such as "You finally find something I like and then you refuse to buy it."

He opens the silverware drawer for a spoon to stir his milk. "Come here, Betsy Ann. Where are the teaspoons? Just where do you keep the teaspoons?" Next comes the disclosure that only four teaspoons came with the new set of stainless steel. Dad is outraged. Nanny enters, still in her overcoat (I don't think she ever takes it off). She says, "Well, why don't you write a letter to the company, Oliver?" and breaks into absolute hysterics. At this point Brooke's hysterics are getting out of hand. "And you be quiet," Dad yells. Next, Nanny repeats her funny, then has to duck an empty milk carton Dad throws at her. With that last gesture, he stalks upstairs only to be yelled at by Mom: "And you wonder where Brooke gets her habit of throwing food."

Today I overheard this about last night's goings-on:
Brooke: "That was the best time I've had in a long time, Nanny."
Nanny: "Yes, that was real fun."

Tomorrow spring vacation begins, and the ten weeks after that will be my swan song to formal education.

I wonder if I will miss the companionship of my peers. It is nice, eating lunch as part of such a large circle. But large circles are transitory things. At the beginning of the year, there was a great going-out-to-lunch craze when driver's licenses were newly-acquired possessions for all of them. Not for me. In California, if you wait till eighteen, you can be a self-taught driver, whereas if you rush into it at sixteen, you have to take state-approved classes, and I am an autodidact in all things.

I find the key to school is being an individual. By never trying to fit in anywhere specifically, I can fit in everywhere easily. I do believe I am the only person in our class who can have a friendly conversation with anyone—from the people who got expelled for taking drugs to the people who got them expelled.

I wonder if it will prove harder to be an individual when not surrounded by other people. Having never succumbed to peer pressure, I hope I won't be affected by life pressure.

Mom told me this morning that she'd discovered the key to peer pressure. She said it was the fault of parents who by excluding children from their world force them into a world dominated by their so-called peers. I agreed with her and thanked her for giving me a perfect life so far.

But for a little while longer, it is nice to be near the dangerous world of peer pressure. For a few last weeks, before I become an independent dot, it is nice to be part of a circle.

M y friends and I were discussing the future today. I do find it a little disconcerting that they can all answer when asked where they want to go to college, but so few have a response when asked what they want to do with their lives.

Of course, I am too harsh a judge because I have always had a response when asked what I wanted to do. I grew up watching my father do everything in life with a steno pad in his left hand and a pen in his right. It seemed an ideal way to live and so I decided that I too would live that way. However, the fact that he never set down a specific time to write, but instead wrote while waiting in line at the post office, while pulling weeds, while talking, while walking, while even driving a car, led to my greatest childhood misconception.

I did not really understand that writing was his profession. I assumed he was kind of a waiter-in-line-at-post-offices/weed puller/talker/walker/driver. And he, as I assumed everyone did, wrote while doing all his jobs. I thought that was the way everyone lived. They had these odd jobs and, of course, always wrote. When I envisioned my future life, it was usually as a farmer (I preferred the profession of farmer to that of waiter-in-line-at-post-offices/weed puller/talker/walker/driver), but of course I would always be writing a new play while feeding the sheep. A great melancholy accompanied the realization that not everyone in the world carried a steno pad. And I still feel that perhaps secretly they all do.

So I urge all my friends to be writers. But none have listened. They are waiting for college to find out what they want to do with their lives. But is that what college should be used for? I thought its main use was for the consumption of knowledge. Yet I have met very few people of any age who recommend higher education for anything but the experience of it. One frank friend of my mother's told me: "I only went to college to lose my virginity and I had to take a year abroad to do that."

I do concede that college is very useful for becoming a doctor, a lawyer, an architect, an engineer, or Madame Curie. But for people without such definite ambitions, college seems more a passageway from childhood to adulthood than a place to learn. And as rites of passage go, it would be hard to find a more expensive one. In general, the parents of my friends are going to be shelling out close to twenty thousand dollars a year. With plane trips home and all the items necessary to make a home away from home feel like a real one, I suspect in a few years an education at a private university will cost somewhere very near a hundred thousand dollars per child. Whereas being an autodidact is open to everyone.

I remember when I was little, watching a program on television (I have found the only surefire rule of bringing up a wonderful child is never to limit the amount of television consumed) that mentioned how much college could cost, and I was suddenly so afraid I might not be able to go (college being, at that tender age, my main ambition).

Yesterday I read that the fear of escalating college costs has made some states adopt a system whereby new parents give the state a certain sum of money at their child's birth, and the state, in exchange, guarantees the child a college education in eighteen years.

What happens if they've raised an autodidact? Why must college be the only choice after high school? I think I am the only one of my graduating class not choosing it, but also the only one whose parents have not limited the choices to college or getting a job.

So many parents seem perfectly willing to shell out all that money for an education, but so unwilling just to provide food and shelter and allow their children the opportunity to educate themselves. Or to get a head start on their chosen careers. Without the pressure to show immediate monetary gain. Or just time to take a look at this life we have been tested on so furiously for so long.

Did you know that the eighteen-year-old leaving for the first semester of college has the highest incidence of suicide among teenagers? We are so terrified that the decisions we make now will decide the rest of our lives. And we feel as if we have to decide everything by tomorrow. That shouldn't be what tomorrow is for. The point of tomorrow is it's a chance to change our minds.

A girl in my class has had to leave school because she has leukemia. All this time I have been thinking I was so much braver than anyone I knew because I was going to be facing life while they were just going to school. And in my all-encompassing self-concern, I had not even realized she was ill.

It was strange in the sense that the news came during a period when I have been obsessed by the fear of losing my grandmother or my dog—my two oldest living relatives.

At school, after I heard the news, I went in the bathroom and cried. I said a few rather clichéd lines like why did it have to happen to her—all of which I meant very deeply—their truth has made them clichés.

I told both my parents what had happened but avoided telling Nanny and Thomas because I thought it would make them so sad. However, as I was telling Nanny good night, I remembered I had to borrow a stamp from her, and Nanny (who is loathe to part with a stamp without a reason) asked whom I had written. I told her I was writing a friend who had to leave school because of leukemia. And she said, "Oh, Kendall, I'm so glad you're writing her. Maybe if you tell her what's happening in school, she won't miss it." I kissed her good night, assuring her Mallory was much too bright to miss school.

And as I was walking to my room, I suddenly realized that in writing the letter today (something I want to do every day), school had validity to me for the first time. At last the fact that my English teacher shakes the hands of people who say brilliant things in class and that I have never gotten my hand shook (thank God) seemed important because it might amuse Mallory.

Mom got a letter today from a woman saying she thought *Life Sentences* had saved her life. A few weeks after reading the novel, she, like the book's heroine, was raped. She said the novel was in the back of her mind, so she tried to react as the heroine did and she felt that was what saved her life.

I guess that's about the zenith when it comes to the effect a novel can have on a life. And how right that *Life Sentences* should save a life since it is a book that makes me want so much to live. And to live so much.

And, heaven knows, it has already begun to make me live more. It was because of *Life Sentences* and the book tour that I had to leave drama, which would have required my presence at rehearsals, and take up painting, which is a more portable art.

And painting has been the great gift of school to me. With a teacher so marvelous I would go to college if I could expect to find more like her. But I'm afraid she's a rarity—an art teacher who does not impose her vision on her students. She saves it for her own paintings.

And thanks to her beautiful introduction to the art, I'll want to paint all my life. As my five-year-old self would have said, I'm changing my profession from farmer to painter, but of course I'll always have a steno pad in hand.

We got a phone call from Texas today, telling us Georgia, my stepgrandmother, has died. And so it's all over. Jack and Georgia are both gone, as is the world they lived in, which I never visited and never quite seemed real to me.

A trailer park. I remember a picture of Jack, walking through the gate to their trailer, which had the words "Sheriff Hailey" written on it, and on the back of the picture it said, "Going out to check for Indians."

I wish I had seen it in a way. I have been fully exposed to the other side of the family, my grandparents on Mom's side, in the middle of Dallas society. I've seen my grandfather Earl's law offices. I should have seen my grandfather Jack's butcher's cleaver. Jack and Georgia came to California three times. Once, Dad flew them out so Jack could see the top heart specialist in the country. One of Dad's plays was opening in Los Angeles, and on the way to the doctor, Jack said to Dad, "I hope it's a failure, boy."

Jack was definitely mean. Nanny (who did not come out of her room when Jack and Georgia visited) told me once, "He was mean as the devil." In the only family videocassette we have of my grandfather Jack, I am sitting between him and Georgia, and I, obviously coached by Nanny, ask him repeatedly, "Why are you such a terrible old man?" But he also had a native wit, which made him, I suppose, colorful/mean.

Georgia told me a story about what he'd done to her just before they came out. They'd been eating in a diner. When she came out of the ladies' room, he was at the cash register paying. He said he'd left his newspaper on the table and asked her to go back and get it. She picked up the paper and out fell all the silverware that he had wrapped up in it. Jack said, "Georgia, I told you to stop stealing silverware from restaurants." She ran to the car in tears but laughed when she told us about it.

And that's the thing about family history. It loses so much of its pain as time goes on. But Georgia gave us all something by loving the meanest man our family ever produced. Every family has a meanest member, but not many are graced with someone who will love him.

It is amazing that so many people have believed in a Heaven when there is no proof whatsoever for its existence. Just a need to be saved from nothing.

The thing that gets you is that all these billions of people already know. Georgia, too, now. To relate it to mundanity for a moment, it's like during finals, when others have been handed the final before you have and seen if the essay question we've all prepared best is on it. Only in the case of life—unlike finals—you can't count on a smile to tell you what you want to know.

Life is working out like Handel's *Water Music.* Filled with joy and beauty.

My friend Mallory is back in school. She looks and seems to feel wonderful so, happily, idiocy is beginning to get on my nerves again.

At the last assembly of the school year, I was awarded the Harvard Book Prize. It is the first year this honor has been given, and I was shocked to receive it since it takes into account not only test scores and grades but things like school spirit and extracurricular activities, and everyone knows I wouldn't touch an extracurricular activity with a ten-foot pole.

And my last painting of the year, a self-portrait, hangs in the central hall of the school, so that practically everyone who goes anywhere has to look for a few moments at my five-foot face. I swear I did not start out to make my face so big. But with the end of the year, supplies were running low and all the smaller canvases had been snatched up, leaving me with one almost as tall as I am. The day I was to begin my painting, I came to class intending to paint my full-length self, but all the good mirrors had also been snatched up ahead of time and the only ones left were too small to show anything but my face. But when I stared into the mirror, I saw that there was a lot more to a human face than I had ever taken the time to notice—so much that I used all five feet of canvas trying to capture it. I don't know who managed to do the original so small. Now when people ask how I had the courage to paint such a large face, I just smile, keep my mouth shut, and thank God for necessity.

I am almost sprung. Tomorrow evening at eight o'clock I will march into my school auditorium, and at approximately nine-thirty I will march out—and then I will be free.

From the moment I got up the courage to tell the old school I was going to leave a year early, I have never doubted my decision.

We start out with every possibility open to us and, slowly, as we make choices, we narrow until we find our own path. I hate the

process of narrowing. More than anything, I want to do everything. But for everything we do, we don't do something else.

Yet, with this choice, I can't imagine what it is that I'll be
missing. It seems as if it is the first step in a path to all possibilities.

I have been free from the bondage of formal education
for two and a half hours now. I adored my graduation ceremony,
though I was almost ill with nervousness beforehand. I had the
audacity to make a speech. I hope the seniors—the real seniors—
didn't object. I think I might have if some phony senior had
butted in on my class ceremony and had the audacity to make a
speech on top of that. But they were awfully sweet and had great
tolerance for a phony senior and her speech:

> I would like to make one thing clear. Just because I am graduat-
> ing from Oakwood a year early does not mean I didn't have a
> wonderful time here because I did, and I have a lot of thank you's
> to make.
> I would like to thank Madame Tokar who taught me French for
> five years and imprinted on my mind forever that invaluable
> French phrase: *"Chewing gum dans la poubelle."*
> I would like to thank Steve Bellon, who, seeing me pacing up
> and down trying to memorize the plot of *The Comedy of Errors*
> before the final, shouted, "Go out and have a three-martini lunch,
> Kendall—you'll ace it."
> I would like to thank Larry Ceplair for everything except the in-
> class essays, which I really could have done without.
> I would like to thank Mimi Flood, who understood my attitude
> about school wilderness trips ("I just don't do that sort of thing"),
> and about everything else.
> I would like to thank Elliot somebody, who taught me math for
> four weeks before our class gave him high blood pressure and he
> had to leave.
> I would like to thank Selma Moscowitz, who has made me spend
> innumerable hours staring at glue bottles, naked ladies, toilet pa-
> per, and myself—and through them all made painting my favorite
> class.
> I would like to thank all of you. For being kind when you didn't

have to be. For being generous when you could have gone out to lunch. For defying the inherent student-teacher relationship by making me feel we were all friends. For your unfailing support, unbelievable understanding, and that wonderful feeling that only parents and teachers can provide, that no matter what we did, you would still be there tomorrow.

Until tonight, that is. Tomorrow has now become a frightening proposition. Where else will we find people who will understand our rebellion without apparent cause, our lack of anything even resembling courtesy, and that dearly beloved quality of defying anything and everything anyone else stands for in the search for what we stand for, and still be intent on making us better people?

You have been too good to us to have prepared us for real life. You have prepared us for a better life, which, now that I think about it, may have been what you were planning all along. And, now that I think about it, I thank you for it.

That is not the speech I gave at all. I just this minute added the last three paragraphs. Why couldn't I have given that speech tonight? Perhaps I couldn't say those things until I was really free. Though I can't believe I couldn't have thought of them a mere three hours earlier. Ah, well, I always knew I would have to rewrite my life. I just didn't know how soon I would have to begin doing it.

WHAT I DID:

Enough.

LIFE
(at last)

WHAT I HOPE TO DO:

What I Want To Do.

I have not been so angry since I left school. I guess that's not saying too much since I only left school yesterday, but I am pretty angry.

I was looking at this book called *Novels and Novelists*, trying to decide what the first literary expedition of my life (which began today) would be. I enjoyed reading the first part about the writing habits of various novelists, and then I began to get mad.

First, Evelyn Waugh is labeled an alcoholic and a depressive, and *The Ordeal of Gilbert Pinfold* called his greatest novel. Really now.

Then, in a section on novels being made into movies, David Selznick is attacked. They talk of the "vulgar energy he was able to inject into his literary adaptations." I should have slammed down the book then, but if I had I wouldn't have known what a huge group of idiots the people who composed it are.

They proceed to give four separate ratings to each novel. A possibility of five stars for four categories: readability, characterization, plot, and literary merit. (It's hard to believe such egoes as these can be housed in this universe—I don't see how there's any room left over for mine.)

What I think may be my favorite of Nancy Mitford's novels, *The Blessing,* is given 4,1,1,2. I have not yet forgotten Grace (I am going to name my second daughter after her), Nanny, or Sigisimond.

The Great Gatsby gets only a 4 for plot, but don't feel bad, F. Scott, so does *Madame Bovary.*

And one of the greatest characters ever—Miss Jean Brodie—gets only a 4.

I cannot put this book down I am so enraged. *Jane Eyre,* tut,

tut, tut, Charlotte, a 3 in character and plot. I am ready to throw up.

I think I'm losing my mind. *Alice in Wonderland* gets only a 2 in plot—but, then, of course, I'm forgetting, nothing ever happens to her.

The Murder of Roger Ackroyd gets a 1 for literary merit. Possibly the finest whodunit ever written. I am ready for a fistfight.

Babbitt rates a 2 for characterization. Considering that name has traveled down to have a meaning all its own in our native tongue, I have to wonder what a character must do to merit a 3.

And poor Margaret Mitchell, turns out Scarlett and Rhett (my, those are unfamiliar names) were worth only a 3—God knows what these people would have thought of the characters once they were combined with Selznick's "vulgar energy."

Did you like *The Catcher in the Rye*? Of course you did (and spare me introductions to the person who didn't), but did you know the plot is worth only a 2?

I am too sleepy to go on with the offenses, but this has been fun. I do think a little hate is good for any life. And nothing is a better target than people who spend their time criticizing literature instead of having enough guts to try to make some of their own. I hope I have not just attacked myself, but I do make it a point not to criticize anything except critics.

When Mom saw me looking through the bookshelves today, she seemed surprised I didn't want to take a break between school and education. But I told her that reading to be tested and reading to read were two such different skills, I felt no need of a respite in between.

Since I have vowed not to follow the recommendations of academics, my first reading-to-read choice is Marcel Proust. You see, Proust was recommended by Mom and Dad. The week before graduation, they both said that I must read Proust. The fact that neither of them has ever read Proust goes without saying. But I like having parents who recommend books they have not read themselves. Just because all the world's riches have not passed directly through their hands does not mean that they hesitate in wanting to pass them on.

It is about 6:30 A.M. and I sit outside in the very early light. It is magnificently beautiful. In such a short time the sky has gone from black with stars to blue with clouds and just one star left. It is so beautiful with the trees and the sky—and I see another star. Sometimes I wonder if it would be better getting up at this time instead of going to bed. But I don't think I'd have the heightened appreciation—two birds have just flown over—I have now. It is so still and calm, as if nothing were ever meant to move. The sun must be beginning to come up, though—I see the orange in one part of the sky.

I feel as if all this light is all mine. With nothing barring my vision of it. No real responsibility in the world and, even better than that, no homework.

Tomorrow the Van Scoyks and the Haileys leave for London on a trip that is a present to me for beginning life. And what a life I've begun! I was conferring with Matthew on packing details tonight (namely, who will bring the Watermark fluid to throw on Uncle Thomas at the airport). And as we were hanging up, I said, "So this is the real life I've heard so much about." And he answered so wisely, "Kendall, don't get confused. What we're living can never be referred to as real life."

Matthew's recommendation about keeping the little paper water cups provided by the airplane covering your ears throughout the flight to avoid jet lag seems to be working marvelously. We have been in London a whole day and have not felt it yet.

Since the flat we have rented accommodates only seven, we have left Nanny and Thomas in their favorite hotel in London. Brooke, Matthew, and I privately refer to it as the dungeon, but

Nanny and Thomas are in hog heaven as long as they are within rolling distance of Woolworth's in the Strand.

Our flat is grand. It is so big that I lost a room between my first and second tours of it. Upstairs is the master bedroom, framed by the roof's beams. Next to that is a dining room and kitchen large enough to hold seven Van Scoyks and Haileys while eating (we tend to expand).

Downstairs is a small, elegant sitting room and a large, thank heavens not so elegant den. Toward the back of the flat are two bedrooms, one for me and Brooke and one for Mom and Dad. (Bobby and Leona get the master bedroom at the beginning of the trip, since Bob has to go back early to earn more of the money Leona gives to Harrods.)

Matthew is all by himself in a little room near the front of the flat. I think this must have been the room reserved for family fights because all the furniture in it is broken. I pointed out that he did have a bathroom all to himself, but he just pointed toward the sink. It does look like its days of being attached to the wall are numbered.

But I like this strange little room. We ended our first day in London in it, all talking together—Matthew lying in bed and Brooke and I balancing on three-legged chairs. Brooke provided subtle underscoring, using Matthew's miniature calculator that also plays tunes. Actually, not too subtle as the only tunes it plays are "The Battle Hymn of the Republic" and "Dixie." A true journalist, he even has a calculator that believes in equal time.

I have been out of school twelve days and I feel it is time to write a novel.

It is going to be about Matthew and me. I have got to remember on paper why I ever liked him so much because I'm sure having a hard time remembering in real life.

I cannot believe I ever wanted Matthew for a brother. My great memory of London is of Matthew's foot as he climbs over anyone between him and a seat in a taxicab. For any distances deemed unwalkable by my father, we hail one taxicab for Thomas and three lucky others (or to put that more accurately, Matthew and two lucky others), and the rest of us go underground on the tube. Of course, distances deemed unwalkable by Dad are few and far between, hence causing the major rift between the adults on this trip. At one point, Leona yelled at Dad, "I thought you had Parkinson's." Dad reminded her of Sinemet, his miracle drug. She cursed the advances in medical science throughout the entire British Museum. I thought she was going to have a breakdown by the time we finally found the Elgin Marbles—she said she had to have a sit-down. Nanny immediately joined the mutiny and dropped to the bench with Leo while Dad paced until they caught their breath.

How often, after that day, in the course of my walks along the "Guermantes Way" and with what an intensified melancholy did I reflect on my lack of qualification for a literary career, and that I must abandon all hope of ever becoming a famous author.

I've only finished the first chapter of my novel, but lack of fame resulting from it is already a great concern. It's so nice to know Proust felt the same way. To read of emotions that reflect our own is the only proof we have we are not mad. And Marcel is so full of emotions that I can always find a few I share. Mom told me Proust was regarded as a failure for most of his life. But, of course, all the time he was being looked on as a failure, he was working on *Remembrance of Things Past.*

I am reading Proust as we head by train to Canterbury. I was sitting next to Matthew, talking, until I noticed he had the dirtiest fingernails of anyone I'd ever seen and told him as politely as I could that they made me sick. I am being rotten to Matthew lately.

Only this morning Brooke and I attacked him for eating two tarts from a newly bought package. We had calculated and decided everyone's fair share would be three quarters of a tart. Le-

ona said Matthew could eat her share. We pointed out that he still
owed us half a tart.

We really get along too badly to ever be brother and sister. I
suppose only husband and wife is left.

If the Hailey/Van Scoyk relationship can survive the
holy city of Canterbury, it can survive anything. Our pilgrimage
preparations began a few minutes before the train was due to
arrive.

Coat on, Proust in hand, I was ready, knowing English trains
like to keep up a brisk pace, leaving minimal time for jumping off.
Mr. Matthew, however, unaware of this, was blithely stretched
out in his seat, cleaning his fingernails to "Dixie."

As the train pulled in, Dad shoved us all out, and only as the
train was chug-a-lugging away did Matthew realize "Dixie" was
still playing in the train compartment.

He went into a frenzy. Leo asked how he could have left his
calculator on the train, at which point Matthew fixes a glare on
Dad and says, "Why don't you ask Mr. Conductor." I thought he
was talking about the train conductor, so I couldn't understand
why Leo slapped him, unless she had suddenly developed a passionate attachment to British Rail.

It must say something about all the good will which has
lingered in Canterbury for so many centuries that by the train trip
home, we had decided a highpoint in the tales of our two families
was the story of "Mr. Conductor . . . whack."

Proust and I love Paris. He did some of his best writing on the boat train there. Listen to his feelings on completing
the description of a steeple:

> I found such a sense of happiness, felt that it had so entirely re-
> lieved my mind of the obsession of the steeples, and the mystery
> which they concealed, that, as though I myself were a hen and had
> just laid an egg, I began to sing at the top of my voice.

Isn't that a wonderful way to describe writing—like laying an egg? So nicely unpretentious for Proust.

Writing is such a wonderful way to live life again. I thank heaven I had the good sense to begin my novel about this trip while in the midst of it. And get to live every day over again every night.

Today was indeed chapter-worthy. As I think we all now know, boarding and deboarding trains are rather traumatic experiences for our group. When Uncle Thomas is involved in the endeavor, it becomes as difficult physically as it is emotionally.

The process of getting a man in a wheelchair onto a train usually comes down to throwing the man in the wheelchair onto the train and then throwing his wheelchair on after him. And next, a prayer that our compartment is not too far away, since it is not easy to drag Uncle Thomas, who manages to maintain his dignity in the damnedest of situations.

We had just thrown in Uncle Thomas and were pitching in the suitcases (trying our best not to hit him) when we looked in to see if Uncle was still conscious (Nanny had been aiming rather carelessly) and saw Leona singlehandedly dragging him down the train aisle. She was doing such a fine job, we thought it better not to throw her off by offering assistance, and have referred to her as Mother Courage ever since.

We were still admiring her when we began to notice that everyone who passed by our compartment was staring in very curiously. We know we are a strange group, but we didn't see how everyone on the train could have figured it out so fast.

Dad stepped out to investigate and saw that the word *Mutilés* had been stamped on our compartment. Because of Thomas's wheelchair. But *Mutilés* seemed a word full of so many more possibilities than one man in a wheelchair could offer. So as the next group of passengers paused and stared in, we all assumed the most grotesque positions we could think up. I do believe we gave them their word's worth.

This day, which I had begun with so many misgivings, was, as it happened, one of the few on which I was not unduly wretched.

Dear Proust, I could not agree with you more. Last night after arriving in Paris, most of the group was pooped, but Mom, Dad, and Matthew and I wanted to go for a walk, and as we walked it began to rain, and though all I did was hold Matthew's arm while he held the umbrella, well, heavens above, this is Paris, and it felt like a great deal more.

When we arrived back at the hotel, I immediately tried to capture the walk in my novel. After I had finished, I was convinced it was the most beautiful thing ever laid down by man or woman, but twelve hours later it read like just about the worst. My work does not stand the test of time.

I was discussing my literary woes with Matthew when he informed me that his novel was progressing very well. I was thrilled to think he'd finally made the switch from fact to fiction, but he told me not to get too excited. It was not going to be a novel for everyone. He had decided to write a cult novel. Dad said he never heard of anyone starting out to write a cult novel. If it is a success artistically and a failure commercially, then maybe it will become a cult novel. But there is no cult waiting for it now.

I found out today that the heroine of Matthew's cult novel is called Mama Betsy. Apparently Matthew is more spellbound by my dear mother than I'd imagined. We have all now started calling her Mama Betsy, and though Matthew still refers to Dad as Mr. Conductor, I've decided to start calling him Daddy Oliver so he won't feel left out—he'll feel left out enough when he finds out he has no place in the cult novel.

Daddy Oliver said today to Mama Leona (who, by
the way, hasn't made it into the cult novel either—I think it's kind
of an ode to Mama Betsy) after one too many pleas for a sit-down
while touring the country place of Louis Quatorze: "Leona, I did
not lay out Versailles." Just because he didn't lay it out doesn't
mean he couldn't have let us sit down.

Though they can be charming, kleptomaniacs make
hazardous traveling companions. Our day began with the cult
novelist being chased through the halls of the hotel by an inflamed
French maid. He had risen early and decided to do some souvenir
shopping. From the maid's cart. He was still loading up on the
soap when the maid appeared. Chase ensued, but he ducked into a
broom closet and lost her.

After Matthew hid the soap in his suitcase, we headed off to the
stamp markets since Brooke, Matthew, and I are all collectors.
Matthew and I are serious collectors. Brooke picks out stamps she
thinks are pretty. We had a lovely time, Matthew and I buying the
stamps we needed to complete certain sections of our collections
and Brooke buying the attractive ones.

We all then went off to have a sit-down meal, which is something of an event in an Oliver Hailey tour of Europe. It was a
sidewalk café (if Dad does make a concession and sits down, he at
least likes to be near people who are walking), a charming atmosphere until our waiter, Pierre, noticed that when we gave him
back his menus, we gave him back one less than he had given us.
The second French citizen we inflamed today.

As we hurriedly finished the croques monsieur hurled at us and
escaped from the café, Leona pulled the menu from her purse. She
had stolen it to protect Matthew's stamps and the angrier Pierre
got, the more afraid she got to give it back. Perhaps Dad is right
and sit-down meals always end in disaster.

I think Daddy Oliver put the Hailey curse on sit-down meals. It is Bastille Day in Paris. Bob and Leona go out in search of an overpriced dinner. Dad, appalled by their behavior, leads Mom, Brooke, Matthew, and me (Nanny and Thomas think room service is the essence of festive) out into Paris, where there is quite literally dancing in the streets.

Mama Betsy, who cannot resist singing in the kitchen, dancing in the streets, or making a fool of herself on any occasion, is tapping her foot (out of the corner of my eye I see Matthew making notes for his cult novel), and soon we are all holding hands with the crowd and dancing in a great circle.

It was the highlight of a life. Or at least of mine—but that's only because I am constructed normally emotionally. The highlight of Daddy Oliver's life was spotting Bobby and Leona, who could not get into any expensive restaurant, at a sidewalk café.

Tonight Mama Betsy proved, once and for all, how she got the nickname Density, and I proved why I may inherit it.

The remaining Van Scoyks (Bobby has departed for Los Angeles—the land of a sit-down meal a day) and the Haileys have taken three rooms in one of the last great wooden-frame hotels in Edinburgh, Scotland. In the wee hours, the fire alarm goes off. Here follows the scene taking place in each room:

Leona and Matthew's Room: They hop from bed and head for the fire escape, Matthew remembering to grab Leona's purse which contains their passports.

Nanny, Thomas, and Brooke's Room: Brooke must have been the one to hear the alarm, since Nanny and Thomas specialize in deafness. On the way to the lobby they run into a hotel staff member, who takes them down on the elevator, realizing how little luck that group would have on the stairs.

Mom, Dad, and Kendall's Room: Dad hears the alarm and dashes for Nanny, Thomas, and Brooke's room, since he assumes the elevators will not be in use and plans to drag Thomas down eight flights. He arrives at their room only to find the door locked

(Nanny doesn't want anybody trying on her shoes while she's gone). He thinks they are still asleep, bangs on the door, but no answer, and is breaking down the door with a chair when a hotel staff member dashes over to save the door with a skeleton key. Dad sees they have all escaped and runs for the lobby himself.

Meanwhile, Mama Betsy and Kendall are putting on their stockings. They casually decide which of their new Scottish sweaters to save and, after appropriate hesitation, decide to save them all, then prance down the grand staircase, and can't quite understand why they are the subject of ridicule.

As Mama Betsy said in her own defense (mine is I was so sleepy I was doing everything she did, and I can take no blame), "I just couldn't believe the hotel was on fire."

In fact, her suspicions were absolutely correct. It was a false alarm. The hotel was not on fire, but had it been, she would have been one charred novelist.

As our trip draws to an end, we had to torture Matthew really well one last time. We are back in London for a final week, which means six more evenings in the theatre. However, Uncle Thomas, after one too many plays that just didn't quite work, has temporarily given up theatre-going so there was no need for a cab after the play tonight (which, by the way, did work —one can never quite give up the theatre for good).

That meant Precious (as we have taken to calling guess-who) rode the tube for the first time. I think subconsciously the Hailey clan must have been out to get him because we all neglected to mention that to be allowed to leave the station, you have to hold onto your ticket until you reach your destination.

Matthew left his ticket on the train seat. His mistake was revealed to him after we had all stepped off when Daddy Oliver asked, "Where's your ticket, Matthew?" Considerate of Daddy Oliver not to ask that question a few moments earlier.

Precious went white, leaped back on the train, grabbed his ticket, and leaped back off before the doors closed and he was carried away forever. Then he was alternately corrected first for leaving his ticket and then for jumping back on and possibly being whisked away to another station just to retrieve his ticket. Matthew said not to worry—had that happened, he simply would have gotten off at the next station, left the foul tube, and hailed a cab back to the flat.

Brooke and I spent the walk from the tube station to the flat waiting for a calm to settle and then screaming at him, "Where's your ticket, Matthew?"

Daddy Oliver, who loves a good torture, decided to join in but showed his superior skill with an original question: "Where's your raincoat, Matthew?"

Precious screamed, "I left it on the tube" and started to dash back when the group took pity on him and pointed out that he was wearing it. He took it off immediately and looked at it. Then he threw it over his head to have, I suspect, a good tube-raincoat-family-life-induced cry.

When we got back to the flat, Brooke told me that at the beginning of the trip, she thought she was in love with Matthew, but after a month together, as far as she was concerned, I could have him.

Frankly, a month together has not exactly done wonders for my relationship with Matthew. But after a month apart, I suspect I'll like him just as much as I did before I lived with him. And, who knows, maybe someday I'll like him as much when I'm with him as I do when I'm without him.

Our last night in London and we saw a stinker of a play, but I'll always be grateful for how much my mind wandered. It wandered so much that I began to wonder what I would do with a beautiful stage like that.

No sooner had I begun to wonder than two characters of my own invention (though bearing great resemblance to Matthew and me), made their entrance. They were on their honeymoon (I went ahead and married us—I felt Brooke gave me permission last night), and they had so much to say to each other that they talked for practically a whole act.

But, of course, before they could finish out the act in any privacy whatsoever, the voices of Mama Leona, Daddy Oliver,

Mama Betsy, Bobby, Baby Brooke, Nanny, and Uncle Thomas were heard from the suite next door. All characters in my play, they had, of course, accompanied Matthew and me on our honeymoon.

So I am abandoning prose for dialogue. I think I was writing my novel because I felt that after graduating high school, the thing to do is write a novel. But I'm going to write this play because the characters started talking and haven't stopped yet. And how lovely for me that we can all still talk together, even after the Van Scoyks and Haileys are living in separate houses again.

WHAT I DID:

Met Proust.

Started a novel.
Abandoned a novel.

Fell out of love (as Matthew's first London taxi pulled
away from the curb and he waved).
Fell back into love (as our car pulled away from the Los
Angeles airport and I waved).

Started a play (to continue where life left off).

LIFE
WITHOUT PATTERN

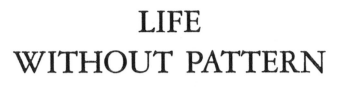

WHAT I HOPE TO DO:

Just about everything.

For the past several days I have been working on my play—if it can be called that—in the morning while my mother works on her new novel. Yesterday she asked me what I was writing. "Nothing," I replied.

Everything else I have ever written I have read to someone within minutes of writing. I have never been more private or protective of anything than I am of this play. Perhaps I should have always been like this. Perhaps my first novel about the sixteen cousins—started and abandoned the summer I was twelve—would have turned out better . . . though somehow I doubt it.

At twelve o'clock tonight, simultaneously, the clock began to strike and I began to read *The Personal History, Adventures, Experience, & Observation of David Copperfield The Younger of Blunderstone Rookery (Which He never meant to be Published on any Account)*.

When I wrote my grandmother (my mother's mother) to tell her I was planning to read it, she replied, *"David Copperfield* is my favorite Dickens—in spite of the fact my mother Bessie paid me five dollars to read it the first time (I was only twelve)."

Brooke just announced that she was "farting paragraphs." How I love living in such a literary family.

Aside from all her paragraphs (Brooke does not like padding and can tell a good story in a paragraph), she also has the most delightful idea for a children's book. The story of our family through the eyes of Puli. Brooke could be very threatening if I weren't so well adjusted.

Puli just got home from a whole week at the veteri-
narian—I hope he didn't miss us as much as we did him. He had
to have a lot of teeth pulled (we're supposed to start brushing the
remainders) and had pancreas problems, but I am happy to say he
has been cured of them. Of course, he now requires vitamins, pills,
ear drops, and geriatric dog food, but other than that, he is most
chipper.

Today I found a book written in 1947 called *Present-
Day Italian,* and I am going to teach myself the language in preparation for future Hailey/Van Scoyk travels. So far I have read
only the part about pronunciation, and I am trying to follow the
instructions very carefully about just where to put my tongue
because there are only three words I know how to pronounce in
Italian: *buon giorno, grazie,* and *prego.* Brooke knows a fourth:
scusi. She discovered it in Venice on our second trip to Europe
when she was three and used it in every country. And needed to,
because she was always stepping on people. It was her favorite
European word next to *pièce de résistance* which she would yell at
the slightest provocation, damaging its meaning slightly.

Dickens said, "I have a favorite child and his name is
David Copperfield." I think he may turn out to be mine, too.
   Dickens is said to create such larger-than-life characters, but I
have never read about ones that seem more real. They live on even
after you have finished the novel, when so many great characters
seem to fade away as you turn the last page. Proust spent so much
time with Swann, but I confess I wouldn't know him if I met him
on the street, whereas I pray every day I'll run into the Aged One
from *Great Expectations.*

Dear me, I thought I was nearing the end of the first
act of my play, but I just counted and I've only written seven

pages. Actually, I don't ever want it to end—I'm having such a good time writing it. When I finish it, I'm going to finish my novel and then, perhaps, I'll jump off my high horse.

I think my days with Italian are numbered. I love English. In this language there's only one way to say "you" and that's "you." In French there's *tu* and *vous,* and if I have read this darn book right, the Italians have three ways. I don't see the point in learning the language if I'm going to offend the first Italian I address.

I have finished the first act of my play. It's a little short, but then I think most things are a little long. A twelve-page first act—well, stranger things have been done. Length aside, I must say, I'm awfully proud.

I sadly parted from David Copperfield today. I loved everything about him, though I was a little shocked that he could be totally in love with two different women. Not that he was in love with them at the same time (this is Dickens, for heaven's sake), but that he could be in love with them in the same life. The idea that you can find two people on this earth you can fall in love with has always bothered me. It seems to go against the theory of true love—the thought that there is one person in this universe for whom you are truly meant, and that person for you. It seems to suggest that if you work hard enough at it, you can be meant for anyone. Though I suppose, now that I think about it, that is the more comforting notion.

Never ponder aloud what you will read next because someone will always make a strongly recommended suggestion. Hence, I am now staring at *The Spoils of Poynton* by Henry James. Worse yet, it was recommended by my father, who has questionable taste in novels. It seems he went through a period when he read all these hideously difficult books—even *Moby Dick,* for goodness' sake—and now delights in recommending them to other people. When Mom was struggling with *Life Sentences,* he ordered her to read *The Green Hills of Africa.* The look on her face as she turned the pages was enough to make me seriously doubt his taste.

Apparently my father is right when he says he's never wrong. He is certainly right about Henry James. He told me he loves *The Spoils of Poynton* so much because James wrote it after five years as a failed playwright, so it has all his lingering dramatic instinct. All I know is, it's so good I may even read *The Green Hills of Africa.*

I guess George Bernard Shaw was right when he said anyone can write a first act. Not that my twelve pages really qualify as a first act, but you should see my second act. Seven pages and I've already run out of things to say. But then I don't seem to be able to do anything twice. I started a second painting tonight (I think of the self-portrait as my first real painting). And I think I made a big mistake painting to the strains of Handel. His music is so alive and vibrant I became convinced my painting was as good as his music. Until the record ended. I only paint to dirges from now on.

Today I told Dad I now trusted him totally and asked where he kept *The Green Hills of Africa,* but he suggested I begin with *A Farewell to Arms.*

As for Henry James, I know there will be more of him in my future, but I feel guilty sticking to one author when there are so many left unexplored.

And I admit a little verbal economy will be refreshing. Several readers were reported lost for years in a Henry James sentence.

I just got home from seeing the 1950's television show *Together with Music* starring Mary Martin and Noel Coward. Watching them perform made me want to so much. You would think talent like that would give one an inferiority complex, but I think it's usually the inept who make one feel inept. Greatness and timelessness seem so easy when you watch Noel and Mary.

I'm afraid it must say something about Henry James that I felt guilty at the mere thought of reading another of his books immediately. Yet directly after finishing *A Farewell to Arms,* I went right to Hemingway's *A Moveable Feast.* Forgive me, Henry.

It is the purple dawn. I'm not being fancy (I wouldn't dare after reading Hemingway), it really is purple.

I had some social contact today, but finding out how little my friends have read this summer has had the opposite effect I supposed—I couldn't wait to get back to Ernest, but that may be more a credit to him than a reflection on my illiterate acquaintances.

These people have lived a whole summer and what do they have to show for it? They are going to return for their senior year tomorrow without having learned a thing.

Julie Reich is one of my closest friends and the most literary of the whole class (proof positive of this is that the only thing she ever submitted to our school literary magazine was turned down). Her total reading for the summer consisted of the first five pages of *Pride and Prejudice.* Not being able to get involved stopped her from reaching the sixth.

It takes only the first sentence to get involved in *Pride and Prejudice.* ("It is a truth universally acknowledged, that a single man in possession of a good fortune, must be in want of a wife.") And after reading the second ("However little known the feelings or views of such a man may be on his first entering a neighbourhood, this truth is so well fixed in the minds of the surrounding families, that he is considered as the rightful property of some one or other of their daughters."), I should think anyone of sound mind would want to follow Miss Austen anywhere.

I did my best to bolster Jane's sagging reputation (it hit its nadir at this gathering), but I seriously doubt whether any of these people will ever see the sixth page of any of her six novels.

Perhaps I am underestimating them reading-wise, but I think I've been overestimating them life-wise.

One girl whom I thought I knew well mentioned casually tonight that she was still recovering from getting stoned two days ago. I was shocked, but then I am shocked too easily to be taken too seriously. How naive can a person be? I suppose I should consider the word "very."

I realize I have always overlooked the use of drugs, alcohol, and sex by my classmates in an attempt not to feel odd man out.

Why are there so few of us who find life exciting enough not to need to hallucinate? Perhaps if what my classmates were facing now was life and not just another year of high school, they would share my excitement. I have a feeling it is conventional choices that lead to unconventional stimulants.

WHAT I DID:

923 pages of Charles Dickens, 196 pages of Henry James, 458 pages of Ernest Hemingway, and 19 pages of my own.

UNCONVENTIONAL CHOICES

WHAT I HOPE TO DO:

Make as many as possible.

Though it is no longer a part of my life, I suppose it should be noted that formal education began again today. I have not had one moment of regret. A fact that stuns me. But I seem to have a knack for life decisions. It is certainly a wonderful thing to go all summer and not worry about school or have cardiac arrest when "Back to School" ads start appearing. Yet I remember school very fondly, which must be proof I left at the right time.

Autodidacts do not get the same respect household-wise that students of formal education do. When school started, Nanny began making up Brooke's bed. I waited for that seventy-eight-year-old to make her way into my room to do mine, but she never came. I followed her to her room and asked if she didn't think autodidacts should get their beds made? She said she didn't. I was offended educationally, but I'm just writing it off to the terrible seventy-eights.

Actually, I rather like making my bed (though I like to save doing it till early evening—you never know when Nanny might change her mind, and I'd hate for the bed to be made the morning she did).

I started my second act for a second time and now all is going swimmingly. I so enjoy writing my play. The thing is, before I write any more of it I must decide what the plot is—not that I necessarily want one, but it does help to give the chatter a direction.

I have decided I like writing at night. I look forward to it all day. It is something to build to. I just hope I am not taking myself catastrophically seriously.

I am in awe of autumn. I just stand outside and stare at trees—and keep a lookout for other members of the family who might very well have me committed. But now that I'm no longer in school, I finally have time to enjoy my favorite season. It is all so beautiful. I feel a bit like Wordsworth walking near Tintern Abbey. I can finally understand how those poets felt.

You know, now that I think about it, it defies understanding to teach the Romantics in a classroom. Sitting in that room, pulling up my knee socks (Brooke has given up on me fashion-wise) and trying to get comfortable at my desk, I had no feeling for any of them.

Though I'm not going to read any of the Romantics right this minute and disprove my wonderful theory, I do feel closer to them in spirit.

An unproductive day ended with me going to bed chanting, "You're a failure, you're a failure"—which produced a curiously comforting effect.

The first acrimony of an autodidact: the fact that there is a barrier to break down every day with Brooke because I have not had to sit through seven and a half hours of school. She hates me a little bit for it. But usually if I approach her very nicely after she's had something to eat, then all is forgiven.

Tomorrow I'm going with Dad to pick her up at school. I have been avoiding doing this because I hate to get so close to formal education again. And I will have to sit on the floorboard to avoid acquaintances and questions about just what I am doing with my life. But I'll risk it to see Brooke that much sooner.

You know, I'm actually lonely for that child when she's at school. I think this is retribution for the way I treated her when she was little. I was always busy doing homework and kept wishing she'd just say hello, then leave me alone. I had an image of the perfect little sister, who would come in, give me a kiss, then leave with our relationship still in a state where I could smile after her —as opposed to her demanding my attention and then crying and screaming and yelling when she didn't get it. I never thought the sins against the little sister could catch up with me.

Just three minutes ago I was in such an indecisive mood about what to read next. But the solution has just come in the form of *The Brothers Karamazov*. I am very excited because, first and most important, it is so much shorter than I expected.

Tonight I went with Dad to the playwrights' group he leads. About thirty playwrights meet every week and read scenes from their works in progress. It all sounded very interesting when I was in school and Dad would come home and tell us about the scenes. Sitting through some of them is a different matter. I suppose I was rather superior and nasty in the car going home (the only people who are ever superior are the people who have no right to be) and we had a small argument, but today he has forgiven and forgotten all (and, worst of all, I may have to go again!).

I have just seen *True Confession* with Carole Lombard, Fred MacMurray, John Barrymore, and Una Merkel. I have been trying to pin down star quality lately—I can't seem to, but it was there in abundance, I know that.

My favorite line was John Barrymore's, to a man who had just insulted him, "Would that life were all as simple as you." I can't wait to say that to Brooke.

I was thinking it's strange being born after people die—I know that's a silly thought, since it happens to all of us, but I mean here I am born twenty-four years after Carole Lombard died and I don't know what I mean. It's just so strange to know first that people have died and then to love them. I certainly do miss her— only a little later than most.

Nanny is the only person who really understands the way I feel about movie stars of our era—our era being the one Nanny was lucky enough to have been born into and the one I have adopted.

She is an encyclopedia of scandal about the stars' personal lives, but her devotion to them remains unshakable. This woman lived through a son crippled by polio at age ten, horrible poverty, a terribly painful marriage, and says the saddest day in her life was when she found out Robert Taylor and Barbara Stanwyck were getting divorced.

I have finished my play and, I confess, I love it. One day when I look back I may not, but I truly hope I never change that much. I'm going to copy it over now—I would be taking myself too seriously if I typed it—and I'm either going to make each act longer or else add more acts. I never realized length would be my great artistic problem.

Tonight I saw, for the very first time, my mother's stage adaptation of her first novel, *A Woman of Independent Means,* based on the life of her grandmother. Barbara Rush was the only actress on stage, yet I came away feeling as if it had been brimming over with people. Her performance has given me my greatgrandmother. A great performance brings another person into the world, and that is what she, with the help of the midwife/director Norman Cohen, has done.

And I want to say something about Mom. I was so overwhelmed hearing her words tonight, I swore I would try to be grateful for her every moment instead of just taking her sweetness, lovingness, and kindness for granted—as is my habit. It worked for a few minutes, but then I just started taking her for granted again. It must be impossible not to take one's mother for granted. Perhaps it is the secret of a really good mother. She gives you everything without ever sending out the smallest signal that you should realize what she's doing. I have certainly been indulged, but as Bess Steed Garner, my fictionalized greatgrandmother, says, "I have found the most loving people are those who have been loved." I just better turn out to be pretty damn loving.

Tonight I finished my painting and promptly hid it in the hallway because I cannot stand the sight of it. And I have given up copying over my play for the opposite reason. I am so in love with it that I don't dare change it. So here I am, scared to use a pen, and too furious at how my paintbrushes have betrayed me to pick them up again.

Hemingway said in *A Moveable Feast* about Dostoevsky, "How can a man write so badly, so unbelievably badly, and make you feel so deeply?"

I haven't begun to feel too deeply yet, but I'll agree with the writing badly part. Dos. does lecture a bit—no one in real life could talk as long as his characters do without being interrupted. So I am being forced to provide my own interruption by going to sleep.

I could live a million years and never finish *The Brothers Karamazov.* I am beginning to have as little respect for novels as Jane Austen's characters do. They only respect readers of history.

Since Dostoevsky could not give me any answers to life, perhaps just reading about the progression of life itself will. I'm in no mood to waste time, so I'm heading straight for the height of civilization. I don't think anyone has ever really found the answers to life we all need, but at least in Greece they were always looking.

Will Durant is going to be the man to provide the basic path to my new world, then I'll do the branching out myself.

I'll read Will to get an overview and then works of the age to decide if I really like these people.

Why Will? Basically, large print and a good marriage. I didn't mind squinting through *Anna Karenina,* but history has got to make the sacrifices in our relationship. And as I read about the Greeks, I'll keep in the back of my mind Will and Ariel. I have always thought they had one of the most romantic relationships in the world. Living all of civilization together. So much more than just spending a lifetime together.

Immersed in *The Life of Greece.* I love a historian who's a person, and Will is not one to be overshadowed by a civilization. He is also possessed of a refreshing, albeit historian-type, wit:

> Anaximander, who, though he lived from 611 to 549 B.C., ex-pounded a philosophy surprisingly like that which Herbert Spencer, trembling before his own originality, published in A.D. 1860.

It is Halloween and I am a wreck. I have never been the most skilled dispenser of Halloween candy, but tonight I have failed more hopelessly than usual. Having had years of experience as a trick-or-treater, I remember how I hated to make the trip up to a house, ring a strange doorbell, and avoid a snarling dog, only to be rewarded with a single Tootsie Roll. So I'm an over-generous dispenser, yelling at little children to come back and let me give them more candy.

Now the other problem: I myself was usually an early trick-or-treater. If I wasn't out of the house and on the road by a quarter past six, my foot started tapping. Tonight, it's after seven and we've had only two trick-or-treaters. I become nostalgic about the good old days and Mom laments that all the children on the street have grown up. Stoically (despite the fact I haven't quite gotten to the Stoics yet), I position myself in the living room with *The Life of Greece,* hoping against hope another little ghost may show up.

A few minutes later I hear chains rattling, and pounding on the door. Three grunting, horribly masked children appear. I am so delighted I give them handfuls. They grunt happily. After telling them how frightening they are, I begin to shut the door. As they move away, I hear a little voice say, "Goddamn, she's nice." It is a high point.

Figuring that was the end, I go back to Greece. All is well. There is not enough candy left for me to be accused of overbuying one more time but there is enough to make the day after Halloween a happy one. My mind slowly drifts back to Pythagoras when . . . need I say it? At least thirty little trick-or-treaters come to the door.

The day after Halloween will not be such a happy one, but tonight was grand—even if I did have to give away all the candy Nanny hides with her underwear.

Using the works mentioned in *The Life of Greece*, I am trying to compile a reading list of ancients. I suppose I should also read some books on Greek art to be well-rounded—oh, and what about language? Hard as I try to visualize it, I just can't see myself learning Greek. The major works I would at least like to peek into are these:

Plutarch's *Lives*. Reason for reading: The concept of examining two lives and then comparing them is so interesting, plus we have the set that belonged to my greatgrandmother Bess (and I respect her enough to think she may have even read it).

Hesiod's *Theogony*, where so much of the ancient mythology is put down, and his *Works and Days*. I love the fact that *Works and Days* was written as a lesson on how to live for his good-for-nothing brother. I feel I ought to read it so I'll know what to say to Brooke in future years. I am having such fun making this list. I'm so glad I'm making it myself instead of asking anyone. Even if I overlook essentials, I so prefer telling myself what to read. Being told what to read by someone else is a violation of basic human rights. Or at least basic literary ones.

Histories by Herodotus, Thucydides, Polybius, and Xenophon. One does have to know what went on.

Pindar (at least one ode).

A smattering of Greek verse. If Matthew can quote Sappho, I want to be able to.

Aeschylus. First of all, I would love to know how to pronounce his name. Only seven of his plays survive, though he is said to have written ninety. I feel the least we can do is read the seven that are with us (let us hope they are among his best). Though since I think we only own *Agamemnon* (the first play in the *Oresteia*), I'll probably settle for that and call it quits. I was wrong. . . . I just looked . . . we have the whole *Oresteia* . . . damn.

Sophocles. Seven plays and a fragment survive, and he wrote well over a hundred. I'll begin with the Oedipus trilogy and start preserving my own fragments by storing the early pages of my play in the freezer section of the refrigerator (a trick learned from Mom, who, for safekeeping, kept *A Woman of Independent Means* on ice until it was published).

Euripides. Eighteen of eighty to ninety plays survive, and I like him best already because he was the least honored in his lifetime. I only hope he knows how well *Medea, The Trojan Women,* and a few of the others are thought of now. I'll begin with the aforementioned and *Alcestis,* too, if I'm in a good mood.

Aristophanes. Eleven of only some twenty plays remain (comedy was hard even in ancient times). I think I may only sample *Lysistrata.* I just have a feeling I am not going to like this man. And my instincts about men are usually right, though I've never dealt with one quite this old before.

Plato and Aristotle. I'd like to know if they're really as bright as I've heard.

Joyously happy. I have been adding to my play. On a whim, I decided to start typing it and find that has started me rewriting it. Problems that never seemed apparent on a legal pad become all too clear on the elegance of a typed sheet.

I heard such a wise thing at the playwrights' group tonight. Laird Koenig, one of the playwrights, said, in talking about a scene, "I get worried when an author likes one character better than the other." I think that's just hopelessly wise and will help my play no end. I've got to stop liking the character modeled on me best.

You know, I misjudged those playwrights. I guess it is hard to be a playwright and not write a bad scene every so often, but, as Dad says, you can learn more from a bad play than a good one until you can write a bad one all by yourself. Then it's time to start learning from good ones.

Truth to tell, I'll always prefer good ones. I think a bad play is like being trapped in the worst that life can offer. But a good play is so much better than life, one sees why there are so few really good plays—life can't take the competition.

I am in the depths of despair about my play. It stinks on ice. And can a full-length play run thirty minutes? Because I can't think up much more. The truth is, I don't know how I am going to go on writing at all, since I am pretty well convinced it's all excrement. But who knows, there is always the vague chance it's just shit. The only thing is, I'm going to have to ask soon and if anyone tells me it's anything but brilliant, I'll die. I type with one hand and hold my nose with the other, but at least I feel I'm getting something done.

Well, you won't believe who I just saw on television. Matthew! He and his school friends congregated to watch *The Day After*, the groundbreaking television movie about nuclear war, and called the media to see if they would be interested in teenagers' reactions. And the media fell for it!

I didn't have the courage to watch *The Day After*. Instead I found my fingers moving toward our cassette of the musical version of *Our Town* which starred Eva Marie Saint, Paul Newman and Frank Sinatra. Thornton Wilder allowed the program to be aired only once on television, in 1955, but after we saw and loved it at a screening at the Directors' Guild, Eva Marie sent us a copy

—a gesture as sweet and beautiful as her Emily. And just what I needed tonight.

From the first time I saw *Our Town*, I have tried to see each day as a great gift and the more I have tried, the more they have been.

I think everyone who has the power to start a nuclear war should be made to see *Our Town* at least once a day—until the last thing they want is the power to destroy life. If they could see how precious one life is, perhaps they would stop seeing nine hundred million lives as an endurable loss.

I read in *The Life of Greece* today that after the collapse of an expedition to Syracuse in 415 B.C., whose failure had been forecast in *The Trojan Women,* captured Athenians were given their freedom if they could recite passages from the plays of Euripides. That's the best incentive for being well-read I ever heard.

I keep seeing myself performing my play in front of an audience who just adores it—but it's going to have to be an audience packed with morons because I can't think of a person I know who could tolerate it. It's obviously time for a little break and a big snack.

I have found an intellectual soul mate. In an interview, Bette Midler said she was plugging away on Will and Ariel Durant, adding her favorite person in history was the man who could fart the "Marseillaise" (I guess she's already gotten to *Rousseau and Revolution*).

Brooke and I began our day with an argument on the subject of nakedness. I find it necessary when going from nightgown to street clothes. Brooke, however, does not. She is appalled by the state and manages to go from one outfit to another without

ever being totally uncovered. We never should have let her learn
to get dressed and undressed by watching Nanny.

The more I read about the Greeks, the more I am
beginning to act like them. I look for signs all the time and I bathe
my feet regularly.

I have just heard the most moving, yet simple short
story—not by a famous writer, but by my yet unpublished friend,
Julie Reich. I never knew anyone could be such a good writer and
not have read Jane Austen.

Julie did not graduate early, and so is now free to take all those
electives with which they tempt you to stay for a final year of high
school. Of course, I have to admit, without all those electives, she
would never have gotten to take a fiction-writing class, and the
lovely story she read to me this afternoon might never have been
written.

But I do worry about any writer with talent being safe in a
fiction-writing class. Certainly, formal education did all it could to
discourage my parents.

The only "B" my father ever got was in playwriting. And my
mother's history is more encouraging still to the autodidact, even
if it did discourage her for twenty years. She took her only cre-
ative-writing course in college, received a "C," and was told by
the professor, who was new to the college, that he would have
flunked her, but he hated to flunk anyone his first year.

And pleasing as it may have been to receive his fan letter for *A
Woman of Independent Means,* it does not make up for the loss of
confidence that took two decades and Dad to regain.

So I am going to protect Julie Reich. She is the first writer
who's been all mine to encourage. My parents have so many writers they encourage. And I read some of the plays and novels that
are left on our doorstep and encourage the writers when I feel like
it, but now I have one all my own.

I'll try my very best to protect her from all the creative hazards of the academic world. And she'll keep me up-to-date on what I'm not missing.

Being of similar sense and sensibilities, she will be the perfect college correspondent.

I HAVE FINISHED *THE LIFE OF GREECE.* I have cracked my first civilization. I now know what went on, in what sequence it went on, and who made it go on. But while governments were being built and philosophies thought up, what were they seeing in the theatre?

So tomorrow, the *Oresteia.* But tonight, *Suspicion* until Cary Grant sells Joan Fontaine's chairs.

Leona just called to say she has contracted yet another fatal disease.

My childhood has been spent watching Dad and Leo trade their fatal illnesses. One would contract something, have it for a while, get bored with it, cure himself or herself of it, and a few months later, the other would have gotten it.

But now that my father really has Parkinson's disease, I know their fun days of dieting, losing a pound, and being convinced this meant cancer are over.

Illness is losing two of its greatest allies by really saddling them with something.

But it is funny how they are still working as a team. Dad got his disease and now, not a year later, Leona has hers. It is one of the mildest forms of lupus, so Dad doesn't think she did quite as well as he.

I hate what is happening to my parents and their friends. A little Bell's palsy here, something undiagnosed there . . . aren't mid-life crises all the fun middle age needs? Must the deterioration of hope be accompanied by the deterioration of the body? Or perhaps that's the reason.

I cannot wait for tomorrow—I'm going to rewrite the last scene of my play. No matter how putrid this play may be, it does have a certain optimism about it and I love it for that. I sometimes think if I did not write I would be a madwoman. Now I am a sane woman with a lot of mad pages.

I finished the *Oresteia* today. For a tragedy, it certainly has a happy ending. I expect it will take the introduction to make me see the true size of it. Because I sure didn't read three of these plays not to see the whole size. Next, the Oedipus cycle. Dad says it shows exactly the way a daughter is supposed to behave. We'll see, Father Brontë.

I do dread for the years to pass and for me to have to look back on my play objectively. During a double feature of *The Philadelphia Story* and *Old Acquaintance*, I think I finished rewriting it.

Earlier this fall I had felt a little lonely staying up so late, but (and I do find this odd) these hours alone have become my favorite (and most productive) part of the day. When I am with just one person, I miss everyone else, but when I am alone (if you don't count the company of my characters, plus Katharine Hepburn, Cary Grant, Jimmy Stewart, Bette Davis and Miriam Hopkins), I feel surrounded.

Just made it through *Antigone*, the last of the Oedipus plays. It is my favorite, though *Oedipus at Colonus*, the second play, will always hold a special place in my heart.

I read it one day when I was sick (and perhaps a little lightheaded) and pretended it was a comedy just to see if it could ever be played that way. Except for the incredibly moving ending, it could almost be taken as a farce—with Oedipus weeping and whining all over the place. By the end, even Antigone (whose

example, I have told my father, I am going to have a very hard
time living up to) is a little put out with him. At one point she
does say, "Enough, Father." I'm afraid I would have said it much
sooner.

I don't measure up to the Greeks' idea of a daughter
and I don't measure up to my own idea of a sister. An older sister,
that is.

As Jessica Mitford says of her eldest sister, Nancy, in *Daughters
and Rebels:*

> . . . I dimly remembered the hushed pall that hung over the
> house, meals eaten day after day in tearful silence, when Nancy at
> the age of twenty had her hair shingled. Nancy using lipstick,
> Nancy playing the newly fashionable ukelele, Nancy wearing trou-
> sers, Nancy smoking a cigarette—she had broken ground for all of
> us, but only at terrific cost in violent scenes followed by silence and
> tears.

The only sacrifice an older sister has to make in an otherwise
easy life compared to that of a younger sister is to break a little
ground. And what happens in our family?

Brooke has already gotten a spade and is breaking away
whereas I, happy with the ground as it is, am stretched out on it
taking a little nap.

We recently had a "call waiting" signal installed on our telephone, which lets you know mid-conversation that another caller
is trying to get through. It is cutting in half the time Dad spends
on boring conversations, but there is a drawback. Whenever Dad
is on an important business call and the beep sounds and he ends
that call, thinking the interruption might be an even more important business call, the new caller inevitably begins the conversation with the words, "Is Brooke there?"

In a state of exasperation, Dad decrees offspring may no longer
receive calls. In an equal state of exasperation, Brooke says she
wants her own phone line. And in a state of total calm (my main

association at this time being with Greeks—who rarely phone), I take a seat for the battle.

All is going as usual—Nanny and Thomas silent but rooting for Brooke, Mom and I speaking up for Brooke, and Brooke screaming for Brooke. But Dad still does a very nice job of holding up his end. Then the phrase I knew was coming is uttered.

Oliver, sensing defeat, but plowing ahead with useless pleas, looks at Brooke and says, "Why can't you be more like Kendall?"

This is a crucial moment in the relationship between sister and sister and father and daughter. Sit back with a smug smile and I've lost a sister. And also, I think, ultimately, a father. Outright, disgusting goody-goodies will not be held up as icons of behavior in days to come.

So, taking a deep breath, I forego my momentary position as perfect child and leap into the fray, making it clear to Dad that I am not being me in an effort to please him, but rather because that is who I am. And Brooke must be allowed to be who she is.

After the fray was over—and the new phone line to be installed next week—Brooke summoned me to her room and said that was the nicest thing anybody had ever said in her defense. But I feel pretty low—the least I can do is come to her defense. I should be leading the offense.

Brooke started on the road to adulthood four years after I did and is gaining on me more quickly than she should have to.

Today I skipped several civilizations and read Robert Browning's long poem, "Christmas Eve." I saw it on the shelf last night and thought it appropriate to the season, if not to my current century. I can still see some of the scenes, he described them so vividly. What an emotional writer. Little wonder she fell for him.

I'd been thinking about the Brownings all day today (Did you know Elizabeth was older than Robert? Remind you of another pair?), and tonight Matthew kissed me for the very first time.

Well, truth to tell, it wasn't really a romantic kiss, but it was—excluding all doubts—a kiss. It was when we were all saying good night after spending Christmas Eve together. He had kissed Mom and Nanny and given Brooke and me his usual embarrassed look. Then Brooke threw herself at him, as she usually does, and he threw her off, as he usually does, and then something happened that's never happened before.

He was standing by the door smiling at me, then he leaned down (he is getting so tall I have decided I need to get a little taller too) and kissed me on the cheek. It is the first time he has ever kissed me. Needless to say, this has been a great year.

Marriage is the topic under consideration. One kiss, it's time to start thinking about it. The question: could I be a part of one?

Dad has only one piece of marriage advice. I've heard him say it to two friends. One of the friends listened to his advice and stayed married, and the other listened to it and then got divorced. All Dad said was that you fall in and out of love with the same person your whole life, and people who understand that stay married, and people who don't, get divorced.

Mom and Dad have stayed married, but I've never seen them fall in and out of love. Maybe they do it when I'm not looking.

Frankly, I don't see why they'd ever have to fall out of love when Mom is pretty much perfect. I don't remember her ever yelling my whole childhood. Dad is the one who gets so worked up (and they tell me he's mellowed).

Their most famous early-marriage fight happened when Mom got a new hairdo apparently so repugnant that Dad was forced, as a way of working out his revulsion, to sprinkle Parmesan cheese on all her underwear.

Yuck! I don't know if I could be married if stuff like that goes on a lot of the time.

I am watching fields whizzing by and imagining myself on a horse riding through them. We are on a train to Chicago to see a production of one of my father's plays.

As I sit here watching the moving fields and thinking how much they look like process shots, I am trying to think up something to write. I read that Ben Hecht wrote the script for *Nothing Sacred,* a great Carole Lombard screwball comedy I have yet to see, on a four-day train trip across the country. Well, I've got a two-day train trip across half the country twice. Which does add up to four days and one country. If only I added up to Ben Hecht.

I am actually thinking of writing a sequel to the Thin Man films. With Nick and Nora aged appropriately. Of course, William Powell is now ninety-one years old. But Myrna Loy is just seventy-nine. The awful truth is I was born about fifty years too late. Sixty-one to be exact. Of course, Nanny was born in 1905, my ideal year of birth, and she wasn't ever buddies with Myrna Loy. You can even be born in the right time and still miss the right life.

Arrived in Chicago in time for a walk before rehearsal. Taking a walk in Chicago in winter means taking a few steps, running into a store (buying something helps to warm up), then taking a few more steps and repeating the pattern till we reach the end of a city block—then turning around and sprinting back to the hotel.

But they say cold weather is better for comedy, since people laugh less when they're hot. So all is well, since the theatre is all-important, and I also have my eye on a gorgeous winter coat (Brooke keeps asking me where I'll wear it in California and I keep telling her to be quiet).

I am sitting in my favorite place in the theatre. Back row, aisle seat, no pressure. Actually, I suspect spending so much time in the back row of a theatre watching actors asked to change

whole performances by curtain time, a playwright pressured to
add a new speech, a director faced with a scene that is simply not
working can either make you want to stay in the back row forever,
thanking God that you take no responsibility for what is happening on that stage, or else make you want to edge a little closer. I
think I'll move up to the next-to-last row.

This trip to Chicago is the first time I have been introduced to a lot of new people since I left school. I hadn't realized
how much more difficult it would be to answer the question,
"What grade are you in?" Eleventh certainly was an easier reply.

Now I let Brooke respond first and hope they'll just forget to
ask me. But after she says eighth, I have no choice but to take a
deep breath and say as quickly as I can, "Well, actually, I've
decided to take a year off between high school and college."

What has amazed me is that the response to this quickly sput-
tered statement is so positive. Nine out of ten think it's a wonderful choice. The only trouble is, I haven't learned how to argue
with the disagreeing tenth. I find myself so politely agreeing with
them that you'd think I'd be spending the next day begging colleges to Federal Express me their catalogues. Of course, I don't
really think there's much point in arguing with the closed-
minded. I have found that no one I truly respect ever disagrees
with me. Of course that makes sense, as I decide after a person
agrees or disagrees with me whether or not I truly respect them.

The play opens tonight, but we boarded the train this
morning. We don't like to stay in a city after the critics have come
out of their caves.

We saw a beautiful last performance. I keep trying to imagine
what it would be like to walk into a theatre and see one of my
father's plays without having grown up alongside them. I can't
help thinking I would be overwhelmed with the feeling that I had
found all I was looking for in the mind of one man.

I always so hate to leave a theatre in which one of Dad's plays
has lived for a while. I doubt if there are any friendships that grow

faster than those connected with a play. Yet once the play is in perfect working order, they seem to end. Or perhaps not so much end as be put on hold until a new play.

As a very well-planned present of fate to cheer us up, we met the sweetest taxi driver, who drove us back to our hotel after the play. He liked us the minute he found out we were not from Chicago. For some unknown reason, he hates all Chicagoans. He asked if we could guess where he was from, and Dad guessed Egypt and hit it right on the nose, and the relationship was sealed. He said he would be at the hotel this morning to take us to the train station, adding his only regret is that he did not meet us earlier so he could have introduced us to his pet snake (the most current in a long line of pet snakes—they keep running away from home, he says, but I think he is getting his revenge on the people of this city).

We woke up this morning to a Chicago looking beautiful but half buried from an overnight blizzard. The usually packed cab stand was deserted, except for our beloved Chicago-hating Egyptian. As we approached, a woman was begging him to let her have the cab. We were within earshot when she made her fatal mistake:

"But I'm a native Chicagoan," she pleaded.

"That is the best reason yet for not letting you in my cab."

He drove us to the station without turning on his meter. He said he wanted no money for the ride. We were friends. He is going to school, getting a master's degree (the first pedant I've liked), and Dad said it was his education that was important and forced the money on him. He mourned again that we would not be meeting his pet snake and drove away. Perhaps the best friendships are the impermanent ones. My first lesson of the year.

I was hoping for a few last night, but I didn't get any. We had a delicious late New Year's Eve supper at the hotel (best food of 1983—smoked salmon, cream of crab soup, beef Wellington, floating island). I was planning some emotional, optimistic, New Year talk, but instead we all listened to Brooke make a list of the friendships she was planning to end in 1984.

If only I could spend this year getting done all the things I want to do. Sometimes I just walk—no, storm—around the house, aching with all the things I want to do. I want time to move fast and yet I want it to stand still. Actually, I want to move fast and make the world stand still. When I am not obsessed by the feeling that I was born too late, I know I was born just in time. Just in time to catch hold of my favorite era. And in some way connect myself with it forever. I just want to take the world and shake it and wring it until I get everything I want from it. In case you've forgotten, I'm still a seventeen-year-old who has not yet come to grips with that fact.

My first educational accomplishment of the year has been to read the entire introduction to *The Complete Plays of Aristophanes*—I have an awful tendency to skip introductions, but this one has led to my greatest ancient-world discovery.

Did you realize Aristophanes was the first known playwright to create his own characters with their own world? The tragedians all used characters from mythology. I wonder how he got the idea. Imagine what a brainstorm that must have been. Somehow it seems as if all the great discoveries have already been made—or does every lazy slob think that?

Soon Brooke will be pushing the wrong button in the train bathroom again and turning that little space into a shower when she only meant to flush. She did it both nights crossing the country heading east, so I don't see why she shouldn't do it going west. I really wish she would give in and just check quickly to see which button she is pressing, but Brooke makes it a policy not to read any word she doesn't have to.

She didn't. She's dripping wet and in a nasty mood. Just the kind of person I've always dreamed of sharing a small space with.

Charles and Katherine (the stage's alter egos of Matthew and me) were born tonight.

No wonder my mother wants to dedicate all her books to my father. I feel the same way. We were sitting alone in the train compartment and, out of the blue, he asked what I was writing (and I wasn't even writing at the time). I said, "Just my thoughts," and then, in a panic, I took out my play and began reading it over to myself. There was not one amusing line there. But I decided to go by the signs from the gods (you see what reading Greeks has done to me). I decided that if the door between the sleeper compartments slid to the right, I would read my play to him.

Well, unfortunately, it flew to the right and, with more courage than I have ever used in my whole life, I said, "Would you like to hear some of what I've written?"

And he said, "I'd love to. What is it?"

"A play," I answered.

And from then on, it was a dream. I couldn't believe I was letting Charles and Katherine live for someone else besides me. I couldn't believe they could live for anyone else besides me.

But they did. Dad called the play a masterpiece and me a genius, and I seriously doubt an upper berth on a train moving across the middle of the United States has ever held a happier person.

WHAT I DID:

Had a bumpy first date with Dostoevsky.
Began to live civilization.
Became a playwright (at least for one night on a moving train).

COMING TO GRIPS
WITH
NO FACTS

WHAT I HOPE TO DO:

Be born in 1905 (1908 also perfectly acceptable).

Home to Hollywood. I just turned on an Alan Ladd/Veronica Lake movie to hear Alan Ladd say, "Besides, that crummy brother of yours needed killing." A little *film noir* has reminded me to pray for a peaceful new year.

I saw some of my school acquaintances tonight—the last night of their Christmas vacation—and was questioned exhaustively about just what I am doing. I tried to answer as best I could, but as my two main areas of interest at the moment are Demosthenes and Preston Sturges, and they couldn't discuss the works of either, we didn't get very far.

They can answer so easily when asked what they are doing with their lives. All they have to say is what colleges they are applying to. It is much harder to explain what I'm doing with mine, yet I want to keep doing it.

Whenever I worried about graduating early with no plans for college, I would tell myself that I was just taking a year off and if I hated my year without school, I could begin looking at college catalogues as early as June and spend the fall practicing the essays for my applications. When January came and it was time to apply, I would be ready. Then somehow I would muddle through the nine months until orientation week.

It is now January of my year off and I have not opened a college catalogue, which means—since school takes so much advance planning—I will now be taking at least two years off from school, and quite possibly the rest of my life.

When I could read the Romantics without emotion in school

and be moved to tears by Hemingway reading him all alone, I find it hard to imagine returning to a classroom. When I can get up in the morning and think about my play as opposed to the tortures of P.E., I know that the life I want is here.

I wish them happiness at all those venerable old institutions they'll be attending, but I know that having tasted freedom, I could never set foot in school again.

Perhaps I will be missing something. Too many people look back on the college years as the best of their lives for me to be naive enough to think they are without meaning. But tomorrow I will be spending with Hesiod. We are separated by twenty-eight centuries tonight, but in twenty-four hours I'll know him well.

I'm being arrogant, I know. But I have found that being a minority leads to arrogance. It's very necessary when faced by twenty people who seem so sure of their life choices. Those who have convention on their side can be good and kind, but lack of convention sometimes leads to severe personality flaws, a theory I'm afraid I often prove.

Brooke and I have been trying to decide which of Mom's looks we find the most irritating. With very little arguing, we both voted for her famous "confused" look. This look occurs when Mom does not understand what we are saying (frequently). The look consists of her mouth puckering in a helpless kind of way, her nose tilting skyward as if in search of an explanation there, and her eyes looking a lot like Puli's when he wants to be let out.

I wonder if we would tease Mom so much if she did not have her professional reputation and gobs of material success to take comfort in.

I remember when Brooke was in a heated argument with Mom (though Brooke was the only one who was hot) and finally screamed, "You're just jealous of my life." Of course, Mom is too kind to defend herself, but I had to interject, "Yes, Brooke, what this best-selling novelist really longs to be is a seventh grader."

It has taken Euripides to show me the real tragedy of Greek tragedy. Tonight I read his *Alcestis* and I loved it as much as Capra's *It's A Wonderful Life*.

Every word seemed to weep. It was heartrending until the ending, when Alcestis is given back life just as George Bailey was.

The play has one of those great situations it takes mythology to provide. Admetus is fated to die but will be spared if he can find someone to die for him. After his parents and all his friends have refused, it is Alcestis, his wife, who says she will.

Here lies the only problem of the play in that it is hard to feel sympathy for a man who mourns so for his wife when she is dying to save him. And yet I think it takes less bravery to die for the one you love than to live on alone.

That has to be the bravest and the most senseless thing any of us is ever asked to do. I have always tried to share the Frank Capra conviction that everything works out for the best, and I can see a point to almost all that goes on in the world except losing the one you have found to love all your life.

So I'll ascribe more noble motives to Admetus than Euripides ever gives him, and I think I may also have to abandon Greek tragedy for a while. You wouldn't expect me to watch *Mrs. Miniver* right after *It's a Wonderful Life*—I'd have to see a little of *Theodora Goes Wild* in between. So I'm heading for Aristophanes.

Aristophanes has cheered me up considerably. I've read *Lysistrata*, *The Birds*, and *The Clouds*. I am ashamed to say he was the Greek I dreaded reading (because I thought he'd be silly—I hate a silly ancient).

What he is is lyrical. Reading *Clouds*, I felt as if I were floating in them. I can't believe that the happiness these ancient works give has been here for twenty-five hundred years and still remains so fresh.

I am falling in love with every Greek I meet.

Add Peter Jennings to the noncollegiate journalist list: a high school dropout. I must call Matthew immediately to tell him. I spend a great many of my waking hours trying to figure out a way to keep Matthew from going to college. How people can realize something is a waste of life and yet still consider it a necessary step is beyond me.

Of course, I am lucky when it comes to my chosen profession. No one ever asked a writer if he or she had a degree, possibly because most of the great ones didn't.

On to new ancients. Today was spent reading Heracleitus, Parmenides, Empedocles, Simonides, Tzetzes, and *Cosmopolitan.*

Typing (when it's not my own work) occupies the mundane side of my brain just perfectly, so the other half is free to think up ideas. I can never think up ideas when I try to think up ideas, but when my brain thinks it is typing a letter for Dad, it doesn't keep such a close watch over the ideas, and a few can make their escape.

All my ideas of late have been appearing because of something I said to Puli (in one of our frequent conversations). He was standing in front of a door, patiently waiting to be let out, and as I passed by, I said, "Puli, if you want out, just say so." Since he so rarely talks, I went ahead and opened the door for him without a verbal request and as I did, I realized that when I talked to Puli, I sounded a little like Alice Brady in *My Man Godfrey.* And I thought, one day I should put what I just said to Puli into a screwball comedy. Then I remembered the genre is dead.

But as far as I'm concerned, great genres never die. I am going to write a screwball comedy, and then after I finish it, I have an idea for a Greek tragedy.

I started a new painting today. The problem with my last painting is that it really wasn't my style, but then so few of my paintings are.

This one probably won't be either. It will be my first landscape or, more accurately, poolscape. Though our pool is not really a normal, well-adjusted type pool. It thinks it is a swamp. It was built when Brooke and I were small, and so is very, very shallow, built more for the small people we were than for the tall people we were to become. However, since most swimming is of a horizontal nature, it really doesn't matter and it is lovely to be able to offer small swimming visitors a whole half a pool to run around in rather than the usual shallow step.

The other reasons our pool thinks it is a swamp are really the fault of Dad. First of all, he thinks trimming any living thing is a very mean and spiteful thing to do. So the ivy has spread the word that Oliver's house is a sanctuary, and we are surrounded by it. It was also Dad's idea that the bottom of the pool should be painted black. It does look much prettier and more mysterious, but I am glad he had the color changed after Brooke and I had outgrown our fear of stray sharks lurking in the pool.

The real reason I want to paint our little swamp is because it is at the center of our living. Our house is kind of like a medieval castle in reverse. There is a bridge (covered, of course, by Oliver's ivy) leading from the driveway to the house, but instead of a moat surrounding our castle, our castle surrounds our moat. At the front of the moat/swamp/pool is the main house, where the kitchen and dining and living rooms and Nanny and Brooke and I all live, though not in too close proximity.

Dad thinks the reason we have all been able to live together for so long is because our bedrooms are so far apart. The bedrooms belonging to Brooke and me are on one side of the house, but the living room has to be crossed to get to Nanny. It seemed a frighteningly long way when Brooke and I were little, and some time in the middle of every night we would feel the need to leave our beds and get into Nanny's. In fact, this midnight crossing seems to be a habit with anyone who sleeps on our side of the house. Reportedly, a former owner used to do the same thing every night so he could get into bed with his children's nanny.

Built on next to my room, but up a long flight of stairs is Mom and Dad's room. It was built up so high so as not to lose a little stream which used to flow underneath, but we were out of town when the final construction was done and came home to find cement everywhere. Dad cursed the contractor, but it actually turned out to be a wonderful mistake because after using the space for Ping-Pong for a few years, we decided to wall in our lovely cement floor and make a new room. And that is what we did and what we have called it ever since. It is part library, part study, mostly playroom, but we can never make ourselves call it anything but "the new room." Until we add on another.

Next to the new room is Thomas's room, which was once a guest house where one infamous former owner tried to kill his wife (good marriages abounded in our house). An act which gives the room great character, we feel. And Thomas's room is connected by a long, winding ramp to the main house, which is easy to navigate in a wheelchair, but hell, I discovered many years ago, on a tricycle.

And so the pool, surrounded by people and ivy, forms the wet heart of our house. I do so want to capture it in a painting that will not have to be hidden in the hallway for reasons of ugliness.

With the first brush stroke of my pool painting, I found rather suddenly that I have no talent for painting water. So I ran for the Impressionists, who have always been my favorites, to see if I could pick up a few hints.

Before I could even begin looking at the pictures, I found another autodidact. Mary Cassatt spent six years of independent study in the museums of Italy, Spain, and Holland before she arrived in Paris. Of course she paints so wonderfully I should have guessed.

I never knew how much there is to be learned by reading about painting. I always thought all a painting had to give could be gotten just by looking. But after finding out the happy truth about Mary, I began to read all those pages I usually skip.

I had no idea that the work of the Impressionists was rejected by the only real gallery in Paris, and their first show was called the *Salon de Refusés.*

Obviously, no one is allowed an easy life.

Bought Hesiod's *Theogony* today. I will never forget the look Dad gave me when I handed it to him at the cash register. When I start buying writers he can't pronounce, I do believe he thinks my education has gotten out of hand.

I would so like to be myself, but I am nothing but a series of other people. Maybe one of them is myself, but I doubt it. I just can't seem to find my best self.

In changing my life course from the one taken by my peers and ruling them out as a measuring stick of my own progress, I have so narrowed the circle of those who approve me. I don't have teachers anymore, who, as Mom used to say, write Kendall love letters instead of report cards (arrogance is becoming rather obnoxious as a survival tactic, don't you agree?).

I love having parents who are at home all day (that may be the greatest gift for an autodidact—to have such a fully populated study), but I can't have a new play ready every day for them to applaud. And I can't have a nervous breakdown every time I find out they aren't perfect.

I think I am coming to a realization. Here I have all along been searching for someone in this family I can rely on to show me how to live. And I have been emulating each of them in their turn and then when I found out the one I was emulating was not perfect moved on to the next. But I think I am beginning to see that, though I love them, they are all human, and I—though unhappily human too—am best able to show me how to best live.

When it comes to gods, I think Hesiod tells it like it was (and is, I suppose, since they are immortal). As the *Theogony*'s Introduction tells us:

The gods of the *Iliad* and *Odyssey*, although not perhaps very admirable ethically (they lie, cheat, steal, manhandle each other, play favourites and commit adultery rather more often than Homer's humans do), are still fully anthropomorphic and civilized, and the poet has erased from their past every trace of castration, child-swallowing, incest, and other primitive behaviour.

So, on to Hesiod who has, thank goodness, not cleaned up a thing. I'd hate a writer who cut the child-swallowing, Kronos's preventive measure against any of his children trying to take over his kingdom.

Sorry to say, Hesiod not quite as juicy as I had hoped (or perhaps it's just harder to shock these days). The most interesting thing so far is how much of the world is the responsibility of gods. In the ancient world Love, Terror, Fear, Order, Peace, Justice, Power, Force, Doom, Deceit, Age, Strife, Work, Forgetfulness, Famine, Pains, Battles, Fights, Murders, Quarrels, Lies, Stories, Disputes, Lawlessness, Ruin, Desire, and Chaos were all gods.   It must have been easy for ancient man to lead a blameless life when all those were gods and not a part of him, and yet also rather terrifying—not to mention dull. I think I prefer being responsible for my own chaos.

Tonight I'm going to count the number of lines in *My Man Godfrey* and then I'll know how many more I need for my screwball comedy. Counting lines may sound a little daft, but I'm getting desperate. My plot ran out ages ago. There are times, though, when I love not having a plot. It is structure that makes for tedium.

Just finished the *Theogony*. Reading it was like lying on the beach, letting the waves and verses roll over me, doing my best to adjust myself to their rhythm without trying to analyze them before they rolled back into the ocean, then picking up the stray seashells and beautiful poetic images they happened to leave behind.

This was my favorite seashell: "And even to the gods/Who are immortal, Death is an enemy." The *Theogony* may not be quite the *Iliad*, but a line like that is worth reading one thousand twenty-one others to find.

Tonight the play version of *A Woman of Independent Means* closed in Los Angeles. But in a month it will open on Broadway. So tonight was a beginning as well as an ending (the stagehands who were so devoted cannot come to New York because of union rules). There was a cake with the chosen epitaph of Bess, the character based on my greatgrandmother: "To Be Continued."

I was painting away when Dad walked over to my easel, looked at my poolscape, and I know I heard him say, "This is turning into a real problem." While I was pondering how he could say such a mean thing, he repeated it and I realized he was saying, "This is turning into a real painting." He also said, "This is another masterpiece." Those words gave me a feeling of freedom I have not known since I finished the self-portrait, my only other "masterpiece" to date. It's kind of awful to have painted one painting everyone in the family likes. Of course, frustrating as it is to have painted just one, it does have its advantages over none.

I wonder how much of Hesiod's *Works and Days* his no-good brother actually read. I just finished it, but then it was not aimed at me. Being reprimanded is bad enough, but to be reprimanded in verse? Find me a worse fate.

However, *Works and Days* is chock-full of good, sturdy, practical advice, such as:

Don't let a woman, wiggling her behind,
And flattering and coaxing, take you in;
She wants your barn.

Hesiod was plenty wise. He knew how much women love barns.

I just saw Gore Vidal being interviewed. He is so bright. I would love to read some of his books. The only thing is, if I stay in this chronological mood I'll be senile before I get a chance.

Sat down to read a few odes of Pindar and fell asleep in my chair after one line. A little Pindar goes a long way.

I finished my pool painting and in a canvas thirty-six by thirty-six inches, I captured the way water reflects in a space of one inch by one inch—but a square inch is better than none at all.

I've had an idea since Christmas for a painting of an embrace shown only with the feet, but I need someone to pose with me. You don't suppose Matthew would be interested? I doubt it, yet I am feeling the urge to paint. I think perhaps a still life for now and then back to people, which are by far the most interesting. Of course, they are also the most difficult. Isn't that always the way?

Herodotus is the most readable historian I've ever read (though he also takes the most liberties with history). And I have also forgotten whether the Greeks or the Persians won the Persian War, which makes reading about it infinitely more interesting.

Brooke and I got in a terrible fight today, and then Brooke asked Nanny to substantiate all the hateful things I had said, and that's just what Nanny did. Substantiate, substantiate,

substantiate. Dad was wonderful. He said I could hide Nanny's teeth for two days.

Still reading and, yes, enjoying Herodotus, but the Persian War was rather long, and I'm trying not to rush through it. Liar. I don't have a prayer of getting through the Persian War any faster than the Persians did.

I have been reading Thucydides whilst dining on frozen grapes—a delicacy taught to us by dear Joan Hackett. I remember when I was little I only knew three people who had died. My grandfather Jack, Larry Parks, and Barbara Colby, and whenever I would think of one, I would think of the others because they were the only three I knew. The saddest part of maturity is that I have now lost count, and I don't remember to think of them all.

Two of our dearest friends are getting a divorce. To think we will never know them as a couple again. I suppose it is better for them not to be together, but heartbreaking for the rest of us. It is hard to go on with a screwball comedy with this knowledge (on that subject, a plot, which I used to regard as such a burden, would be damned helpful about now). So much of life is turmoil. I shall eat ten more chocolate-chip cookies and then go on with the part that isn't.

Thucydides' rendition of Diodotus' speech about the Mitylenians is such an eloquent argument against the death penalty. Matthew wrote an editorial for his school paper recently using the exact same argument. I always knew he was as bright as Thucydides. (Or should I say Diodotus? When Herodotus does a rendition of a speech, you can always be sure he is making it up, so he should get credit, but with Thucydides there's always the off chance he's telling things as they really were.)

Just tried to call Matthew. He is always out (after swearing to me he doesn't socialize), and as Irene Bullock (Carole Lombard in *My Man Godfrey)* would say, "probably with some woman on his lap."

I have everything I want in the world and yet I am miserable because Matthew has not returned my call (I wanted to tell him about Thucydides). If I ever do marry him, the first thing I'm going to do is punch him right in the mouth.

He called. At most I'll give him a friendly clip on the chin. We talked till midnight—of everything from NBC News to CBS News (quite a jump for Matthew) to dodging visitors when we are in our bathrobes. We probably would have talked all night, but *Made for Each Other,* written by Renee Taylor and Joe Bologna, was on, so I insisted we watch (the title didn't hurt either). As we hung up, Matthew said, "I know we'll laugh at all the same things." I think that's my favorite thing he's said yet.

I am appalled by Plato. That anyone could write a book like the *Laws* (which denies free thought and places all authority with the state) and still be considered a great philosopher is shocking. He was no more than an ancient Hitler—listen to this:

> The best of either sex should be united with the best as often as possible, and the inferior with the inferior; and they are to reap the offspring of one sort of union, but not of the other; for this is the only way of keeping the flock in prime condition.

I am certainly glad I read about the old fool, so if his name ever comes up I shall not have to be quiet out of undeserved awe.

Though the chance of Plato coming up in conversation with the people I run with is doubtful.

I spent this evening looking through some of Mom's old scrapbooks. I was trying to find my favorite picture ever taken of her, which I have to look at every so often. In it, she is a one-year-old with a page-boy haircut and is being chased by this huge baldheaded baby twice her size. It says so much about her character.

But what I found instead were her old college scrapbooks. My God, what a scholar. And what a wonderful shock it was to find this paper on Plato. I read the assignment and thought, my heavens, I could never do this. I should give up being an autodidact and head for college because I don't really know anything about Plato. How nice to know that my mother, despite having studied him in college, didn't either. On the final page of her paper was written "totally unacceptable."

On that reassuring note, good night.

My screwball comedy is almost finished. Some of it has plot, some of it doesn't. Some of it needs massive rewriting, some of it is just about perfect. Some of the roles are good, but the roles written for those born before 1910 are better. I set out hoping to pay tribute to my favorite actors and actresses, I ended up writing another film for them.

I am so drawn to Aristotle it is embarrassing. What amazes me is the time he took to think and reason. He is also firmly convinced the philosopher's life is best, and he is a wonderful philosopher because of it.

I have never enjoyed a book as much as I am enjoying his *Ethics* (sometimes I step back and listen to what I am saying and just about faint, but, you know, it's the truth). Listen to what he says about an opinion of Plato's he disagrees with:

Yet surely it would be thought better, or rather necessary (above all
for philosophers) to refute, in defence of the truth, even views to
which one is attached: Since although both are dear, it is right to
give preference to the truth.

He makes me wish I had not been so mean to Plato, though I
do still hate him, but not as much as I love Aristotle.

Aristotle has given me the ending to my screwball
comedy. I wanted to say something at the end about what those
great films have given to me. Little did I know Aristotle (who
must have gone to the movies more frequently than any of us
could have guessed) had already described their effect on my soul.
Here is my favorite thought of Aristotle's, describing a way of
living that my favorite actors and actresses had already taught
me:

But we must not follow those who advise us, being men, to think of
human things, but must, so far as we can, make ourselves immortal
and strain every nerve to live in accordance with the best thing in
us; for even if it be small in bulk, much more does it in power and
worth surpass everything.

Because I think part of me will be forever Greek, I know
enough to leave when I get the proper sign and not to continue
too long, reading less and less.

That quote of Aristotle's is it. It says everything I have always
wanted to say, and though I do believe Aristotle's *Ethics* is the
best book I ever read, I think I'll make it a point never to finish it,
for to read it all would be to know that everything worth saying
had been said.

Of course, I'll never really finish with Greece. I have every
suspicion that reading about Greece is the same as riding a bicy-
cle, and that it will be quite easy one day to pick up Demosthenes
just where I left him (in the middle of a speech—I suspect that's
where everyone leaves him).

I hope I have opened a door . . . which only the foul wind of lifelong laziness can shut. Of course, I've often felt that breeze, but it is one I'll try to avoid.

For now, on to Broadway and then to the place where all roads lead (even Forty-second Street, in my case) . . . Rome.

Today was the first preview of *A Woman of Independent Means* at the Biltmore Theatre in New York. It was a matinee filled with old ladies who would all kind of sigh in unison after their favorite lines. When Bess, in her final moments, says, "And I mustn't forget to call Sam," after Sam has already died, one huge "Ohhh" came up from the audience. It was wonderful to watch them love my greatgrandmother (whose soul now inhabits Barbara Rush) so much.

I confess I had not wanted to share her with them. I remember when Mom announced that producers from New York had seen the play and wanted to take it to Broadway. I stamped my foot and said that was the biggest mistake in the world. This is a beautiful play about nothing more than life—when was the last time you saw one of those on Broadway?

I stamped my foot on her optimism in practically the same spot where I had jumped for joy seven years earlier when we found out *A Woman of Independent Means*, her first novel, was going to be published.

My mother's amazing success in novel writing has left me an innocent in that area. I am the happy harborer of the illusion that success plays fair when it comes to prose. But thanks to my father, at seventeen I know more than anyone should about the rotten odds of the theatre. I know so much there's not a lot of room left over for hope.

We took a train from New York to Philadelphia today to see my father's freely adapted version of Strindberg's *The Father*, which is being done by the Philadelphia Drama Guild. When we looked in *The New York Times* this morning, he and Mom had side-by-side ads, which must be some kind of marital advertising record.

It is his first adaptation, commissioned by the artistic director of the theatre because he saw so many parallel themes between Dad's *Father's Day* and Strindberg's *The Father.*

Dad asked for a literal translation of the play and worked from that. When he finished his first draft, he showed it to Betsy Palmer, for whom he had freely adapted the role of the mother in *The Father.* And it was really she who urged him to say a few of the things even Strindberg had not dared. An idea as bold and right as her performance.

It is certainly a gift to know the people for whom you want to write roles. And then there's other casting that just happens by luck. I nearly fainted over my bagel as we sat in the deli across from the Biltmore when Dad told me who was playing the role of the wet nurse. Ruth Nelson, the widow of John Cromwell, my favorite film director.

I confess, when I heard, I was most excited to meet her because of who her husband was. But when I saw her in the play tonight, that became secondary. She is an actress of such skill and passion.

Our train back to New York after the play was delayed for a fiendishly long time, which gave me a chance to ask questions of the first person to have really been a part of my favorite era.

I had always wondered what happened to John Cromwell's career between his great films of the thirties and forties and *The Goddess* so much later. Ruth Nelson told us tonight that just after she and John Cromwell were married there was a huge spread in *Life* quoting Adolphe Menjou, who had accused John Cromwell of leading the Directors Guild down the red river or something to that effect.

She said the accusation was ridiculous, and he could have easily cleared himself by giving the names of already well-known Communist sympathizers. These names would hardly have been news to anyone, but he would not even discuss the matter. He gave up an incredible new contract and, she said, was never bitter for a moment. I just knew it took a great man to make great films.

All my life I'll treasure getting to hear Ruth Nelson talk about John Cromwell. Everyone reacts to loss in his or her own way. I remember meeting a widow who could never talk about her husband without bursting into tears, and then I found out later that at one point in their marriage she'd had him sent to prison. So I've since been a little suspicious of anyone who bursts into tears. But Ruth Nelson spoke of John Cromwell with such joy. His presence was there, and she seemed to continue to take strength and happiness from it.

One of the last things she said about him was, "John always said he had three favorite women. Fanny Brice, Carole Lombard, and me." How wise he was.

I just returned from the Claudette Colbert Tribute at Lincoln Center, which I had been reading about and wishing I could attend for so long. By the luckiest of circumstances and the best of press people, we were able to go. And I am still in tears—a way I never expected the evening to end.

We walked into expectant photographers disappointed to see we were not celebrities. Then we watched limousine after limousine pull up, but no CC in sight. We took our seats and I thought I was going to faint, I was so excited waiting for her to enter. Brooke bet she would be in red and she was—a gorgeous dress. The tributes were beautiful, and Claudette still has the same wonderful laugh. To say nothing of the fact Miss Colbert wasn't listening when God told all of us aging was part of the deal. When Barbara Rush found out where we were going tonight, she said, "Claudette Colbert . . . the woman time forgot."

At the reception afterward, Dad found us the perfect spot from which to view her. We were close enough to spit (we did not).

I couldn't believe that here, in person, was the woman I can usually fast forward and rewind at will. She put on a beautiful red cape to leave and suddenly she was coming right past us. She looked up and smiled. And I said, "We love you." She looked right back up at me and said, "I can feel it." So of course, I had to burst into tears. But I do like to give life the emotion it deserves.

One of the producers said backstage tonight that when he goes into other New York theatres, the stagehands come up to him and say, "We hear you've got yourself a hit at the Biltmore."

Could it possibly be true? Of course, I've always had a wonderful time with my father's Broadway plays, until opening night when we fly home before the reviews come out.

As I sit in the back row of this beautiful empty theatre, I think how much fun it has all been. I love sitting in an empty theatre. It is like seeing the world before it began.

Our last preview. So many bravos you could barely hear the clapping, and one man stood in his seat and yelled, "Thank you."

Opening Night. What are the memories I will choose to take with me from it? That the guests ranged from Yoko Ono to Lillian Gish (whose hand I got to shake, and who sweetly protested as I told her how magnificent she is that I wasn't old enough to know who she is—she doesn't know how old I really am)? Or that I got to watch Pia Lindstrom (a New York critic and Ingrid Bergman's daughter) watch the play and see her mother's smile light up her face because of my mother's lines? Or that her review, which was the best we got, was not enough?

We weren't sure what the fate of the play was going to be until after we got to Sardi's for the opening night party. I've heard tell that when you get good reviews (God knows my poor family would know nothing about an occurrence like that), they are brought in to you, and now I know for a fact that when you get bad ones, nobody says anything and you slowly begin to figure it out.

My father figured it out before anyone. He said he was feeling terrible and had left his medication at the hotel and could we go? I couldn't believe he was asking Mom to leave her own opening night party, but then as we walked back to the hotel in the pouring rain (I hope it was a sign that the gods were as furious as we were) with no one saying anything, I knew.

Finally, Dad just stopped in all the rain and said to Mom,

"Well, it turns out you're as good a writer as I am." And we all began to laugh.

I knew then we had won again, despite the fact a lot of space is going to be wasted in the papers tomorrow trying to tell us we failed.

Even if you know you've won again, the day after a play fails is a hard one. I feel as if all the promise in the world is gone. We saw a matinee of the play, with Barbara giving her best performance yet. I wish the world would get to work bottling that strength. Mom and I passed a woman in the lobby at intermission, tears streaming down her face, mumbling, "Thank God I don't listen to the critics."

Home. I miss the companionship of adjoining hotel rooms, but I am surrounded by Romans. Though they are less fun at night than Mom and Dad.

In my first day of reading, I found my favorite: Ennius, a poet, who, as Will Durant tells us, "announced that the soul of Homer, having passed through many bodies, including Pythagoras and a peacock, now resided in Ennius."

I came home all ready to start a new play, sat down this morning, and could not. I just can't visualize a stage without feeling hurt. However, I will not be conquered. It may not seem a big step forward in the battle of life, but I will write another play, despite the fact I have just seen one beaten to death before my very eyes. Besides, my dear characters, Eudora (for Eudora Welty) and William (for William Powell) are waiting to make their entrance.

Just talked to Julie Reich and heard where all my former classmates are going to college.

I listened, as Ingrid Bergman says in the last lines of *Gaslight,* "without a shred of pity, without a shred of regret." Actually, the pity was there. Julie spoke of houses that should have been wreathed in black, so many rejections had come to the door. The tension of thin letter versus thick letter from the college of your choice. Thin means rejection. Thick means here's the forms, kid, you made it. I'm not sorry I'm missing the thick or the thin of getting into college.

I am now well-acquainted enough in Rome to know just whom I want to really get to know.

I am going to read the history and the literature at the same time, which I think will be slightly more effective, as I did have a tendency with the Greeks to forget who people were by the time I read what they wrote.

Roman Authors Whose Royalties I Would Like to Increase (in the best chronological order an autodidact can manage):

Plautus wrote twenty-one comedies, twenty of which are extant. I was shocked to learn that all are adapted from Greek originals. What kind of people were these Romans? I was hoping for a little more originality.

Terence was very fond of the process of *contaminatio* (combining two or more Greek plays to form one Latin one). He seemed to spend most of his time translating Menander, but I was touched to learn that, according to one account, he died of a broken heart when all his translations were lost at sea. There is obviously as much love in transforming words as in writing them down for the first time.

Cicero was the greatest of orators, and I am a good listener.

Lucretius wrote *De Rerum Natura,* which gives us a whole philosophy of life in seven thousand lines of poetry. But he sounds a little like an existentialist. I thought in a society of so many gods one could get away from the existentialists.

Catullus was a great poet, especially when it came to love and a dame named Lesbia.

I began to like Virgil when I read that his *Georgics* (poems of farm life, inspired by Hesiod's *Works and Days*—these people could not keep their eyes off the Greeks) were written at an average rate of less than a line a day. And I grew crazy about him when I discovered that on his deathbed Virgil asked that the *Aeneid* be destroyed because it was so unpolished. The Emperor Augustus, however, asked that it be published as Virgil left it. Poor Virgil. To think that he cringes every time someone reads the *Aeneid.*

I almost turned on Horace when I read he went to the University of Athens. Though I do think it's amusing that the only university-educated Roman I've encountered so far is also the only one described as second-rate. I'm too mean to the college-educated, I know.

Livy is the greatest historian of his era. According to the *New Gresham Encyclopedia,* "Polybius, painstaking, meticulous, and impartial, is only read by specialists; Livy, careless, inaccurate, and prejudiced, is widely read and admired." Even history needs style.

Only two books of Tibullus' verse survive, each dealing with love and country life and each dedicated to a different mistress. Sad to think only two mistresses are extant (goodness knows how many there were).

Ovid's *Heroides* are letters from heroines of legend to their husbands or lovers, which is a great idea if I ever heard one. His *Ars Amatoria* is about just what you think it is. I must get it for Brooke immediately. Finally, a classic she will enjoy. And his *Metamorphoses* will be my only school textbook allowed on my autodidact Greek and Roman shelf.

Petronius is the author of the first novel, so he is to blame for the fact that ten years ago my mother started writing novels and we started getting frozen waffles.

Pliny the Elder penned *Historia Naturalis,* which doesn't seem very me. However, some of it is so inaccurate, it is often referred to as *Historia Unnaturalis.* Which sounds like more fun.

Tacitus. This man is hugely respected as an historian but sounds dull. After Herodotus and Thucydides, I really prefer a little fiction mixed in with my facts.

Juvenal writes biting, Brooke-type satire. I am especially anxious to read the second and ninth of his satires, as they are usually omitted from school texts. They deal with vice, are said to be revolting, and I can't wait.

Pliny the Younger's letters are supposed to give a wonderful picture of the era. He has been accused of writing them with a view to subsequent publication, but show me a writer of whom that isn't true.

And I have decided the best place for Plutarch is at the end of my classical world, as his *Lives* compare a Greek to a Roman. The *Lives* are thought to have had a greater influence on the revival of learning than any other book, so I feel they should have an equal influence on my beginning of learning.

And finally: Cnaeus Naevius. One of Rome's earliest authors, his work survives only in lines, but his name, thank God, has traveled down to us in its entirety.

Seventeen authors. If I'd just read one a year, I'd be done by now.

I just stepped on the scale, something I feel I should do every so often, and I was so shocked at the number I saw that I could only pray Brooke had hopped on with me. But she was nowhere to be seen.

Food has always been one of my very dearest friends. But it is definitely time to start seeing less of it. And it will be a test of my fulfillment in being an autodidact to see if I can do so.

Food and homework always held hands in my world. But since I am now reading for pleasure, I should be able to cut down on eating for pleasure. I am leading exactly the life I want to lead, and that should be fulfilling (and filling) enough.

Will Durant on the Roman husband and his wife: "He could condemn her to death for infidelity or for stealing the keys to his wine." Doesn't it make you think of *Notorious*? If only Claude Rains had known! What he would have done to dear Ingrid Bergman, who did both!

SUMMER NOT SO DIFFERENT FROM FALL

WHAT I HOPE TO DO:

Enjoy summer without school as much as I've enjoyed fall, winter, and spring without it.

I have not spoken of Matthew much lately. That is because he is working on the Mondale campaign and has time only for people who can advance his political career.

My heart aches night and day. Here I am reading about all these Stoics, and all I want to do is weep. I console myself with the fact that he's not going to marry anybody else without at least consulting me.

I was planning to call Matthew up, but decided it would be wise first to talk to Uncle Thomas about just what is happening in this country politically since, of course, I haven't got the faintest idea (in the political struggle I care about, Pompey is the man to watch), and I have just escaped from the talkative Uncle's room after what seemed years of political anecdotes.

In a way, the use of Thomas' voice has taken the place of the use of his body. He can't run to the door of his room and throw himself in front of it to prevent exiting while there are still political anecdotes to be told. But he can say, "What was I going to tell you?" and "I've got a story for you" till he has forced his listener to the brink of madness. Did I say madness? I didn't mean it.

I love my mad uncle. It is quite a gift to know someone who has gone my whole childhood without running out of conversation. And it is because of him that I know about the baby Brooke and me, Sherlock Holmes, Roy Rogers, all the adventures of Tom Sawyer and Huckleberry Finn and Becky Thatcher that Mark Twain forgot to record, and, of course, along the way, a little more about Watergate and Bobby Fischer than I ever really wanted to know.

But I must always remember not to take my family too seriously. It's just no good wanting rational, civilized human beings for relatives. The whole idea of loving someone unconditionally just because they have the same blood coursing through their veins is so irrational that you can't expect the people who abide by such a notion to be especially sane.

There is nothing as good for dieting as a Carole Lombard movie. I have lost ten pounds due solely to her films. The secret is to eat as little as I can of anything that appeals to me and all I want of things I just hate and watch three of her movies a night. A viewing schedule that may interfere with the reading of Rome, but is wonderful for the figure.

I am furious with Mom. An unusual state, I agree. Sometimes I run up so hard against the wall of knowledge that people aren't perfect, I want to cry. Of course, I rebound against the wall of knowledge that no one is all bad and so I bounce along. But I do wish people were without faults. I want someone who doesn't disappoint. Someone to love without any shield because I know they'll never hurt me. Someone for one brief moment not human for those moments when I am all too human.

Actually, that is just a general need, not really brought on by my irritation with Mom. We barely even had an argument. I was the one who started, fought, and finished whatever there was of one. She glides peaceably through life.

The simple truth is she's a plagiarist. And I'm afraid it's me she's plagiarizing. In friendly (or so I thought) conversation, I told her about my Carole Lombard diet and the minute I finished, she started writing it down (you are never safe in a family of writers).

I said to wait, that I was using it.

"Oh," she said, disappointed.

"Well, if you want to take it, go ahead," I said limply. I always start out firm, but then I always wither.

And the next thing I know Ms. Motor Pen is writing away.

Mondale lost the California primary today. Poor Matthew worked so hard for him. Personally, I could not care less. Callous, I know, but as my character Eudora says of her political-minded husband, "I always considered governing the people a very transitory thing to do with one's life."

Am sitting here, exquisitely happy. Had a lovely conversation with Matthew. Of course, I had to commiserate about Mondale (I faked it). We talked for three and a half hours. I took responsibility for changing topics the first half of the conversation, he the second—an unsaid kind of agreement. Unknowingly, he gave me just the piece of information (a detail of what it's like to lose a primary) I needed for my play. Sometimes I wonder if we will ever get together, but luckily I write plays in which we always do.

There is something about reading a letter that makes you feel it arrived in today's mail even if it was posted over two thousand years ago.

I spent the day with Cicero and his correspondence, which, twenty centuries later, still reads fresh out of the envelope or, rather, like just unrolled papyrus.

Thanks to Cicero and his personal point of view, I finally understand how the world got from Caesar to Augustus and why. History that far away seems so close when it's seen through the eyes of someone who was there at the time.

Imagine reading the mail of a man who had Julius Caesar for a houseguest: ". . . we were human beings together. Still, he was not the sort of guest to whom you would say 'do please come again on your way back.' Once is enough!"

Though Caesar seemed to have much respect for Cicero, saying, "It is better to have extended the boundaries of the Roman spirit than of the Roman empire," it wasn't too mutual, for Cicero says, rather bluntly for such a basically sweet man, "How I wish you had invited me to that superb banquet on the Ides of March!"

I'm reading Caesar's *The Conquest of Gaul* next, so I'll see how I like him (I think it's easier to judge a man by his writing than how he ruled an Empire).

Certainly, it is not hard to adore Cicero. He is so dear about himself ("Would you ever have believed it possible that words fail me . . ." he says at one point) and honest ("a letter does not blush"), but perhaps it is better we are separated by so many years, for as he says, it is difficult to deal with a wife and philosophy at the same time.

I will be eighteen in ten more days and feel absolutely unprepared.

I started a portrait of Nanny today. I was sitting in the living room and she walked in and leaned against a chair, striking such an interesting pose that I shouted at her not to move. Of course, the minute I shouted, she, having the nervous system inherent in all the Haileys (i.e., one on the brink of disaster) jumped ten feet into the air, landing, to my torment, in a different position.

I kept trying to re-pose her just as I saw her. Finally, I gave up and am painting a variation on her original pose. I've only done her feet so far, but all is going exceptionally well. It is irritating, though, how many sit-down breaks you have to give seventy-nine-year-old models.

Independence Day. The day, quite ironically, Mom finished the first draft of her novel about her marriage to Dad.

Since I am the kindest person in the family, I am Mom's first editor—though I don't think Dad knows this yet. He may still think he is. I am not quite sure how I got to become the first reader of her work. Actually, I think the seeds of my new preeminence were sown when Dad read the first hundred pages of this novel and told Mom to throw them away. She did, wrote a new first hundred, gave them to me to read, I loved them, and now I get to read everything first.

Mom finished the book just before we headed to the Van Scoyks' Fourth of July party, where Leona makes a Roman banquet look like child's play. It was a swell party, culminating in a second kiss between me and Matthew. It happened like this: Matthew gave me a birthday present, and I said, "I love it. Oh, thank you" and moved a bit closer to him. He moved a bit closer to me, and I kissed him on the cheek.

I wonder if it is not a grand farce of an idea that we could really coexist peacefully together, but sitting in the kitchen, the last of the guests to leave, all of us laughing, I realized I just wanted to be near him twenty-four hours a day—just like that—sitting in the chair next to him, knowing I wouldn't have to go home at my father's command.

What amazes me about Matthew is that he is the person I get most nervous and worked up about seeing, and yet I feel more comfortable and at ease and more myself with him than with anyone else. I seem to be someone else with everyone else, myself only with Matthew.

I need to get back to reading—Romans tend to calm one down.

I practiced driving again today. By waiting till the age of eighteen to get my driver's license, I am avoiding lessons . . . from a certified instructor, that is. Even an autodidact cannot escape driving lessons from her father.

Streets were being torn up and I couldn't figure out how to make this left, so I just made three rights instead, and suddenly I had such respect for Caesar for conquering all of Gaul.

However, I disagree philosophically with Caesar from the first line of his book about the conquest of Gaul. This great warrior is under the delusion that being continually at war is what signifies bravery.

He can't see the courage of peace, but he can, indeed, write. And I share Cicero's respect for the literary side of Caesar. He said of his *Commentaries*:

They are like nude figures, upright and beautiful, stripped of all
ornaments of style as if they had removed a garment.

But I wouldn't have wanted him for a houseguest either.

Today I unveiled my "Portrait of Nanny." I finished
it a few days ago, but it looked so out of proportion (much more
out of proportion than even the real Nanny) that I decided to
cover it up and pray it'd look more human in time.

And you know it does. As I hesitantly pulled off Brooke's old
bed sheet (from her days when she liked to sleep covered in jungle
animals), I jumped for joy at how like Nanny it looked. Nanny's
reaction was less enthusiastic.

If anyone took the time to paint a portrait of me, I'd be pretty
darn thrilled, but all she says is, "It doesn't look much like me."
(As Picasso said to Gertrude Stein when she complained his portrait of her didn't look much like her, "It will.")

Dad keeps telling me to change the portrait so we don't see her
face—I can't decide whether that's a slap at my face-painting
abilities or at Nanny's face.

Dad's enthusiasm about our playwrights' group tends
to run over into the car ride home where he continues to talk
about what makes a good play. I love listening to him, so the rides
would be heaven if only I did not see every word as a direct attack
on my characters, William and Eudora, even though he has no
idea they exist.

But everything he says a play should have, I scramble to find it
in mine. Everything a play shouldn't have, I quickly slam through
my ideas and make sure it isn't there. It is quite a test to put a
barely living play through. Most of the time it fails on all counts,
but I keep writing it, which must count for something.

A woman is going to be the next Democratic vice-
presidential nominee! I am usually the least political of people (as

everyone but Matthew knows), but I wanted to cry when I heard the news! I had been rooting for her—Geraldine Ferraro, as the history books will tell—all along. Matthew, who is going to be working at the Democratic Convention, kept telling me it was going to be someone named Bumpers and had me convinced she didn't have a chance. Well, it is just past midnight—and she is in!

It is now officially July 12, 1984—my eighteenth birthday. I didn't want to be eighteen until this very moment. Awfully old, I kept thinking. Now it seems just the right age. I can cast my first vote for a woman—and the man bright enough to choose her.

It's almost hard to go back to the ancient world when the modern one is working out so well, but nevertheless today I read *Amphytron* by Plautus. It was hysterical—as wonderful as Aristophanes. Plays about the gods are always fun. It is so comforting to think such cut-ups are running the universe.

I am floating on air—in my head and in real life.

We are on a plane headed for a very un-Hailey spot, Hawaii. Since this is a vacation which is to involve relaxing, we are all, of course, a little tense because we aren't very good at it.

Sadly, Nanny and Thomas have decided to sit this tropical vacation out due to the fact it involves not only relaxing but also charting new territories. Nanny and Thomas prefer proven trips. A few years ago, Mom, Dad, Brooke, and I journeyed to Honolulu, decided it was a perfect spot for Haileys, and made a second trip to show it to Nanny and Thomas.

But this trip is to see Maui and the big island of Hawaii, so Nanny and Thomas are again awaiting our verdict before they go out and buy new bathing suits.

Pliny and virgin piña coladas by the pool do not mix.

When I read that no serious attempt had been made to translate Pliny's letters since 1746, I felt heartbroken that he had been neglected all this time. Now, I have just finished reading a few of his epistles, and I'm beginning to understand why.

Despite the fact that, as he so modestly informs us, "there are very few people who care for literature without caring for me too," I am very tempted to mark him "return to sender."

Thomas has had a cerebral hemorrhage and is in intensive care. Really we don't even know if it is a cerebral hemorrhage. All we know is that Nanny found him this morning in a comalike state and we can't get home to be with them.

We have called home every other day to check on mail, phone calls, and Nanny and Thomas. Usually we call at night, but today we called in the morning.

Thomas always answers the phone, but today Nanny answered. She told us about the mail and the phone calls, and then we asked to talk to Thomas. And she said, "He looks like he's in some kind of a coma. I can't get him to talk to me and I don't know what to do."

When Dad told us what had happened to Thomas, Brooke let out a piercing scream and ran to the balcony of our hotel room. I saw her throw something out toward the ocean, then I realized it was the piece of rock she picked up touring a dormant volcano yesterday. Ancient superstition said that bad luck would follow whoever took a rock from the volcano. But Brooke had picked one up and dared the gods to get her.

Dad told Nanny we would take care of everything and we called our nearest friends, Neal DuBrock and Michael Healy, who called the paramedics and then raced over to our house. Then we called Nanny again and told her Neal and Michael and the paramedics were all on their way.

While Mom ran to the lobby to pay the bill, Dad called the airport. There was a plane leaving for Los Angeles in three hours, and we were a three-hour drive from our side of the island to the airport.

We lived that phrase "throwing everything into a suitcase." I threw everything in but the sweater Matthew gave me for my birthday the night of our second kiss (I tied the sweater around my waist and I haven't untied it yet). Then we ran to the car and Dad started speeding toward the airport.

We got to the airport in time for the flight, but it was full. We were given emergency priority if there were any cancellations, but there were none. And the flight left without us. There is only one flight a day, so here we are, stranded for a night.

As soon as we realized we couldn't get out, we checked into a hotel on this side of the island and called home. Our friend Neal was waiting for our call. Michael had taken Nanny and followed Thomas and the paramedics to the hospital. Neal told us a blood vessel burst inside Thomas's head, but they don't know yet how serious his condition is. We gave Neal our number at the hotel, and he said he had once stayed there. Dad didn't tell us that till later, but it gave me a feeling of safety to know that a friend had once stayed in this place which only held fear and pain for us.

The second call we made was to the Van Scoyks. We told them what had happened and that we couldn't get home and to take care of Nanny. Nanny loves the "Van Squirks," as she pronounces their name, as much as they love her, and that is saying something because Nanny does not have much use for people not related to her by blood.

We have reservations on the flight tomorrow. There isn't anything we can do tonight. Except sleep or not sleep, yell or pray to God.

As we sat on the plane this afternoon, waiting to take off, I suddenly thought, "This plane is never going to leave the ground." Then we began moving down the runway and, just as we were about to ascend, the plane blew an engine.

We came to an abrupt stop and a disembodied voice quickly assured us another plane would be brought over right away, but meanwhile dinner would be served. Then after dinner, the same voice told us the other plane had been delayed and there would be no flight until tomorrow.

At that moment, Brooke let out another of her piercing screams and said, "I've got to see my uncle." Four Haileys who have had it up to here with fate are not pleasant to deal with, and at last the airline managed to get us on a plane to Honolulu, where we would have better luck getting a flight to Los Angeles.

The Honolulu airport was a blur of trying to get four seats on a plane to Los Angeles and calls to the hospital, giving permission for one test after another.

Now, at last, we are on our way home. It was night when I caught a glimpse of the Honolulu lights as we boarded the plane. With the length of the flight, plus the three-hour time difference, it will be early morning when we arrive in Los Angeles. But our faithful friends, Neal and Michael, said they would be at the airport to meet us.

In that last conversation, they also told us that Thomas isn't recognizing anybody. I won't lose Thomas. I won't lose one of us. I'll get him back. I'll make him know me. I'll call him every silly name I've ever called him and I'll call myself every silly name he's ever called me. I'll say, "Jack Toma, it's your Jalapeño Palomino Pal." And he'll know me.

All this time I hadn't cried. This morning we finally got home. And as we opened the door, Leona and Matthew and Nanny emerged from the bedrooms. I hugged Nanny and I hugged Leona and, then, as I hugged Matthew, I burst into tears. And in that moment, it seemed as if there were no space between Matthew and me, and no space between my grief and the rest of the world's.

We went straight to the hospital, but somehow I got separated from the rest of the group and walked into intensive care by myself. I didn't know which room Thomas was in, and so I had to look in all of them.

The first room I looked in, I thought maybe that was Thomas. The patient was all curled up under the sheets in a helpless-looking way, but I didn't know, I thought maybe that was Thomas. I almost went in, but something kept me walking and in the next room there was Thomas, sitting up in bed, his usual handsome redheaded and bearded self, and of course, he was talking.

He recognized us all, but every once in a while, he'd say, "Would someone hand me my telephone?" and we'd have to remind him he was not in his room, but in the hospital. He looked so well, and seemed so happy that it didn't really frighten me when he didn't know where he was.

But now I'm home and it does. Every time I lie down, I get so frightened. But if I want to go back to the hospital tonight, I have to try to sleep now.

I am just going to lie down and repeat again and again and again, "Everything is going to be fine," and not think of anything else. And that will work. The mind is a genius at creating tortures, yet so simpleminded when you make it be.

I was sitting with Thomas in intensive care, but Thomas fell asleep in the middle of a political anecdote, leaving me only my book for comfort. I reached into my bag expecting to pull out *Auntie Mame,* since that is the kind of woman you need in intensive care, and found in my nearsighted stupidity I had picked up Pliny instead. I decided to give him one more letter and found this:

> Send me some words of comfort, but do not say that he was an old man and ill; I know this. What I need is something new and effective which I have never heard nor read about before, for everything I know comes naturally to my aid, but is powerless against grief like this.

We have just come out of intensive care and something is going terribly wrong. Thomas didn't understand what we were saying. He didn't want to talk at all, he just kept falling asleep.

Nanny was holding his hand and talking to him, and I glanced over and saw she was crying. I never thought Nanny would be any good at brave fronts, but I was wrong.

What do the Fates have against Thomas?

It is like some awful game and they will not be satisfied until they've crushed him. But he has not been crushed yet. During every football game I've ever watched with him, whenever there is a brutal tackle, he always shouts, "Cripple him for life." And then, of course, we both begin to giggle.

Late tonight, Thomas had brain surgery. I was spared some of the worst hours I could ever have lived through because I didn't know it was happening.

After seeing the way Thomas was slipping away this afternoon, Mom and Dad brought us home, then called the doctor and told him to meet them at the hospital. Then they left for the hospital, telling us they just might sit with Thomas all night and not to worry.

When they got to the hospital, the doctor was already there and said he had scheduled Thomas for brain surgery immediately. He had hoped the medication would have prevented the burst blood vessel from forming a blood clot, but it hadn't. A blood clot had formed and he'd have to operate to remove it.

There was nothing for Mom and Dad to do but wait. So they called the always near and always there Neal and Michael. And our close—at heart and in distance—friend Fred Sliter, who has sat through surgeries, deaths, births, and Broadway openings with this family. And they all sat and waited together, knowing at any time the doctor could walk into that waiting room and tell them Thomas had died.

But Thomas pulled through yet again. And he is going to be just fine and it is all finally over.

I spent all day with Thomas, his one-week anniversary of "major brain surgery." As he said to his doctor, is there such a thing as "minor brain surgery?" He is still without hair, but they saved what they shaved off and he is advertising it as "one bag Robert Redford–type hair." He is himself again.

All I want to do now is live. But as it's late and everyone else is asleep, the most convenient and quiet way to live at the moment is to read.

Though, actually, I'd better forego Pliny for bed while Puli is still asleep. He is sleeping with me while Thomas is in the hospital, and I would hate to ponder the consequences if I woke him up. I always thought one of the advantages of being a dog was the ability to sleep soundly, but I was wrong. And I'm afraid even the pleasure of Pliny would be reduced by spending the rest of the evening listening to Puli try to get comfortable again.

Today Dad offered to give me a practical education by teaching me to do all the things Thomas usually does. Turns out all this time Uncle Thomas thought he was just typing scripts and handling finances, he was really getting a practical education.

I began with the stockmarket. I looked up all our stocks in the paper and wrote down how much they had gained or lost, then I added up the total and found we had lost an incredible amount. I was so depressed and Dad nearly had a heart attack when I told him. I am not really that bad at addition—what happened was Dad had sold several stocks, whereas I thought we had lost that amount.

I hoped I might be fired after such a heinous mistake, but Dad said he'd give me another chance. And handed me a just-finished script to type.

I love reading it and I type at about the same speed I read (very, very slowly). I have not actually calculated just how many pages I can do per hour because I know that would depress me, but tonight I typed for two hours and went from page one to page six. Any further calculations are up to anyone but me.

But truthfully, I am glad I am getting a practical education. I've had a whole year of pretending I was Milton, doing only what I wanted. Frankly, any more totally carefree years and I'd probably turn into the tyrant he did. A little recording of stockmarket profits and losses would have helped his character a great deal. I know it will help mine.

When I was little, I would only do household chores for a fee. Thomas was the only one who would pay my prices (Nanny did once, but after she got the bill, never again). Twenty-five cents to empty a wastebasket, fifty cents to clean the bathroom sink, a dollar to dust a table, seventy-five cents for most chairs, a dollar fifty for sweeping, and a whopping three dollars to dust the table where Uncle Thomas displayed his chess sets (chess sets included in the price). It was always easy to clear twenty dollars in his overfurnished room.

Today Thomas moved to a private room and I began writing a mystery novel in his honor because he loves them so.

I am going to let my play ferment for a while before finishing it. It is in quite a mess. My biggest problem is I sent one of my major characters offstage at the beginning of the play and it's almost the end of the first act and I haven't been able to get her back on stage. All my characters are in turmoil, and they have reduced their author to the same state.

I want some characters who are fun to be with and don't have a lot of crises. Which is why I am writing a mystery. It has always seemed to me that whereas in a play or novel, the main thrust of the story must be the emotional conflicts of the main characters, in a mystery the main thrust of the story can be the mystery, and the main characters can just sit back and enjoy themselves.

Turns out my characters don't know how to sit back and enjoy themselves. Well, they did for the first chapter, but after a chapter of pure enjoyment, we were all ready for a little tension.

So I picked out a victim and killed her off. The reason this is going to add tension is that the victim is an actress. And the murder and solving of the crime all take place in a theatre. I think I may like writing about the theatre even more than being a part of it. After all, today I did something Dad has always wanted to, but in all his years in the theatre never gotten to: murder an actress.

Most irritating person in ancient history: Vespasian. He may have saved Rome from the effects of a few Caligulas, but he also established the first system of state education in the classical world. Unforgivable.

Maybe I should thank Vespasian because Brooke is now looking forward to school. I don't think she's the autodidact type. She tends to lie around moaning that she doesn't know what she wants to do with her life. Which of us does? But most take it better. Or do they?

She was pining for school (her favorite phrase these days is "I'll be glad when school starts . . . so I can get away from you") with such fervor yesterday that I dreamed I was being sent back, and I have to confess it was a nightmare. The world has become my teacher and I can never accept a go-between again.

I am too happy being busy without anyone ordering me to be, but then I have always been like that. I remember when I was very little my favorite word was "productive"—I used it all the time, assuming that what I was doing always was.

Brooke is not as obsessed by productivity as I—she is more content. Also wittier and a better person, but aside from that, I think you'd prefer me.

Last night I reread my screwball comedy. I had lost all faith in it, but after I read it again, I was so excited I danced in the living room. So today I am showing it to Dad. I didn't think I should show it to him until I at least knew what I thought of it. Last night I seemed to see very clearly for the first time where it was strong (a few places, believe it or not) and where it was weak (a huge chunk). I could never before differentiate between the two. I have not gotten a lot more intelligent recently, so I suppose it's just time, which is a great editor.

It was 2:14 A.M. when my heart jumped—I heard Dad coming down the stairs. It was so late I was convinced he had fallen asleep while reading my screwball comedy. I wasn't mad at him for going to sleep. He was hardly expected to know that my life rested on what he said. No matter how strong one's inner confidence—and mine is shaky at best—it vanishes in the face of another opinion (any other, to say nothing of Dad's).

And to make me more nervous, it had not been an easy day with Oliver. First, I was supposed to call Howard, our honest stock broker, who spends most of his time telling my father to calm down, and ask how much faith he had left in some stocks that have plummeted in the few months we've owned them. I woke up after he had already left work (embarrassing, to say the least).

I gave the pages to Dad after we came home from the hospital for the night. He was going to read them then, but I begged him to wait, why I do not know. Then, convinced I had ruined my life by putting off the moment of judgment, I ate three sloppy joes and tried to go on.

I was really a wreck because there was this *film noir* on and no one would watch it with Dad except me, but I would have done anything at that point. I am so easily depressed by bad movies, and at the end of four hours (a double feature of mediocrity) I very much wondered how I was going to get through the rest of my life.

I was in awful agony and by 1:00 A.M. I was sure I would have to wait till morning for an opinion. (Oh, I forgot to tell you, at 12:30 A.M. I hear footsteps. Dad! He has come to tell me not to miss tonight's *Alfred Hitchcock Presents.* It looks great, he says. It's about a woman who stuffs people. Just what I was in the mood for.)

Then at 2:14 A.M. I hear a noise. My heart actually skips a beat. Then silence. I am appalled at myself that I am so nervous my heart is skipping beats. Then I hear the door opening. With each stair my heart pounds.

Moments later I was again dancing around the living room. Dad said I had done things which hadn't been done since the thirties. With tears in my heart, I ask what more could one possibly ask for? What thrilled me practically as much, though, was when he spoke the names of my characters. It was as if they suddenly really existed—no longer just part of me. I hope I can spend my life writing and going through agony and perhaps joy and then writing more and going through more, and if I am very lucky, it will never stop.

It is 10:28 on a rainy morning and I don't know what's wrong with me. My friends left for college today. Does that have anything to do with it? I have barely kept in touch this year, but still, to see them go is hard. The people it's hardest to see go are people I didn't know very well but liked being around. Because I don't know if I'll ever see them again. I just hate finality and letting go—I hate those two things more than anything else.

I am not exactly having doubts about my own life, but sometimes I wonder. I want so much to change the world, but could I get through a day that started earlier than one in the afternoon? And you have to get up earlier than that to change the world. I suppose what it comes down to is it's almost as frightening to stay home as it is to leave.

It is 5:16 A.M. and I've just checked on Thomas and Puli. Thomas is home and they're back together—pretty cruel to make a man who just had brain surgery sleep with such a neurotic dog, but they'd missed each other.

I left them both sleeping soundly, which is what I now plan to do. I tend to check every hour through the night and Nanny will be up in about forty-five minutes. No one has told us to check so often, or that there's any need to at all, but when you know where your happiness is, it does seem foolish not to check on it every once in a while.

═══════════

WHAT I DID:

Realized What I Had.

═══════════

FRESHMAN YEAR
FROM
A DISTANCE

WHAT I HOPE TO DO:

Love So Much Today I Don't Need Tomorrow.

Today I received my first college epistle from Julie Reich, the short-storyist turned collegiate, at Tufts outside Boston.

Dear Kendall,
The official colors of Tufts are brown and blue—disgusting.

I'm not having as great a time as I thought I would, and I don't want to face up to it, so I debated writing to people . . . but I thought about it and decided I'd like to have people other than myself feeling sorry for me. No, actually, it's not *that* bad. I'm just feeling a little lonely—I miss L.A.! Everyone is from *heah*! I've started thinking in an eastern accent.

I'm looking forward to classes starting. I don't feel as if I'm developing any lasting relationships, and I think they'll be more lasting with people who are in my classes.

Okay—here's what I'm taking: English I (I couldn't get out of it), French III (I ended Oakwood in French IV—what does that tell you?), art history, and calculus. You know why I'm taking calculus? Because it fulfills the science requirement and I'd rather take math than science. The calculus book is two inches thick. I'll never survive two inches of calculus.

I hope you're doing whatever it is you do—you know, you never elaborate!

I'll write you when I have more to say . . . until then, why don't you write me?? *Please* write to me!! I hate seeing an empty mailbox.

Love,
Julie

Calculus. I don't know how she'll do it. I myself am taking geometry this year. That is, Brooke is taking it—it just feels as if I

am. The more I help her, the more I am convinced she is mentally
retarded, and I'm afraid the feeling is mutual. I don't know what
it is, but Brooke, geometry, and I simply do not form a workable
triangle. You know, I rather enjoyed geometry when I took it, but
the second time around it absolutely confounds me. I'm just terrible at it now, and Brooke keeps giving me these looks as if I never
should have been allowed to graduate at all, much less a year
early.

Brooke and Kendall saying good night after another
geometry fight:
    Brooke: Get out of my room and shut the door.
    Kendall: What if, after I leave your room, I trip and break my
neck? Do you want those to be your last words to me?
    Brooke: Good night, Kendall. I hope you don't trip.

Sex at Smith: A tale of the first morning, as told to me
by my friend Amy Balser.
    On the first morning Little Amy went to use the communal
bathroom at the end of the hall. She took out her retainer and put
it in its case on the ledge above the sink while she brushed her
teeth. She noticed another case on the ledge and was surprised
anyone else was still diligently wearing a retainer. Finished with
her ablutions, she trotted back to her room and was popping her
trusty retainer case back in its drawer when she realized she had
picked up the wrong one. Anxious to see how much trouble somebody else's teeth were in, she opened the case and saw she had
picked up not a retainer but a diaphragm. Which she still has.
Retrieving her retainer would have meant admitting that all she
was trying to prevent was an overbite.

Today I finished painting my background for my new
painting of Mom, and tomorrow I'm starting on Mom. Dad said
tonight, "It's going so well why don't you just leave your mother
out of it?" Encouragement, encouragement, encouragement.

At the moment I am at odds with my father. Mom is now rewriting her new novel. And though Dad has a lot of ideas, he always says that finally she must follow her own vision.

Then, directly after telling her that, he runs down here to tell me how to paint my painting, even using a throw rug to cover parts of the canvas he feels should be banned from human sight forever.

It's different in writing. I listen to everything he says in that area, but the man has no firsthand experience with painting. And I'm not even sure I want to paint the "masterpieces" he wants me to paint. I like to paint to capture the way I saw us and that may not always lead to a masterpiece.

I've discovered the sweetest writer—Saki (the pen name of the Scottish writer, H. H. Munro). We met in the most roundabout way.

Dad came running down at about 11:15 last night, saying there was a great *Alfred Hitchcock Presents* on. It was indeed—with Hermione Gingold, Pat Hitchcock, and such a dear story.

The credits at the end said it was based on a story by Saki, and today Dad found another of his stories, "The Lumber Room," for me in a collection. It was full of truth and laughter. When I read the notes on Saki at the back of the collection, I saw that one of his books of short stories is entitled *Beasts and Superbeasts,* and suddenly I remembered reading Cole Lesley's book about Noel Coward and writing down that very title because Noel Coward loved Saki so much. I was in school then, so I never followed up on it, but I am so glad I didn't lose Saki a second time.

I keep worrying that there are so many people I miss. Education is, I think, the meeting of kindred souls. I am kindred with Terence (his *Phormio* certainly makes for a fun evening), can get nowhere with Lucretius, and buddies with Saki. Tomorrow I sink my teeth into Catullus. An overflowing life.

Good mood almost spoiled by drive with Dad. I think my driving skills peaked two days ago. Since then I have had so many near collisions it is unfathomable. I've even started bumping into things as I walk through the living room.

Life and I have not been getting along lately. Oh, we get along most of the time, but there are little spats. I want to talk to Matthew. We haven't talked since he started school. It's been about two weeks and I am rather miserable. It's awfully disloyal of my emotions to hinge so on someone else.

Had a lovely talk with Matthew. We seem to talk without words and yet we use words. That makes no sense, I know, but it is the way I feel.

If there were rules to life, we'd all be a lot better at living it, but I've never yet made one that hasn't been broken.

Last night, armed with the knowledge that if I did not like what I did, I could quite easily re-create what was already there and the realization that I love my father more than the painting of my mother, I attacked that canvas.

I hate to admit this because it breaks my favorite rule of life (don't listen to anybody), but the painting looks twenty times better. Suddenly the whole canvas is one and little things that were never noticed before now can be. I have three more sections to do and if it all works out, by the end I will have used every piece of advice Dad gave me when he demonstrated with the throw rug.

He was absolutely right on every count, and after quite a while I realized it. My goal now is to reduce my pouting period.

Julie Reich has gotten over her college depression. I got a letter addressed to Kendall Hailey, bum, filled with news of men and wine coolers.

Dear Kenny,

First I'll answer your question:

Q. So, are you a lot smarter by now?

A. Yes. Tons.

Classes Update:

English I has turned out to be an exact repeat of ninth to twelfth grades. Well, maybe I'll remember the stuff this time. I understand *rien* of French III. We're supposed to speak all in French, and eighty-five percent of the class understands and I, along with the other fifteen percent, keep quiet. Art history is faintly interesting, and I have not understood enough of calculus to tell you anything about it.

Now, on to a more interesting subject: men.

Number one: freshman; lives down the hall; left-handed, like me; blond hair; excellent dancer. Problem—has girlfriend. Depression sets in.

Okay, here's Number Two: Senior. He asked me to dance at a frat party and we danced for at least seven songs, then we stopped and he said he wanted to dance later, but I haven't seen him since. He told me he thought I was a good dancer twice. I don't remember exactly what he looked like because he's about six feet tall and I had trouble looking up at his face for long periods of time. I memorized his jacket, though. Problem self-evident . . . no hope.

Besides my men-problems (they are no longer boys), I'm okay. My last letter probably sounded depressing, but I like it better now than I did then. I'm getting into the swing of things. I got drunk two nights ago. I talked to my mom yesterday, and she asked me if people drink at the parties. I said, "What do you think?" Then she asked me if I'd tried anything. So I told her I had wine coolers (one third wine, two thirds 7-Up)—I didn't tell her I had four of them and went to sleep feeling nauseous. Anyway . . . have fun studying Rome, if you can.

Love,
Julie

Catullus reminds me of Brooke. They have the same thing on their minds most of the time. So I decided to read her some poems by her soulmate. Brooke's response: "If I had a choice between perfect thighs [she has as near to perfect thighs as any I've ever seen] or Catullus never having lived, guess which I'd pick."

Should I have left home by now? That is the question I have been asking ever since the mail arrived.

I was putting the finishing touches on Mama Betsy's portrait (I have once again created a masterpiece and once again my model is complaining that it does not look like her) as Mom and Dad were going through the mail and mumbling that I should "fix the face" (I hate that phrase, probably because I hear it so often) when Dad handed me a letter from our friend George Furth.

I knew before I opened it what it was going to be about. The last time he talked to Mom and Dad, he asked them to put me on the phone so he could discuss my life plans. Fortunately, I was in the shower at the time, and Dad was probably as relieved as I was since he doesn't like outsiders advising me how to live.

But there was no way to avoid the letter. I love George for taking such time and care to write, and I'm sorry that I am not nearly as fond of his advice (head for college, or if I choose to educate myself, do it away from home) as I am of him.

Why do people think you have to leave home to become an adult, happy human being?

I talked to Julie Reich the other day. She called me long distance and the last thing she said was, "Kendall, do you think I'm still the same?"

I mean there she is, independent, breaking away, and she asks me that. I told her to drop out and come live with us. Some might say that her initial period of unrest is necessary to eventually become a stronger, better person, but in a world where I could be struck down tomorrow, I'm not going to spend one moment being lonely without an emotion-back guarantee that I'll be better for it.

You can't say something like this without being eyed as a Brontë girl in the making, but I love my family and I don't ever want to be without them. A line from George's letter said, "I see in you much youth that will lift as soon as you can relate to people your own age who also love what you love and you will be you instead of the daughter, the sister, the niece, granddaughter, etc."

But what I want in my life are more of these roles, not fewer. We are made up of who we love, so the more people I love, the more complete, the more I, I will be.

This was his last paragraph:

> See, you are shy. And you are sheltered. And you are suspicious. And a little bit fearful. But so is everyone. But going off on your experience into newness will eliminate all that. I guess what I'm saying is either go away to college or go away to explore. But move. You have it in you to nest and hide out and stay protected and the reason for this letter is to beg you to begin the journey in your mind that soon you will begin in your life. *Move* figuratively and literally.

He's right when it comes to shy, sheltered, suspicious and fearful—I am a little of all four, but as far as moving, I'll let Eudora Welty answer for me. I don't suppose I ever read a book as slowly as I did *One Writer's Beginnings*. I would read each line again before going on to the next, but the last were my favorites: "As you have seen, I am a writer who came of a sheltered life. A sheltered life can be a daring life as well. For all serious daring starts from within."

There is my friend Julie Reich, away from home, in a new city, surrounded by people her own age, and scared to death in the middle of her four safe subjects. While here I am, surrounded by five safe people, writing as many different things as I can (from novel to play to screwball comedy to mystery) and reading the same way (from James to Juvenal to John Van Druten) and feeling so courageous. As if the world is not some place far off I have to conquer, but sitting right next to me in my other armchair, waiting for me to take another poke at it.

So I hope I won't sound like a coward when I say that I think

George is wrong, that in my view what I've done takes a lot more guts than to head for a "small college" as he advises—though not at first glance and not at first.

I didn't have to face the little terrors of leaving home and finding new friends and adjusting to new ways. And I don't yet have to face the huge terror of making enough money to provide the food, shelter, and clothing I have always taken for granted. But I do have to face a certain kind of terror—life with no schedules and free periods and tests to break it up and show me what to do with it.

I have been given the chance to live my own best life, but no instructions were included with the chance. So I haven't been exactly sure how to do it or if my efforts have been any good. I certainly don't know who I am the way I did in school. I don't suppose one is ever as secure as one is in school because there are such easy standards. An "A" is the best and if you get an "A," then you're the best. And if you get all "A's," then you couldn't possibly be doing more with your life. In the life I've been living, it hasn't been as clear as that.

It's funny, when people go to college, they often have a hard time adjusting at first, but everyone advises them to stick to it. With autodidacts, the period that's hard is after the newness of freedom has worn off, and you begin to wonder what you should be doing with this freedom. But even if the struggle to get the most out of my freedom is sometimes hard for me, I don't want to stop struggling.

I know that for certain now. I've seen too much of life, and even if I haven't loved all I've seen, I've loved being able to see so much. I don't ever want the days to slip together in some terrible way and I'll look back and life will be gone. I want to feel something every day, even if occasionally it happens to be a little misery. Even if at times I feel a little lost, I want to find my own way.

When I was in school, my life was what was due next week, and that's not enough for a life.

Another Halloween, we're all a year older. I remember when I first saw *Meet Me in St. Louis* and heard Marjorie

Main (who I always wished lived at my house) say that line, I was so shocked. I didn't think time could be measured by anything but your birthday. The thought of time passing with each moment is a concept I have yet to accept.

The little trick-or-treaters this year give the impression they have rolls of toilet paper waiting if they don't like what you're serving. One asked me as I was bending down to dish it out (there was a day when I was short and everyone else was tall), "What is that, anyway?"

I don't know why I feel so emotional about Halloween. I suppose because it's the one holiday that really changes as you grow up. No matter how old you get there'll always be Thanksgiving and Christmas presents and Valentines (I suspect that holiday gets better) and Easter eggs (or at least you could eat your children's), but I'll never be a trick-or-treater again.

It's not even that I was ever that crazy about trick-or-treating— in fact, it made me kind of tense. It's just that I'll never be short, and I'll never be a trick-or-treater again.

Ever since I read that Handel was a manic depressive, I've been thinking that I've become one too.

I have been considering my life a lot lately. You get a letter from someone you respect telling you you're living it all wrong, you do wonder. I keep trying to picture myself alone, on city streets, but every time I picture it, I see myself about to cry.

I don't think I am scared of being alone, but for one who's been as happily surrounded as I have, well, it's just not exactly something one yearns for. And yet I don't want to miss anything. I want to try everything.

Just came from tucking Mom and Dad into bed (you can't do that if you live alone). Made my way through the steam to kiss Brooke. If that child gets the sniffles, she plugs in the vaporizer. Tonight she was barely discernible through the fog, but I made it. As I leaned down to kiss her in her sleep, she said,

"Don't kiss me—my throat's sore." I don't think that child is ever fully unconscious.

I got the most heartbreaking letter from a college friend today. Ever since I had known her she wanted to be an actress, and so after graduation, when I was afraid I would not see her again, I wrote to tell her what a wonderful actress I thought she was.

She wrote today that she did not get into the acting school she wanted to, so she is giving up her dream of being an actress. It takes so little to destroy a dream.

I sometimes look at adult people and wonder how they could have ended up so sad, and yet here I am at the formation of what may be some very sad lives. We are changed people once we let go of what we hope for.

Most of my dreams are pretty silly, but I will not let go of one of them, no matter how much of what is laughingly referred to as "real life" gets in the way. As Ruth Gordon said, the key to success is: Don't Face Facts.

Mondale lost. It was so sad when he made the speech the next day saying he would never again seek elective office. I hate to see a good Democrat give up and face facts.

When Thomas was in the midst of his cerebral hemorrhage, I was so terrified he wouldn't know me anymore. Now, he is practically recovered, but I feel I no longer know him. He is so angry. When I asked him today if he was ever going to stop being mean, he said he was through being "milk-toast" Thomas.

He is being unfair to the man he was to label him that. Thomas has never been anything but strong. He survived the effects of a childhood disease without bitterness, and I mean without any bitterness. Dad used to wish that he had been the one who had gotten polio, since he never had any love of sport as Thomas always did. But after he got Parkinson's, he said he now knew he never could have dealt with being in a wheelchair the way Thomas has all these years.

And God knows a man who has been through polio and a cerebral hemorrhage has a right to be angry. He has a right to be furious. But living with what people have a right to be is no fun.

Spent tonight reading Tibullus and listening to Schubert, Mendelssohn and Mozart. I am so lucky to live in a world where so much wonderful stuff from all the centuries exists.

It is amazing how much a little culture can do for just about anything. Washing the dishes is washing the dishes, but washing the dishes to Dvořák's *New World Symphony* (it times out perfectly if you have six in the family and a corresponding number of dishes) is something to remember.

As is Tibullus. I have always loved to read poetry, but it has taken the Romans to remind me I do.

How I loved this line: "Be careful how you do mischief to a girl love guards." What a wonderful image of love . . . that it guards and keeps you.

And the way he speaks out against the death-courting heroics of battle. Imagine finding a pacifist so lyrical in an age when there was a god of war.

I am about to finish my mystery and I don't want to.

In my father's playwrighting group a few weeks ago, a very bright woman told about an article which outlined the similarities among all geniuses. I went into a panic, thinking what if they all have red hair or brown eyes—what if that's the link and there's no chance of me ever becoming a genius?

Well, as anyone of real genius material might have guessed, the similarities are anything but that specific. The one that struck me most is that all geniuses try to "delay closure," which, the way I interpreted it, means to think about and mull over things as long as possible. Not to stop letting things develop.

So perhaps all this rebellion against ending the mystery is just delaying closure. Or is it a sanity tactic? While seeing a very boring play yesterday, convinced I would never come up with another idea to write after I finished the mystery, I had my first anxiety attack—a sure sign of maturity.

At the moment all is well. I was ordered to help Nanny take out the trash, but it gives her so much pleasure I felt I had to refuse. Oh, I took out the last can, but then I saw she'd run around to the backyard to find some more. One man's trash is Nanny's afternoon entertainment.

Saw Matthew tonight. He did not kiss me passionately and declare his undying love forever (which is redundant, but pleasantly so). Sometimes I think he just puts up with me—though when I'm with him I don't even notice life, I'm so in love.

My friends at school—well, not really my friends at all but people within hearing distance—would say of someone if they thought her unworthy of a future, "She'll probably be married at eighteen."

Well, here I am at eighteen and that is exactly what I want. Just to have someone whose hand you could take at any hour of the day and they would know why you'd taken it.

I now have had firsthand experience with cooking and bookkeeping and though I am bad at cooking and good at bookkeeping, I think I could make a go of both. I could probably even learn not to toss and turn in my sleep, but that would take work.

I often wonder if my movies aren't trying to send me a message. In a great majority, you know, it is the woman who tells the man she loves him.

Woman Tells Man	Man Tells Woman
A Man and a Woman	I can't think of any, but
Two for the Road	I may just not be trying.
My Man Godfrey	
Mr. Smith Goes to Washington	
The Ex-Mrs. Bradford	
It Happened One Night	

Bringing Up Baby

Could one person care as deeply as I do and the other not care at all? He must care. Could he? I have no idea. But I do know that what is great is to love. Not to be loved.

I was rocketed out of my dream this morning (my best movie dream yet—I was playing tennis with Katharine Hepburn) by a call from Matthew. We talked for about an hour and a half until he had to leave for the orthodontist. It is hard to talk too seriously of love with someone who still has to go to the orthodontist.

It is now 3:19 A.M. and my room is finally neat. Will there ever exist a day in which I get to do everything I want to? Including straightening, reading, writing, being nice to people, and not equating sugar with happiness. I did straighten and I did read. Unfortunately, I also ate, and I did not write, and Brooke, on going to bed, said the only person she could equate me with was the devil. That about sums up my accomplishments.

Though I did read a lot. I'm up to the Augustan Age. I finished reading about Caesar and Cleopatra and Antony and their wild goings-on just in time to watch Claudette Colbert in De Mille's *Cleopatra*, which is really very true to history—truer than I ever imagined.

I always thought Cleopatra being carried in to meet Caesar rolled up in a rug the clever, if a bit too cute, idea of the screenwriter. Little did I know that was the clever, if a bit too cute, idea of the real Cleopatra.

The film also does a fascinating job of playing out the parts of history nobody knows. History tells us that Mark Antony went to Cleopatra to take Egypt away from her and, after their meeting, not only let her keep Egypt but came away promising her foreign lands.

And not even those historians who make up what they don't know can imagine what went on in between. I will take De Mille's explanation, but I doubt Cleopatra had as much charm as Claudette Colbert.

As I lay in bed this morning, I could not think of one good reason for getting out of it, and so I knew it was time to call Michele Arian.

I have not seen enough of her since I left Oakwood, which we attended together, after attending all of grade school together. And I haven't seen her at all since her graduation from Oakwood. For it would not be likely to find Michele Arian at any of those Oakwood gatherings I occasionally attend due to the fact that most of the class is terrified of her. But I have always found that beneath any slightly frightening exterior lies the sweetest of souls.

For a long time, the company of Romans has been enough, but now I'm in the mood for some friends and countrymen, and when it comes to those, Michele Arian is as old as they come. I met her in kindergarten, we made a few poisons in the backyard during second grade, we compared and refined our pre-test study patterns during all of eighth grade American history, we paced off our anger at the stupidity of everything our eleventh grade said about *The Great Gatsby,* and, throughout the years, I have always known that no matter how depressed I might be, I could count on her to be more depressed.

She was.

Or perhaps all autodidacts live on the edge of life because it turns out that she has become one too! When I saw her at graduation, her plan was to take a semester off and then go to art school. But now she's decided not to go to art school. I said this meant she's an autodidact, but she said she didn't really feel she could accept the title, not having read a book since graduation.

We talked mostly about this feeling that we want to help the world. And yet we don't know where to begin.

She talked about joining the Peace Corps, but is not sure how long one has to sign on for. In school, our convictions seemed to be pacified by simply mocking our fashion-conscious classmates.

But now it isn't enough to exist simply by mocking. Plus the fact we haven't seen our classmates for six months—they may have picked up a few convictions.

We are definitely two disturbed autodidacts, but I am beginning to think there's more to be said for being disturbed than satisfied.

A letter from Julie, the collegiate, today. Nice to know she isn't perfectly adjusted either (though homework does give life a certain sanity).

Dear Kendall,

Right now I'm in a good mood. I fluctuate by hour! I guess I'm in a good mood because I feel sort of "in"—like I fit in. At dinner I ate with some people I don't usually eat with. I had a conversation with this girl who I thought didn't like me—but I guess she does, and she's nice. Little things like that put me in a good mood.

I also have another reason to be in a good mood. I like this guy (he's a new one) and, for once, he might like me too. I met him at a fraternity party last Friday night, and we talked for two to three hours. I was really open and frank, so I feel a sort of spiritual attachment to him, I guess you could say. That's really stupid-sounding, but it's true!

Anyway, he asked me for my phone number, and I got his. He didn't call me, so I got up my guts and called him last night. He was really nice. I asked if he wanted to meet for lunch today (aren't I brave?), but he couldn't because he was going home for Rosh Hashana until Friday. But he said he would call me Friday when he gets back. I hope he really does! If he doesn't call me, I don't know if I should call him because that might be pushy. *Je ne sais pas!*

I had my first French examen on Monday. I probably got a C+ or something, but only because I didn't study right. (At least I think that's why). We're having our first calculus test on Monday, and I'm already shitting bricks. There are three review sessions planned before the test, and I'm going to all of them! English is horrible—it's so boring—now we're doing political articles, which I couldn't care less about. Today I ditched English because it was raining and I was wearing shorts. Reason enough.

I can't seem to keep my mind off that fellow. Ugh! I can't let myself get infatuated because I'll just end up depressed.

Write back and tell me the Studio City gossip! Sometimes I watch Johnny Carson because he talks about L.A. —I kind of miss that smoggy metropolis. I haven't really been into Boston yet—I should go one day before graduation.

I can't think of any more exciting news, so I'll go and do my homework now—it's about time. I've been so bad about doing my homework—I feel like I don't do it half the time. I guess that's because a lot of it is reading, so I'm not actually *writing* something.

Anyway, enjoy whatever an autodidact does. Oh, we had a power failure yesterday. Have you ever been on a completely dark college campus? Chances are, you have not. It's pretty scary.

Okay, I'm really going to go now. I may even do my homework. Talk to you later.

Love,
Julie

Just came from seeing Thomas, who said he had been crying over what a good brother Dad is to him. I am happy to say that Thomas is back to being wonderful "milk-toast" again. His emotions, which were dammed up by anger for so long, are now overflowing. As I was leaving Thomas's room, I saw a light on in Nanny's, so I dashed down—she was up with arthritis. Now we both have Ben-Gay Extra Strength greasiness on our hands (it feels like it's *giving* me arthritis). I live such a textured life. Most of the time it is happy, some of the times it is painful, and rarely it is so happily painful I want to cry. (But I put on *Mr. Smith Goes to Washington* instead and go on.)

I finally solved my mystery. I had gone for such a long time without writing it that when I sat down to end it today I had forgotten how the clues (or rather, clue, as I could only think up one) are put together to catch the murderer. And I just barely remembered who that was.

M̲y grandparents are celebrating Thanksgiving with us. I think that after being with me, they are now primarily thankful for my cousins Alexis and Mimi, who will both soon be off to college.

My grandmother Janet said to me, "If you don't stop reading all these books, you're going to be overeducated. I think you should go to college."

I fear many things, but I've never yet feared overeducation. I really do think it's last on my list of things to worry about.

It's so odd, too, that this remark should come from Janet, since she makes great works a part of daily life better than anyone I know. She's always taking a course in some aspect of literature, history, or art.

I pointed out that she, too, was in danger of being overeducated, but Janet said she had spent all these years trying to make up for dropping out of Vassar to attend art school in Italy two years before graduation.

She's read more than anyone I know and is one of the few adults I can discuss great literature with because she is one of the few adults who reads it now instead of having read it fifty years ago. I wonder if any of those dames who graduated in Vassar's Class of 1934 have read *The Divine Comedy* in the last ten years. My grandmother has. And I am as proud of her education as she is worried about mine.

My grandfather Earl is more baffled than worried. A couple of weeks ago he sent me these articles about the Constitution that had been sent to all the members of his law firm. He wrote that perhaps I might find them educational. I was very touched at his unexpected broadening of my studies.

Though the broadening of my education was another point of contention. My grandparents worry that I might turn out lopsided concentrating on history and literature, and pretty much ignoring science and math. But I pointed out that college wouldn't necessarily correct that. A friend of mine about to graduate from Yale has yet to take a science or math course, and many such progressive colleges no longer force a student who's happy with the humanities to take math or science.

People are always arguing in favor of college, that you are made to read things you would never read on your own, but it's hard to take joy in the things we are made to read. And I think following the path of what really interests us will eventually branch out into all knowledge. After all, the Greeks led me to Isoceles and his triangle and the Romans led me to Pliny the Elder and his *Natural History,* unnatural though it was.

I think I finally persuaded the grandparents that I will not make a total mess of things, but they would be more persuaded if I told them this on a postcard from Stanford.

And I do feel for them. My grandfather was the first person in his family to go to college. His father thought he was very foolish to leave the farm. But he knew he had to, the same way I know I don't have to.

I have been fighting quite a bit with Dad lately. It is very hard to be good friends when one of you is still teaching the other how to drive, even after she's passed her driver's test (though with admittedly the lowest score I've ever gotten on any test in my life).

I think Dad is experiencing anxiety over my taking the least little control of my own life. But I wish he would try to curb his emotions. I'm sure even the Reverend Brontë made an effort.

Dear Ken,

Sorry I haven't written for so long, but I was too busy dropping calculus. Home for Hannukah in less than two weeks. I'm spending my time signing up for next semester's classes—I hope I'll get into a creative writing class. Also, philosophy, French, art history. See you soon.

Love,
Jules

P.S. Hi, Brooke—this being a postcard, I know you're reading it.

I have just seen the most inspiring documentary on Eleanor Roosevelt. One of the hazards of being an autodidact is that sometimes the world can be very small—limited, quite frankly, to your very own problems and concerns. And sometimes it takes Eleanor Roosevelt to make you realize just how many people there are in this world.

I think the best solution to not sinking back into my self-obsessed pit is some kind of charity work. I remember in my first year of autodidatia, calling a public service number at 6:00 A.M. (just when they opened—just as I was going to bed) to volunteer my services at an orphanage, only to be told orphanages do not exist anymore—foster homes now. I guess I've seen one Shirley Temple movie too many.

Ironically, I think the very place for my services may be my old grammar school, where I spent the most awful seven years of my life (life does get better and better). It is the one place I still fear. I'm making it sound like the Charles Dickens Academy. It wasn't really. It was a very good school, but I was a very disturbed child. And it would be nice to help some poor kid who's taking kindergarten as badly as I did.

My first day back at school.

Grade school, I leap to clarify. The biggest shock was that rooms and playgrounds and halls that used to seem so gigantic now seem so conquerable.

Not nearly as traumatic reentering the old halls as I thought it would be. I rather like to shake and tremble with emotion like old Proust at every event, but Hemingway must have made me slightly hard-boiled.

I was assigned to help everybody who had not finished their math and I never dreamed seven take away six could have so many answers.

Puli has died. He was so old and blind that every time we went out, I'd come home praying he'd still be alive. But I always thought, somehow, that my family was invincible. That much as I might fear it, nothing would ever really happen to us seven.

I'm glad Puli was here to see Thomas through his cerebral hemorrhage and after. Thomas may have yelled at us, but he knew Puli, at least, was always good at heart.

Brooke is home all day every day because of Christmas vacation. To have her here with no concerns but her appearance is such happiness.

Brooke is just a bubbling stream of natural talents. She can do everything in the world and also cook. We made breakfast together this morning, and then afterward I put away the jelly and Brooke did the dishes. She did keep berating me with little remarks that I might not be doing enough, but, ah well.

I take such pleasure in guiding her (though she will not be guided anywhere she doesn't want to go). But I do take full responsibility for her character. Mom and Dad are not really guiders. I mean, Mom swoons she loves Willa Cather so much, but she never orders you to read her.

I suppose I am not much of a guider either (Proof Positive: The child has never read Hemingway or watched *My Man Godfrey*), but I do think she respects me enough that she might take my future guiding seriously. She told me today that I'm the only person she knows who's read Livy. Though, now that I think about it, she didn't really say it as if it were something to be proud of.

I've begun a new novel. With a heroine who knows as little about life as I do, which is why I am writing it . . . so we can figure it out together. Finally, I have found a place for all my worries and torments, a much better place than in my head, where

they just keep bumping into each other and frightening themselves even more.

C̶hristmas Eve. Matthew did not kiss me like last
year (though I gave him every opportunity—maybe I gave him
too many), but he did recommend reading the Romantic poets,
which is something, I suppose.

Kisses or not, I do love him. Who else would lead me from the
party to the poetry anthologies to read Blake and Coleridge
aloud? Brooke says we're phony, but if we live in fear of phoni-
ness, I think we hit mundanity.

Even though I am older, Matthew seems to be. There is a bit of
the father figure about him, which I've wanted ever since I first
read *Little Women* and began modeling myself after Jo. I planned
then to marry a much older man. How nice to have found one two
years younger than I.

I used not to be able to go to sleep on Christmas Eve for the
excitement. Now, if I could just wrap the rest of Nanny's candy
and get to bed. Ah, maturity.

I think of children who have never even seen toys and yet I
can't help hoping I get great presents tomorrow. Merry Christmas.

I am just about to plunge into the Romantics. I was
determined to read them sitting outside, as it seemed only fair to
such nature lovers, but it is so cold and wet I have compromised
and am sitting inside looking outside.

I have fallen in love with those I used to hate. In
school I thought the Romantics a bunch of sissies who I wished
would come out of the forest and be sensible about things.

Today, thanks to Matthew, I adore them and feel surrounded
by new, young friends. George Furth told me I needed to be with
people closer to my own age, and the Romantics are much
younger than the Romans.

I read Wordsworth first. *Intimations of Immortality,* especially, I felt so close to, and then I read that this poem is regarded as his very finest. It's not that I was happy because I spotted it (though I am impressed with this little autodidact), but more that the emotions in the poem which had affected me so closely had affected so many so closely.

From school I remembered only that Coleridge was an opium addict, but he's also awfully sweet and tender. His poem "Kubla Khan" was very hard for me to follow and when I read that it had come to him in an opium-induced sleep, I felt much better.

Apparently, he took a bit of opium, fell asleep, had this incredible dream of two hundred to three hundred lines, set down what we know of the poem, then was interrupted by the now notorious "person from Porlock." And when he came back to write the rest of the poem, he had forgotten it.

And yet I wonder, was it better that Coleridge was a kind man, "a wonderful man" as Wordsworth described him, and took the time to be sociable to the "person from Porlock," or would it have been better had he shut the door in his face and finished "Kubla Khan"?

Had I dreamed "Kubla Khan" and that person interrupted me, I would have been so mean to him he would have raced back to Porlock. Actually, I suppose I would have either asked him to wait and felt terribly guilty or had him in and felt worse, knowing "Kubla Khan" was slipping away. What did Coleridge feel?

I must remember to ask him when I get to Heaven. Though I suspect in Heaven, he has remembered the rest of "Kubla Khan" . . . which is a more frightening thought. Think how much there will be to read when we all get to Heaven.

Dinner tonight was worth all the trials and tribulations, all the fights, all the grunts, all the everything of family life.

At our table Mom and Dad sit at one end and Nanny and Thomas sit at the other with Brooke and me more or less center. And Nanny and Thomas, though they refuse to acknowledge it, are both quite deaf, so that news announced at the beginning of dinner by Mom and Dad is usually brought up as fresh news during the middle of dinner by Nanny and Thomas, who have not heard a word that has been said at the other end.

Tonight we decided to root out just where the trouble was. We played that game where someone makes up a message and you pass it along the whole line and then see what shape it is in when it reaches the original whisperer.

Dad whispered to Brooke, who whispered to me, who whispered to Thomas (he had to turn completely around so I could get his good ear, which didn't help much), who whispered to Nanny so loudly the neighbors heard, who whispered to Mom, who whispered to Dad a sentence pretty much the same disregarding things like subject and verb. After analysis, we detected Nanny as the troublemaker.

These are such precious days, before any of us dies or leaves home (which to my father is nearly the same thing). To have us all six gathered around the dinner table is the true ripening of a family. We are at our best. We finally know each other, have almost stopped hating each other, and come close to valuing each other, at least from six to six-thirty every evening.

WHAT I DID:

A novel (the beginning).
A mystery (the end).
A little bit of life (the bumpy middle).

THE SECOND HALF
OF FREEDOM

WHAT I HOPE TO DO:

Leave home without leaving my room.

A letter arrived from Julie Reich today that has reminded me that I really do prefer worrying about life itself, as opposed to the details of it.

Hi . . . (said sullenly)

Guess what happened *again*? Yes—my plane was delayed. I am now somewhere between L.A. and Denver, shitting in my pants, wondering whether or not I'm going to make my connecting flight. Right now there is turbulence, and I feel as though I may vomit. I hate the airlines for doing this to me. My dad says he's been flying for ages, and he's never had a problem with late planes. Of course —*of course*—it happens to me. I am just the most perfect person to be the recipient of personal traumas. I, who cry at everything and anything. Especially when airborne.

Later. I'm in the Denver airport now. Guess what? I missed my plane. The next one is at 12:50 (it's now 12:04, I got here at 11:15). It's not nonstop to Boston. It stops in Chicago, where I have to change planes again. I could've gone on a nonstop, but I wanted to be on the same plane as my luggage. I almost started crying when I was talking to the woman at the customer service desk. I went in the bathroom to cry, but there were people waiting, so I couldn't emit a sufficient sniffle. I look like a schmuck walking around Denver airport with tears in my eyes. Plus, I have a cold, and my ears are plugged, so I can barely hear anything. I've got a permanent lump in my throat when I talk to people—I thought it was bad enough on the way home when this happened to me, but this is twenty-eight times *worse*. I have to take a cab to school from the airport, and I'll probably get raped. Oh—when the stewardess was giving me my hot tea, she spilled it all over my carry-on bag. I knew I was destined to miss my flight when the breakfast turned out to be cheese omelette and sausage (I don't like either).

Much later. I'm at school now! Thank God! In Chicago I found

out that the plane I was supposed to catch was delayed, and that it
was in Milwaukee, and they weren't sure when or *if* it was coming!
I wandered around the airport checking the TV monitor every five
minutes. My ears were still plugged up, so I couldn't hear anything. I called my dad, crying hysterically, and *he* almost started
crying when I told him what happened. *Finally* the plane came in.
I had been calling my roommate all day but there was no answer,
so I called once more before I boarded and she was there, and her
boyfriend said he could pick me up at the airport. On the plane my
ears hurt, and there was lots of turbulence, but at least I was finally
headed for Boston. And I would not be raped before I got to Tufts.
And that was enough for me.

Love,
Julie

I just finished reading the first book in Livy's 142-
book history of Rome. Only thirty-five books are extant, thank
God. I was surprised to learn the ancient Romans were as overwhelmed by Livy's productivity as I am. According to the introduction, his history's very size "deterred men from reading it all,
so that at an early date abridgements of it were made."

I have always pictured the ancients as having all the time in the
world to delve into these great masterpieces. They probably would
have loved the Viking Portables.

As for me, no offence to Herodotus, Thucydides, Xenophon or
Polybius (I suspect they were a very sensitive group), but I have
never read a more compelling historian than Livy.

Of course, he also made up most of his beloved history, but I
have found that always helps. I think he was really a novelist who
found a good plot in Rome.

I have decided to introduce myself to one classical
composer a day until I know them all. Or am I trying to bring an
order to my education because I can't do the same for my life?

Mom is going to have a hysterectomy and I am scared to death.
It's not even the operation that really scares me. It's that she'll be
in the hospital—away from us—for a week.

I am beginning to take loss of any kind so badly (though not half as badly as I'll take cooking dinner). I dreamed about Puli last night. I had tried so hard to put him out of my mind because I miss him so much. And I don't want Brooke to go back to school. Her Christmas vacation has given me some of the happiest days of my life. Even better than summer vacation in a way because it was such a short time. I put away all writing and books and devoted myself to her. We play Go to Texas (like Monopoly, except with oil, cattle, and cotton, which appeals to our blood and bones) all day long.

And yet as we played tonight, I thought even if we played Go to Texas all our lives (which does bring us together), could I ever be as close to her as I want to be?

That seems to be the problem of my life and the reason I need to get back to my novel. Not only do I possess my characters, but I seem to be able to possess everyone I write about. What does it say about me that I never feel closer to my family than when I'm alone in my room writing about them?

We're about to leave to take Mom to the hospital and then spend the night at the Van Scoyks since they are much nearer the hospital, and the operation is scheduled for early in the morning.

And nothing will happen to Mom. I know that. Nothing will happen. And nothing will happen between me and Matthew. I also know that. I used to dream of romantic encounters between us in all kinds of places—where would he choose to tell me he loved me? Now, we're going over there and I can't think of one romantic situation. I am simply worn out—even though we're spending the night under the same roof, something we have not done since I got rid of my bunk beds (did I ever make a worse choice when it came to decor?).

I used to think life would change forever if he told me he loved me. I have now come to the realization that life will probably always be the same, I will just have someone else to shower my affections on. And about time. The family is pretty well drenched.

But I feel awfully guilty talking about that when my mother is here. I should be talking to her. Asking her something.

I have been through so many emotions today I am pretty well wrung out. And unlike my friend Wordsworth, "emotion reflected in tranquility" is not my favorite state. I prefer emotion reflected in emotion.

Emotions of the day:

I woke up happy. Strange as that is. I like going to bed in strange places and I like waking up in strange places (maybe one-night stands should play a bigger part in my life).

The next exact moment was panic. Dad, Brooke, and I were sleeping in the study because no one wanted to be in the guest room alone, and I looked around the room and thought Dad and Brooke had gone—but they were just under their covers. I have a terrible fear of waking up late and finding everyone else has already left, perhaps because I am always waking up late and finding everyone else has left.

The next hour was sheer terror. Deeper terror than I've ever known—I didn't know how terrifying it was until it was over. If you can get through the surgery of someone you love, you can get through anything. I think. I'm so glad that waiting is over. I thought such terrible, deep, dark thoughts. I never once imagined Mom living. I just thought of a thousand different ways we could be told she had died. Last night, Matthew had given me a copy of his school literary magazine which he edited and all through that deep, dark hour of surgery, I read it. I couldn't do anything else. And though the pieces were wonderful, it was not the pieces I was reading. Every word was a part of him and I was reading them as fast as I could. I wonder, no matter what happened between us, if he would ever depend on me like that.

Relief and Joy and Thanks. Mom's surgeon came out with a huge smile—I barely even heard what she was saying I was so relieved. I have such respect for the medical profession. To be a doctor is the noblest calling there is. I thought about it long and hard today. That doesn't sound characteristic coming from someone as rotten as I am, but that is what I would like to be. If I could take it. But then I say to myself, maybe everyone shouldn't try to become a doctor. I mean, what if Carole Lombard had decided to become a doctor? What would the world have lost? But what would it have gained? The happiness Mom's doctor brought us in her warmth and kindness and reassurance is equal, in an equation all my own, to *My Man Godfrey*.

We waited an hour and a half or maybe two while Mom was in recovery—and I couldn't say anything. Our faithful friend Annie Raymond was with us and I kept thinking, what kind of a person are you, Kendall? I wanted to talk to someone so badly inside, yet I could barely get out one-syllable answers to questions. Why am I so different on the outside from what I feel on the inside? That's something I must remember the next time I really detest someone on the outside.

Then came real relief—Mom was brought back from surgery and once I saw her, I could finally talk. That first rush of relief stayed all day long. And everything we did had great importance just because we were all there.

I just discovered Matthew is taking out another girl. There have never been any declarations between us, just a deep friendship which, at least on my part, had grown into something more.

If I were in a movie, I'd cry. But I'm in a hospital room with Mom on one side and Brooke on the other, so I can't.

Would you like to know how I found out? Leona had come to visit and, mid-conversation, asked Brooke if she dated. Brooke answered the question by asking if Matthew dated. Does no one protect anyone? I spend my days protecting people. I won't hum a tune if I think it might stir an unpleasant thought. And Brooke asks a question which has a fifty-fifty chance of really hurting me. And she won. It really hurt.

I take comfort only in the fact that I am living life in a way Brooke will never be able to. I have fallen in love with so many people and places and things over the years. There's no way to judge anyone from anything but the outside, but as far as I can see, Brooke has kept her heart. I have given mine out to a thousand different people. Today, one of those parts came back shredded to bits. But it is only a part.

The awful thing is I love Matthew and more than anything I want to rationalize and compensate for and forget this piece of information any way I can so I can still love him.

And I still want to love Brooke. I almost took her out in the hall and asked her if she wanted to hurt me because she'd really done it. But it would hurt too much for other people, at least at this moment, to know how hurt I am. Maybe they think I didn't hear, I don't know what they think. But I don't want them to know anything else. At least not right now.

Exactly what Leona said was, "He's taken this one girl out to lunch a couple of times because he really likes her as a person." I don't know what the second part of that sentence is supposed to mean. I should hope he likes her as a person. What was she supposed to say? He can't talk to her, but he likes her breasts?

I'm sorry to be vulgar. I want to be like Irene Dunne. What would Irene Dunne do?

I feel like crying. I can't believe I heard what I heard and I can't believe this is my life. It seems like play-life. It's certainly play-love. It's easy to say you're in love when all you have to do is say it. No sacrifices, no fights, no conflicts. You just say you're in love. Today has been the first day being in love has been hard.

Now, I will either write some of my novel or read Horace's *Odes and Epodes.* I'll probably take the easy way and read Horace's *Odes and Epodes.* Imagine a life where Horace's *Odes and Epodes* is the easy way.

I thought I would be able to go to sleep without telling you, but I can't. I thought I had lost the Frank Capra conviction that everything works out for the best, but I haven't.

Today I realized my independence from Matthew. I'll always care about him, but tonight I realized my life does not hinge on him. I also saw quite clearly that I had subjugated a great deal of myself to please him. Just in little ways, but I see it now.

I never thought I'd say this today, but I am so grateful to Brooke. I always thought my world would fall apart if Matthew loved someone else instead of me, and, well, maybe he does, and it hasn't.

It irks me to think what a ninny I had become in some ways— agreeing with everything he said, barely speaking up when around him. But as of today, if I do marry someone, I'm not going to lose any part of myself doing it.

Right now I am sitting in the hospital room with Mom, whose recovery has been miraculous. I suspect that woman will feel like making dinner pretty soon. I know I certainly hope so.

Actually, I lie. The closest I have come to food preparation is opening a menu. We eat near the hospital every night, so we can come back and stay until Mom falls asleep, or stay even longer and read in the bathroom with the light on if we don't feel like going home, which sometimes we don't.

I do hate to see Mom go through all she has had to go through (she said yesterday that standing up wasn't so bad, she just had the vague feeling her insides were going to fall out every time she did it), but I have to confess I have enjoyed every minute of this.

It is a lovely Catholic hospital, and though we are not Catholic, they don't seem to mind. Everyone is so sweet—perhaps the thought of eternal damnation tends to make you that way. What an awful thing to say when everyone is really so very genuinely kind.

And how I love sitting in Mom's room and working and seeing visitors and then driving home with Dad late at night. And our talks.

I value Dad's every opinion as if it came from a sacred god, which it very well might. He is certainly my kind of god. Funny, sweet, honest, and with a certain originality to his vengeance. No one is as laughingly honest as my father. Last night, as we were driving home, I confessed what a fun time I had been having, and asked if this reflected pretty badly on my character. He said not to worry, it is always fun to have your life shaken up. I do hope God is as wonderful as Dad.

Still feeling pretty guilty, so today I confessed to Mom herself how much I liked this time at the hospital. She said I couldn't possibly have liked it more than she has. Breakfast in bed, a little nap till lunch, an afternoon of visitors, family, and no thought of preparing dinner. Then talking till she fell asleep, with Dad, Brooke, and me reading in the bathroom most of the night and reducing the nurses to tears with our devotion. In fact, she's a little upset to be going home tomorrow.

My parents have definitely put my mind to rest about my character problems. Those two really do remind me of Mr. and Mrs. God. Which is how I have come to see God. God is not a man or a woman. God is a marriage.

I have discovered that it does not really matter if I write, read, or am nice to people. All that matters is that I lose weight. I lost two pounds yesterday by watching *The Thin Man* three times (Myrna Loy works as well as Carole Lombard—and the title didn't hurt either).

For me, the key to happiness lies in writing. I lied when I said losing weight. Right now I'm writing and eating peanut butter and am much happier.

Last night, I gave Matthew up for good. We talked on the phone for the first time since the "revelation," and he hardly said anything. Other women and a bad conversationalist—I was just through.

Then today Dad talked to Leona and she said that last night they found out Bob had to go up on his insulin again to treat his diabetes. She said Matthew was so depressed and my call had cheered him up so much. Maybe he does rely on me a little.

Trust an Arbiter of Elegance to write a filthy book. I am reading the *Satyricon* by Petronius, who was Elegance Arbiter at Nero's court (and I suspect if there was ever anyone who needed to be told what elegance was, it was Nero).

Petronius must have been a perfect choice. Since one of the characteristics of true elegance is that it is hard to mock, perhaps an arbiter of it should know what is mockable. Of course, Petronius assumed everything was. He certainly had no qualms about giving it to the Roman world. A character of his says, ". . . our part of the world is so full of watchful powers that it's easier to run across a god than a man."

I was fascinated to find that Nero was almost as responsible for creating the form of the novel as Petronius. One of the great advantages of beginning the new genre was that it would not pose a threat to Nero's literary gift, which was neo-Alexandrian verse.

I am so glad I did not know Nero. Living under an empire ruled by him sounds like living under one ruled by Brooke.

Nanny is eighty years old today. As Dad says in one of his plays, "It's quite a feat to be loved at eighty." And she is going to continue being loved for a long time. Her astonishing health is a tribute to the nutritive benefits of white bread and chocolate.

Nanny's idea of a perfect three-meal day is coffee and two pieces of toast for breakfast, a piece of toast and a slice of cheese for lunch, a grilled cheese sandwich for dinner, and all the chocolate she can eat in between.

If you ask her if this is really all she ate, she'll quickly reply, "I drank a Coke with lunch and dinner." The only nutritional advice I've ever heard her give is "finish up your Coke."

I have this absolutely wonderful life, yet there are times when I can see no wonder in anything. It usually helps to pinpoint the behavior of a beloved relative as reason for this and turn on them for a while, but, unfortunately, that never works for long as a solution.

I tell myself to read or write or walk or paint or watch a little Jean Arthur. But it is hard to get involved in reading or writing or walking or painting, and though Jean Arthur always makes me feel better, there is still a lot of life left over between films.

I think back to the beautiful ending of *Anna Karenina*. That life-conquering last page written by a man who spent so much time in despair. Did Tolstoy ever regret staying on his estate and educating himself? Did he ever ache for the scheduled and orderly life the University of Kazan would have provided? I hate to say it, but I sometimes do.

I received this letter from Julie Reich today, but I knew before I read it the danger of a writer going to college.

Dear Kendall,

I just got back my first story for creative writing class.

They weren't graded, but the teacher all but said he hated it. You know the tone I use in my stories—sort of passive. Well, he found it to be "bland." Also, he's big on plots. So maybe mine didn't have much of a plot, but it had lots of details. I guess he doesn't like details either.

His criticisms really upset me because it made me realize that not everyone is going to like my writing and this horrible experience is just the beginning of many to come. Then that made me reflect on my life. That *really* depressed me.

I realized I hate the person I've become. I'm not kidding. I'm a self-contradictory person. I think one thing and do another. I really think like a nonconformist, but I do things that conform. Also, I wish I was a little more outgoing. When I go to parties, I try to be really friendly, and make new friends, or talk to people I know, but not really well. It's okay, but that's not *me*—I don't like acting like something I'm not, and I especially don't like making a huge effort that seemingly goes unappreciated. I just don't know how to deal with people anymore. It was easier when I was younger, because you know how little kids become friends—they just sort of *do*, you know? But now it's an effort to make a friend, and I don't like that.

I'm just depressing myself. I think I should change the subject. Today I'm going to Harvard Square to exchange some stockings I bought which came with a hole in them. My God, everything that happens to me is depressing.

When you write back, suggest possible story ideas. I need *stories,* not *situations.* I guess I've never written a story—just a lot of situations.

I think the real problem is, at the age of eighteen, I've run out of things to say. My brain hurts because I've been *thinking* so much lately. That sounds crazy, but this is what I mean: When I got my paper back, it started me thinking, and I ended up analyzing my life and every aspect of myself. I'm *sick* of myself. I can see how someone else could get sick of me if I get sick of *myself!* I'm lost within myself, and I'm struggling to get out . . . I thought that writing could be that rope that pulls me out. But now I find that I can't even express myself through my writing because I don't know *what* I want to express! I have no message!

This guy in creative writing wrote three short pieces about himself and his cancer. This guy had cancer! And he's cured now. So he hopes, through his writing, to convince at least one person to quit smoking. Now, I think that's worthwhile. But me—I don't have any message or idea or philosophical thought that I can use as a theme in my writing. And that *sucks*!!!

Love,

Jules

P.S. How is *your* life? I kind of neglected to acknowledge you in this letter, and I'm sorry.

I wrote back immediately to remind her she was writing for herself and strangers. Gertrude Stein said nothing about creative writing teachers.

Just when I thought that at eighteen I knew all life had to offer and was even a little sick of all life had to offer, I saw *Claudia.*

Some things in this world are just meant for each other. And I was meant to see Rose Franken's *Claudia.* If I thought I was kindred with Terence, well, I just hadn't met Rose Franken yet.

Immediately after the movie was over, I found a copy of the

play among Dad's collection and read it right away, while the voices of Dorothy McGuire, Robert Young, and Ina Claire were still so clear in my head.

A whole living stage was being preserved in that slender text.

Have been walking around the living room a lot tonight. I would definitely have to list pacing as one of my recreations. Long after I am gone my restless spirit will march around that living room still trying to make life decisions.

Here is my latest: Deep down inside of me I want to be an actress. I want to step on a stage. And I want to do it tonight.

There are times I can't wait for life to begin and yet in a way I suspect the very best life I will ever lead is here, in my own room, ranting around, mad with all my plans and dreams. I sometimes wonder if even being able to do it all would make me as happy as planning it all.

Mildred Dunnock once said to me about being an actress, "It's an awful business, but if you have to, then there's nothing else."

It was during the filming of Dad's television movie, *Isabel's Choice,* in which she starred with Jean Stapleton, Richard Kiley, and Betsy Palmer. She had just finished filming a scene and was heading for her trailer when we arrived. And Dad took me by one hand and Brooke by the other and ran with us so we could meet her.

I forget just what we said to her that prompted her to say that about acting. I have an image that she said it before we had time to say anything to her. As if it was a piece of information that had to be passed on without delay.

I hope that besides writing, there is "nothing else" but acting for me. And yet how do I go about it?

Most of the actresses whose careers I've studied became Mack Sennett Bathing Beauties first and then went into silent pictures. I don't think that's still the most popular route. And Julie Harris, when asked in a television documentary what she had learned in acting school, replied, "I didn't learn a thing."

If I'm not going to regular school, I don't want to go to acting school. What I have got to find is a way to be an autodidactress.

As soon as Rome falls, I'm going to head for another time in history—Broadway before it fell.

It is hard to know what to read to be educated. Anyone can read *The Brothers Karamazov* (except me, I never finished it). There's more to be said for following your passions.

And I want to study what I want to do. At least I hope it isn't possible to read as many plays as I plan to and not learn something about writing one. And I suspect reading all those lines just waiting to be said means I can learn something about how to say them.

Not that there is nothing to learn from the Greeks and Romans. In those dusty old books (I always like to think of the ancients as being in dusty old books, despite the fact I read them in paperback reprints) probably lie all the secrets of life. And it is always so exciting just to open a book and have a whole era step out, alive and well, for anyone to join.

That is also what happened when I read *Claudia*. And, thank heavens, because just like the ancients, so much of the theatre's history seems to have disappeared without a trace.

The stage artistry of Duse is as lost to the world as the military skill of Caesar. All we know is that it existed. And it is only by immersing ourselves in the atmosphere surrounding such genius that we begin to be able to imagine it. This means, in my case, a path from the battlefield to the stage, both of which are plenty bloody.

I'm almost finished typing the final version of Mom's new novel, and while I type I think a lot about my own. It now has plot, characters, and conflict—the only three things it lacked before.

And thinking about the novel and writing it has changed and

given me my life. Only now am I really beginning to start the novel. It must be an inherent Hailey trait that we throw away our first hundred pages. Actually, I kept my first page and threw away the next ninety-nine. I always liked that first page, but the ninety-nine after that brought me no closer to my character. Only now do I know who she is. At last I can see and hear her. And I just couldn't voice my own soul through her until I knew her.

Thanks to all my strange writing genes, my methods are very mixed, and I find I am trying to write a novel using the techniques of a playwright. You see, Dad has written his best female roles picturing particular actresses playing them. And that is just what I am doing. But while Dad usually writes roles for actresses he knows and loves personally, I could write this novel only for an actress I had never seen before. I had never seen Dorothy Mc-Guire before I saw her in *Claudia* last night. And when I did see her, I realized that was who I wanted to imagine saying all the things my character will say. So whereas Dad has written plays for Eileen Brennan and Barbara Colby and Carole Cook and Betty Garrett and Arlene Golonka and Marian Seldes, I am writing a novel for Dorothy McGuire.

I have to tell you I stopped helping at my old school. I feel awful deserting those little kids because they were so sweet. They gave their hearts so quickly. And I didn't really help them at all. I just ran away.

The first day I was there the teacher made one of them cry, and I knew then I'd never last. I didn't have the courage to do anything about it, and I didn't have the courage to stay and not do anything about it. Maybe kindergarten should be hell. Maybe that's what makes you an autodidact. And the hell of kindergarten was worth being an autodidact now.

I still want to help people, though. That's the best thing in the world anyone can do. And yet, in a way, helping at that school was running away from what I needed to do. Running away from being a writer.

I remember after a party one night when I had done my usual mumbling in answer to the question of what grade I was in, Dad said in the car going home, "Why didn't you just say you were a grade-school teacher?" He didn't mean there to be, but there was just the smallest hint of condescension in his voice. Writing will always take precedence over being kind to small children in the Hailey scheme of things. And I hate myself for that, but it's true in some very terrible way. If I spent my whole life just being kind, I'd probably end up thinking I'd wasted it. I wonder.

Today I finished typing the final draft of Mom's novel, *Joanna's Husband and David's Wife*. The main reason for this final revision is that the book needed more conflict, but I never guessed one of the sources for this new conflict would be me. Listen to this passage I just typed (for the purpose of fiction, Dad is pretty much David and I am pretty much Julia):

> For the first time in our marriage I know I have a legitimate rival. When David tells Julia how beautiful she is, I hear words he once used to praise me and me alone—and I react with a mixture of jealousy and pride. How can I feel such a sense of competition with my own daughter when she is my creation as much as his? Perhaps because she contains within her own unique persona all the unused possibilities of my younger self. It is not just David's praise of her youth and beauty that I covet, it is the long, still formless life ahead of her.

How could she feel that way? Of course, everyone related to a novelist has to understand that fiction is fiction. But, heavens above, I know from trying to write my own novel that fiction is chock-full of truth.

But even worse than the jealousy part is that Mom has changed the whole ending of the book so that the leading character, who is as much Mom as a character could be, is about to have another baby, who, she says, she knows will be a son.

I just can't believe that Mom, who I always thought was real saint material, has so betrayed me by wanting something in the way of children I can't give her.

I confronted Mom about all this and got the "fiction is fiction" talk I expected. All the same, I have turned on her.

Tonight I ordered her out of my room. After dinner, Mom likes to sit in my room and read the paper. She thinks that's being together. But me sitting and her sitting and her reading the paper and me reading a Roman and not talking to each other is not my idea of being together.

I don't know how to be together with her anymore. And I don't care to be.

That's a lie. It is so lonely not to get along with a parent. Tonight I see why kids turn to drugs and alcohol and everything else. Because it so lonely when the one relationship that we are led to believe is such a sure thing is not working out.

In the great tradition of Hailey writers, I have just upset my first relative. I read Brooke a passage in my novel about the two of us. She laughed throughout and said she loved it, then suddenly burst into tears. Of course, I had cried writing it, but I cry writing almost anything, and I was surprised at her emotion until she wailed, "Nobody in this family can capture me on paper."

She is as upset about *Joanna's Husband and David's Wife* as I am, not because of what it says about her but because of what it doesn't say. When she read the first draft, she complained about what a small part her character played in it. Mom said she would try to come up with more for her in the second draft. She remembered a charming childhood story about Brooke not understanding that planes could land and thinking you had to ride giant birds up to board them in the sky. Mom told Brooke she was going to put that in the novel. We all rejoiced, but then Mom realized that according to the chronology, the story could really be used only for my character. Brooke felt this was the final blow and at that point suggested having the second daughter just die at birth.

Directly after drying her eyes tonight, Brooke began her own book (and I quote from the opening paragraph):

"I love Kendall's book so much, but I just cried because she did not capture me. I also cried when I finished Mom's book because she not only did not capture me—she barely mentioned me. I've really got to write a book about myself."

She is absolutely right. The problem with trying to capture her is that just writing down her occasional remarks about great literature makes her come off (in her own words) as "dumb." And just writing down how much I love her and miss her creates the same feeling of distance an audience has in a Shakespearean comedy, "where all the laughing is going on onstage."

How do I capture the fact that she's the brightest person I've ever known? How do I face—let alone capture—the fact that she is without walls—honest in her hate, which is terrifying, but also honest in her love, which makes it worth it. I can't capture her. All I can do is read her book.

Though, on second thought, maybe I won't read it. Look what happened between Mom and me because of her writing, and now Brooke and me because of mine. I wonder if Gertrude Stein was aiming the remark about "writing for myself and strangers" at Alice B. Toklas. If she was, she was right. Only strangers should hear the secrets of your soul. Close relatives can't take them.

Today we began readings of Dad's play, *The World and His Wife*. It is the history of the world through the relationship of two people. Dad and two of his favorite actors are going to begin working on it, leading to a staged reading before an audience.

Rick Lenz is the world, Kres Mersky is his wife, and I am sound effects from the beginning of time to the present. I impersonate mammoths during caveman times, I scream a lot during the Crusades, shoot arrows while doing Indian war whoops during Pilgrim days, fire cap guns in the Revolutionary War, and bang cymbals for the atom bomb. I do all noisy events of the last hundred thousand years.

I was so in awe of my father after spending yesterday afternoon listening to his play (when I got a chance to listen, that is—though I do have a nice rest period before I do my torture squeals for the Inquisition) that I decided tonight, on the way to the playwrights' workshop, to question him deeply about his theory of playwriting.

We were talking about how great writing comes out of great pain when I began to think about a scene I had recently written. Last fall, Paul Kent, who runs the Melrose Theatre in Los Angeles, came to the playwrights' group and asked if they'd be interested in writing a series of scenes all set in a bar. Being playwrights and smelling an actual production, they of course said yes. And in a great act of taking myself too seriously, I tried to write a scene for the "bar play" too.

Talking to Dad, I realized that the scene I wrote dealt with something I really don't know about. It was about two college kids doing a sociology report on why people go to bars. It wasn't the fact that my characters were in college that made me feel I didn't know my material. I know enough about school to know what it's like to go to college. And I have Julie Reich at my disposal as technical advisor. It was the fact that I was writing about two people who had acknowledged that they loved each other.

I don't know how that feels. I don't even know, if acknowledgements started being made, if Matthew and I would have anything to acknowledge. And there is pain in that. It may not be up to the standards of full-length-play pain, but I think it's pain enough for a scene.

And it's unfair to the scene (and to me) if I don't try to be like my father and make people laugh with all the pain that is in me.

We are in the mountains. Light is just coming up over a night that has surprised us with snow. I have not yet seen a sunrise that has not filled me with awe of life which is, I suspect, exactly why we have them.

In staying up all night and watching the sun rise, I somehow feel I am witnessing the secrets of life everyone else misses. My worst childhood fear was to stay up so late I saw the sun rise, but now, in the cold and gray that will soon be dawn, I have the illusion I know all. How I wish I did.

A friend of ours was stabbed to death in a park yesterday. He saw a boy mug an old couple and began chasing the boy who turned around and stabbed him to death with a screwdriver.

I only hope by writing down what happened I can stop seeing it. Dad has the most ominous way of announcing tragedy. He says, "Something terrible has happened to one of our friends." He thinks he's preparing us, but in that moment every friend flashes through my mind.

He told us all together—a tragic family meeting where he told the details and how he had heard because he said he couldn't tell it more than once. As he was telling us, I didn't really feel it.

It was only after seeing the snow this morning that I felt it. I was looking out at the morning, and as I looked at the shingles on the cabin, half covered with snowflakes, I thought of him.

In the briefest, longest moment, the unparalleled beauty of the sight and the unparalleled loss were one. In that moment, everything beautiful and terrible was blended together and it was right somehow. As horrible visions come back to me now, nothing seems right, and I suspect it never will again, but for a moment I had a larger vision.

I have lost faith in the possibility of any real depth to human relationships. I just don't seem to connect with the people I live with in a day. I wish I could stop seeing every relationship from the outside and thinking, "Oh, that was a meaningful thirty minutes . . . thank God, now I can relax." Maybe all my turmoil is because I never really went through adolescence. Maybe this is some strange, late-hitting form.

I'm not an existentialist, but perhaps there is a strength to be derived from realizing that on a terrible, basic level we are all alone. And be grateful for those moments when we are truly with another person, rather than mourn all those when we are not.

There is so much I can say on this topic (don't shudder, I'm not going to), but somehow I would rather say it in my novel. More and more, more of me is in what I write. I was almost frightened by how much of me was going into my novel until I found out what Flaubert said about that very subject. He said, *"Madame Bovary, c'est moi."* And if he can be Madame Bovary, then surely no character is beyond a writer's reach.

Today, thanks to Matthew, we met the woman who made such wonderful history, or rather, herstory.

It was a fundraiser for Mayor Bradley and Matthew, who had been a volunteer worker on the campaign, was playing a major part (or at least he always manages to give the impression he is). Bradley is being opposed by a candidate named Ferraro, so Geraldine Ferraro had come to offer the mayor her support. After she made her speech for Bradley, Matthew led us to a back room to meet her.

Of course, since she first appeared the scandals have scandalized, and she has been brought down to the level of flawed politician, but since I never pay much attention to current events, nothing printed in the newspapers I don't read could dim her light in my eyes.

All I could think about was the day when we heard she was the one. Though the race was over long ago, shaking her hand today, I felt the same elation—as if we were still in the midst of it—which we are.

Today I went from history to the stuff it breeds . . . satire.

When we were studying Jonathan Swift in school, we had a lecture on satire, and I remember hearing repeated and repeated, "Horacian satire is laughing and lightly mocking; Juvenalian satire is sharp and biting." It was repeated throughout the lecture and then before the test and then before the final—repeated so often that it is still with me. And so, never having read either Horace or Juvenal, just hearing them used as adjectives, I always assumed I would adore Horace and be slightly frightened of Juvenal.

Well, it's amazing how attitudes can change when you really read these people. Reading Horace is like being reprimanded—being constantly tapped on the knuckles with a ruler. It is a very light tapping, but I find it rather irritating all the same . . . whereas Juvenal reminds me of me. We both get quite worked up and irritated about a great deal of the world. And though I may not always agree with him, I still feel that we're basically on the same side and it's not me he's after, but the world.

I've just finished with the first and second satires of both Horace and Juvenal. I'll confess now that their second satires are also their bawdiest. Funny they put them so early in their collections. I guess they knew what it takes to hold the attention of readers, modern and ancient alike.

However, I was a little shocked at a bit of editorial prudery. Listen to this footnote: "The scholiast attributes his pallor to his habit *inguina lambentis et stuprum patientis,* a diagnosis which, though probably correct, is perhaps better left untranslated." To tell the truth, I was glad to be spared, though I am curious. I'll ask Matthew. He knows Latin. I'll ask him if he's ever *inguina lambentis et stuprum patientis* and see what kind of look he gets on his face. It'll tell me a lot about Latin and a lot about Matthew.

It is amazing that those second satires actually made it down through what have been a lot of rather puritanical ages. I do worry about the poor monk that had to copy them.

But spicy as Juvenal and Horace are, this was my favorite sentence of the evening, from the introduction to Horace's works: "If originality is thought of as the invention of new genres, then Lucilius [creator of satire] had no rival in Latin literature—except, perhaps, Petronius." Do you know why I love that sentence? Because I got it. I knew Petronius created the genre of the novel. I love that sentence because it just may prove what I have been hoping, that I am becoming a literate Latin.

Today Brooke whispered in my ear that for all future fights with Dad it would be useful to have a T-shirt that had printed on it, "I know you have Parkinson's," since during any disagreement recently, no matter how minor, Dad can be counted on to say, "You know I've got Parkinson's."

I think his miracle drug has stopped working miracles. He has begun to have occasional tremors, he has to take naps for energy, and when he gets nervous, his words stick in his mouth a little.

But worse is that he is being forced to think constantly about what is wrong with him. He takes three to four pills a day. All or none of them may "catch," as he puts it—work effectively and save him from constant tremors and the drain of energy that means.

If all the pills work, then it's a good day. If some don't, then it's not too good a day. And if none works, then there's nothing I find myself wanting more than an "I know you have Parkinson's" T-shirt.

D ad's doctor has given him a new drug. Can one disease have two miracle drugs?

A few weeks ago I did a rough draft of a television script for Mom and Dad. Dad thought it would be good experience for me (sometimes I think I am a serf working in the name of experience).

Actually, I adored doing it. It is such a good idea for a television movie that I have my doubts it will ever get made. A couple is going to have a baby. Conception is set in 1890, but every month of the pregnancy takes place in an ever-advancing decade of the twentieth century, so the baby is born in 1980.

Finally, I could put my movies to a more profitable use than just keeping me sane. My constant viewing of *Life With Father* helped me no end with the 1890's scene, and heaven knows most of my vernacular comes from movies of the 1930's and 1940's. At last I could have a character say "swell," and they wouldn't sound like me, the living anachronism. I also got in a stunning Myrna Loy reference.

So, to sum up, I thought I'd done a swell job. Tonight I read Mom and Dad's version.

I had expected to be hateful about every line of mine they had taken out. Well, about three of mine were still in the script but I feel nothing but awe for my parents.

This is the first emotion I've ever had that is better than the one I imagined. Usually, I think I'll be hateful and I am, or I think I'll be nice and I'm hateful.

Their script was just so wonderfully written. If it hadn't been I would have been hateful. You can bet on that. I think this is the first time in my entire life I've ever been objective. A new and interesting feeling.

Of course, humans weren't really made to be objective. So I'll confess. Not only was my Myrna Loy reference left in, but Dad even enlarged upon it.

Tonight Mom was cooking a dinner we all like and she hates: country-fried steak, biscuits, and gravy. She was muttering, "All this country food . . . I feel like Jessica Lange." And I said, "You look more like Marjorie Main." And she still let me eat dinner.

Watching a documentary on Ethiopia tonight, I saw something I'll never forget. A young girl dying on-screen. The people at the Relief Center tried to give her water, but her throat muscles were paralyzed. I looked at her face and thought she's just as sensitive and bright as I pretend to be, and she could live as good a life as I could or better, and she just died, while I spent tonight trying to decide among Doritos, cold pasta, and Corn Flakes, and ended up with all three.

I hate watching things that are horrible, and I turn the channels faster than anyone when they start showing pictures of people starving. But tonight I watched and I saw her die and I thought why did I watch this, I'm never going to be able to forget it. Then after it was over, I didn't feel pain, but almost a kind of strength.

And I was glad I had seen it, and perhaps started to do my part of sharing the pain of the world.

I have been reading the newspaper, but it has sent me into such a depression I have got to stop. How can I risk loving a future journalist when the real world upsets me to this extent?

Yet I have got to look, but in my own way. After failing with the newspaper, I thought back to that young girl. I owe something to her. More than food, shelter, and clothing. I don't know what, but I know I do.

Dad's new drug isn't working. And neither is his old one. All the books warn that the effectiveness of Sinemet, the drug he has been taking, begins to wear off after three or four years. And now he is faced with a progressive disease and no barrier of medicine. What must it be like to have a progressive disease?

Of course, it is a progressive disease in a progressive life. Our bodies are constantly changing, peaking and deteriorating on us. But it is a slow process and, as it all happens at life's pace, can almost be ignored. It is only with a disease that speeds up the process that the changes have to be recognized—and faced. And to face head-on the processes of life is to be driven crazy. How has Dad stayed sane?

Of course, to most, I'm afraid he seems rather insane. He wins the overprotective-family-member award every year without fail. Mom is convinced he encouraged her to be a novelist so she wouldn't have to leave home to go to work. And it is an accusation that rings true.

Dad definitely believes it is better to have loved and never lost. But not because, as with some, he is more afraid of losing than he is good at loving. And that's why comparisons to the Reverend Brontë are really slightly unfair to Dad. Granted, Father Brontë never wanted his girls to leave home, but I don't think he gave them much reason for wanting to stay home either. Whereas Dad has a way of so lighting up the homestead that there is little to coax one onto the moors.

Another light has been turned on in the homestead. Mom and Dad, model parents that they keep proving themselves to be, are giving Brooke and me their treasured acquaintances. Tonight, they gave us Teresa Wright.

Dinner with just Mom, Dad, Brooke, and me, and Teresa, which is a wonderful way to treasure a treasured acquaintance— parties provide too short a glimpse, but this way there is so much more time.

Teresa told stories of Dame May Whitty and how she would say of a weak actor, "Acting with him is like acting with tracing paper." She told us nobody knew *Mrs. Miniver* was going to turn out to be a classic, but with everyone coming home from the war as they were filming *The Best Years of Our Lives,* they kind of had a feeling they had something with it.

Dad said how much he loved one of her pictures in which she accompanied a man she discovers is a thief across the country. And Teresa laughed and said, "That was a reaction role. In the first scene I said, 'You stole a hundred dollars?' Then in the next scene I said, 'You stole a thousand dollars?' Then in the next scene I said, 'You stole this car?' "

As I listened to Teresa talk, I realized I was sitting right next to star quality and suddenly I knew what it was.

The difference between an actress and a great actress is that an actress acts, and a great actress reveals her soul in her acting. And the difference between a great actress and my favorite great actresses is that a great actress reveals her soul, and my favorite great actresses reveal what happen to be great souls.

So the first step to becoming a great actress is goodness of heart. My first lesson as an autodidactress, which I learned looking in the eyes of Teresa Wright.

I knew that it was Frances Starr who played Dorothy McGuire's mother in the original Broadway production of *Claudia,* but I never thought I'd run into anybody else who did. Tonight we had dinner with two more treasured acquaintances, Norman and Peggy Lloyd. At last I have found two people who share my references.

I was beginning to think there was no point to the knowledge I had stored up, except to tell Brooke, who does not listen. And I was beginning to simply overflow with information because I remember nearly everything I read about the theatre. With the Greeks and Romans (though not exactly hot conversational topics either), I have such a hard time remembering details, but ask me how many performances *Tobacco Road* played and I'll tell you (though no one can tell you why).

And finally I have found friends who share my period. Frances Starr's name came up when Norman was telling a story about David Belasco, and forgot the name of Belasco's favorite actress (I already thought he was probably talking about Frances Starr, but I didn't want to risk making a fool of myself). Then he said she played Dorothy McGuire's mother in *Claudia*. I said, "Frances Starr." Norman turned to Dad, pointed to me, and said, "Who is she?" I do think even Brooke was impressed.

Not only did I feel, at last, there is some point to my file of theatrical facts, but tonight I also discovered, to my great relief, that the way I watch my favorite movies again and again and again, trying to learn about writing and acting, is not just a twist of character particular to myself. Mom was telling Peggy about my odd viewing habits (I think trying to find out if she is the mother of a troubled child), and Peggy said when Ina Claire was doing *Biography* on Broadway, she had gone to see it twenty-nine times.

What I so envy about the Lloyds is they've really lived their lives. The evening was filled with stories of Charlie Chaplin, Bertolt Brecht, Jean Renoir, and everyone else so surrounded by legend that I always wondered if they really existed in this life. But hearing the Lloyds talk about them, I knew they did. At one point in the dinner, a couple Dad knew approached the table and Dad stood up to greet them. After they had gone, Norman demonstrated how Charlie Chaplin would stand up to greet people and, with a very steady hand, continue eating his soup at the same time.

Then Norman told a favorite Alfred Hitchcock story. Norman

was the executive producer of *Alfred Hitchcock Presents*, and appears in *Spellbound* and *Saboteur*—it is Norman who falls off the Statue of Liberty.

He said Hitchock loved practical jokes and told about one of his favorites they used to play together. They would ride in an elevator and wait for someone to get on. Just as the doors would open to let someone on, Hitch would say, "And I took the knife out of her back . . ." and then stop suddenly, pretending he hadn't wanted the stranger, usually an elderly woman, to hear. And the elderly woman would get very jittery and then just as she was getting off, Hitch would say, "The only real problem was the blood, you know—cleaning it all up."

There is only one thing I envy more about the Lloyds than their lives, and that is the way their lives intertwine. When Norman was telling about one of their early experiences in the theatre, I asked if that was when they had met. And Norman looked at Peggy and said, "I was born knowing Peg."

The most wonderful thing in the world has just happened, but the thought of it makes me so nervous I'm alternating between breaking down in tears and being terribly sick to my stomach.

True, I had been acting like something of a saint all day. First I held a garbage can on my head so Dad could rake leaves from the roof into it (definite saint behavior), and I'd just agreed to chop something green for Mom when the phone rang.

It was Peggy Lloyd. When I was talking to her last night about the actresses I watched again and again and again, I said not a night went by that I didn't watch Dorothy McGuire. And today Peggy called Dorothy McGuire and told her the Frances Starr story, and she said Dorothy McGuire wanted to meet the girl who knew that. That is the kind of woman Peggy Lloyd is. She is as generous with her friends as she is with her friendship.

Today I really got to meet the woman whose voice and face I have been using to express my deepest thoughts. And

I'll never be scared again to meet someone I've loved without meeting. Because people are what we hope they are. At least Dorothy McGuire is.

There is only one reason I would like to be famous, and that is so some rotten little kid could idolize me and I could give back what I was given today by being as kind to them as Dorothy McGuire was to me.

She told me about her first audition for *Claudia,* and how she was so upset about not getting to be in a play called *Liberty Jones* that she didn't even care whether she got *Claudia* or not, and she told me how she didn't want to fall in that fountain in *Three Coins in the Fountain* and did her best to convince the director her character just wouldn't do such a thing, and when I told her I watched her in *The Spiral Staircase* (a movie in which she never says a word) last night, she said, "And I haven't stopped talking since you got here."

She shared with me so much of her life. I guess it's just an inherent trait that great actresses are that generous. They give us every part of them. But to be given so much, so very personally was the greatest lesson I've ever had in generosity, taught to me by Peggy and Dorothy.

My secret ambition to be an actress was put to the test tonight. At four this afternoon Brooke informed me, rather fiendishly, that a playwright from Dad's workshop had just called because he couldn't find a girl for a scene, and Dad had volunteered me.

My first thought was should I play it as Dorothy McGuire or Teresa Wright? And then I thought, no, I should play it as myself. And reveal my own soul, instead of pretending I have theirs.

I only saw the script thirty minutes before going on, and I only figured out how to say the first and second lines a minute before going on. The two actresses that influenced me most in my frenzied preparation were Marian Seldes and Nancy Walker.

I have never seen a more gloriously theatrical performance than the one Marian Seldes gave in a play called *Painting Churches.* One of the things that impressed me the most was the way she would break up sentences, letting her thoughts form the periods and not grammar. I only managed to break up one sentence, but I never would have done it without Marian.

And I thought constantly of how Dad told me Nancy Walker never stops exploring lines, trying to make them funnier. He had told me that on closing night of *Fallen Angels* on Broadway, she came offstage and said, "I think I found a new laugh for tomorrow night. But now I'll never know." So, knowing I had only one night, I thought of her and explored my heart out.

We idolize actors because they give us some of the best moments of our lives. I learned tonight that we give them some of the best of theirs.

Everyone was so wonderful. People I have absolutely idolized in that group were so wonderful to me—gosh! And two actors from another scene came up and we talked for a minute and then they said, "We just wanted to hear your voice. To hear if that wonderful voice is really yours." I was sure for a moment I had been transformed into Jean Arthur.

One of my dearest playwrights said I need never take acting classes. I thought that was a magnificently sweet thing to say, but I take classes every night. Every time I watch *Love Is a Many-Splendored Thing* and Jennifer Jones says that the cablegram said, "I have stopped biting my fingernails," I always laugh and cry with her as she says it. And I'm going to keep watching until I figure out why. Until I find a more specific explanation than that Jennifer Jones is such a fine actress.

Everything I know I've learned from watching and listening. Yet when I looked at that script for the first time I was sure I didn't know a thing. It was like, as Jean Arthur says in *Mr. Smith Goes to Washington,* "a forty-foot dive into a tub of shallow water." But one I absolutely adored taking. What a way to spend one's life.

Maybe I really am becoming an actress because I forgot to give any credit to the writer. Much as I love any actress, give her a bad script, and that's a movie even I can watch only once. Bill Chais is my playwright's name. He is the son of the

writer Pamela Chais and the grandson of the writer F. Hugh
Herbert. And sitting at his typewriter, he gave me one of the best
nights of my life.

Well, now that I really am an actress (one night on
stage, but I tell you I feel like an actress), I think it's time to start
working on another ambition. I always like to keep at least one
secret ambition brewing.

Here it is: I want to be a photographer. Photography, to be
honest, is an art I had never paid much attention to (probably due
to writer parents who have an inborn hatred of the saying, "One
picture is worth a thousand words"). Then I met Dorothy Mc-
Guire.

She was married for thirty-six years, until his death in 1979, to
the photographer John Swope. And his pictures fill their home.
Every one was a view of life I'd never seen before. And that he
had captured. A huge blow-up of one of his pictures hung in their
living room—a picture of a young African boy with such a defiant
look on his face. It was clear a great soul lurked beneath that
nameless face. And John Swope had revealed it. And saved it.

So today I borrowed Mom's Instamatic (which does everything
for you, but still makes it possible for Mom to cut off everyone's
head in a family snapshot—I have great photographic genes).
Though as of yet, I have only come to a greater spiritual understanding through my photography of the squirrels in the backyard, I already love the profession.

When she was telling me about their travels in foreign coun-
tries, Dorothy McGuire said, "We would walk and John would
take pictures." And when she said that, I realized photography
must be the most wonderful profession in the world. There is none
other that pervades life more perfectly. To have your work always
strapped around your neck—I cannot think of a better existence.

It is also a private art. People don't often collaborate or make
helpful suggestions. It is there and unchangeable. I don't want to
seem a bad sport about criticism, it's absolutely necessary, but
constant feedback can make one crazy. That's the reason I finish
writing something before showing it to anybody, and why my

family's kindly meant, but rather constant, comments have turned me into a nighttime painter. To be judged brush stroke by brush stroke is something I detest. That's what I love about photography: You can't be judged snap by snap because there's only room for one eye at the lens.

Photography is also the only art with at least the possibility of unity of time. I know some photographs must take hours to set up, but, on some occasions, it can take the same amount of time to take a photograph that it takes to look at one (though the hours needed for some photographs can be equaled by the hours you can spend looking at one). Plays, books, movies, concerts, and ballets, on the other hand, almost always take much more time to create than is ever used to appreciate them. A photograph is somehow a fair deal, and I suspect photographers are basically well-adjusted people because of this . . . which is probably the most important reason I should be one.

Matthew leaves tomorrow for a week of looking at colleges in Washington, Boston, and New York. Tonight Brooke and I helped him pack. We took turns picking out ties for him to take, and he graded us on how our taste corresponded to his. Personally, I don't see how he will ever wear so many ties in one week. I think he must have taken to wearing two at a time. I only pray all the colleges turn him down flat and send him home immediately due to severe overdressing.

But what shall I do if they don't?

I guess I didn't set him a very good example as an autodidact because he certainly doesn't want to be one. He has one more year of high school, and then I suppose he'll be heading for points east.

Could I survive that? Could we survive that? What does "we," in our case, even mean? A politically oriented, constantly busy boy, no doubt on the way to being a hugely successful man of the world who cares about the world. And a girl who is so consumed by her own world that she has trouble remembering what day of the week it is, let alone whether anything of national importance happened on that day. Does that make a "we"?

The difference between us is that Matthew wants what cannot

be found within the walls of his own room, while I, if surrounded by enough books and cassettes and writing paper and pencils, have the ability to be content within that space for perhaps too long a time.

Perhaps he will be the one to lead me from my room to see the view. What could I give him in return? Maybe I could show him how many views there can be in one room.

Tonight was as big a disappointment as my first acting attempt was a triumph. After I read the scene last week, I was immediately booked by other playwrights to read their scenes.

But tonight I lost the audience from the first moment and never got them back. Every ounce of confidence I had from last time is shattered.

There is nothing more wonderful than a house laugh and nothing worse than thinking you are going to get about twenty-six and not getting one.

I detest comeuppances. I wasn't nervous in the least bit. Though I did keep worrying that, according to Frank Capra, Jean Arthur vomited her guts out before and after filming any scene. I wish I'd done that today. It certainly couldn't have hurt.

I have been trying to write. I hate my novel. I hate writing. I hate acting. I am ashamed and embarrassed and void of any talent whatsoever. I make my own self sick.

I hate the theatre and I want to write plays and act in them. I have nothing against novels except I hate the one I am writing. I am a failure at everything but eating potato chips.

Tonight I have reached my artistic nadir.

I've regained my confidence. I was watching one of my favorite actresses and I thought, "Dammit, I can do that." And I can. I know I can.

Confidence has nothing to do with real life. It is something we have that even real life cannot defeat. I was without it for nine hours tonight. I'll never be without it again. Never. Goodness, I spend a lot of time encouraging myself but one simply has to.

I have found, through tears and tribulation, that there is nothing one can depend on. Tonight, it is only me, Carole Lombard, and Norma Shearer. We three. And I think John Van Druten and Mark Twain. Five. Of course Jean Arthur and George Bernard Shaw. Seven. Lindsay and Crouse and Kaufman and Hart. Eleven. Tolstoy, Dickens, Jessica Mitford, and Nancy Mitford. Evelyn Waugh and Ernest Hemingway. Seventeen. Which reminds me of Booth Tarkington. Louisa May Alcott and whoever wrote *The Bobbsey Twins, The Hardy Boys,* and the Nancy Drew series (because they were all written by the same person). Twenty. Aristophanes and Rose Franken. Petronius and Paulette Goddard. Plautus and Preston Sturges, George Orwell and Gregory La Cava. Frank Capra and Shakespeare. Thirty. And Hannibal and Oscar Wilde. Thirty-two. Pissarro, Cézanne, Vuillard, Manet, Monet, Renoir, Van Gogh, and Mary Cassatt. Forty. Marie and Pierre Curie. Greer Garson and Walter Pidgeon. Ellen Terry, Dame Sybil Thorndike, Maude Adams, Ethel Barrymore, Katharine Cornell, and Tallulah Bankhead. The Lunts. John and Lionel Barrymore and Ina Claire. Jessamyn West, Jane Austen, Lillian Hellman, Eudora Welty. Gertrude Stein and Alice B. Toklas. Sixty-one. Dashiell Hammett and Frances Goodrich and Albert Hackett and William Powell and Myrna Loy, who all brought Nick and Nora to the screen. I'm also counting Nick and Nora. Sixty-eight. Victoria and Albert. Robert, Elizabeth, and Flush. Dostoevsky, Chekhov, and Turgenev. John Donne, Irene Dunne, and Proust. Fredric March and Florence Eldridge. My great-grandmother Bess. Ingrid Bergman. Handel, Bach, Loesser, Gershwin. Rosalind Russell and Auntie Mame. Norman Krasna and Ovid. Dame May Whitty and Aristotle, equally wise. Franklin and Eleanor Roosevelt. Helen Keller and Martin Luther King. Anne Frank. Geraldine Ferraro and Abraham Lincoln. One hundred.

We all know where Scarlett got her strength (from the red earth of Tara—Vivien Leigh, one hundred one, Margaret Mitchell, one hundred two). Now you see where I get mine.

I just discovered that the custom of carrying the bride over the threshold is in memory of the Sabine virgins being carried away in violence and not of their own free will. I'm afraid the romance of that little custom has just been ruined for me.

A postcard arrived from Matthew on his college tour today. He said he'd run into Alan Cranston when inspecting the Senate, then reminded me in parentheses, "Alan Cranston is your Senator." My attitude about current events has always been that the really important ones would become a part of history and I'd catch them then.

Dad's doctor told him today that there is a new drug for Parkinson's, but it is available only in England. It has a less than fifty percent effectiveness rate, so it is not profitable enough to be produced in our country.

I got my third chance to act at the playwrights' workshop tonight. And I got to act (though I don't really feel right applying that verb to me) with Marcia Rodd. I have seen her on the stage and on television and in the movies and loved every minute of her. But tonight, actually getting to share a stage with her, I felt even closer to her than I do sitting right next to her on our living room couch. And I was so close to her art as an actress that I could peek and see a little of how it worked.

Some day I want to give another actress what she gave me. For if acting is like a good game of tennis, then here was our tennis game: I had the first line, so I hit Marcia a serve that bounced twice on my side of the court, and then on its third bounce somehow made it over the net. She returned it with a perfect hit landing right at my feet. I gave her a wild return, almost going out of bounds. She returned with ease, again giving me a beautiful ball to hit back. No matter what kind of faulty return I gave her, she always came through to save us both.

On that stage I felt like I was in battle. With all the thrill and almost all the terror (the next worse thing to losing your life is losing your audience). And Marcia was a hero.

We had the staged reading of *The World and His Wife* yesterday. I thought it all went over perfectly, but Dad began rewriting this morning and, twelve hours later, the play is totally revised. I don't know if I have the stamina to be a playwright. I barely have the stamina to be a playwright's typist.

Today was my parents' twenty-fifth wedding anniversary. They spent their wedding night in a theatre, so it seemed only fitting they should spend their silver anniversary in the same place.

Dad took all of us to an early run-through of *The Bar off Melrose*. I'm sorry to say a scene by me was not part of the evening.

I have tried. Ten failed times, to be embarrassingly frank. However, rehearsals don't start for six months. The playwrights are taking the summer off, then will spend the fall honing the collected scenes into a play. Of course, they'll hone under the guidance of Bill Cort, who is going to direct the play. He is one of the nicest, least temperamental men I've ever met who's chosen to spend his life in the theatre—which I think is the first qualification needed to direct a play by thirteen playwrights, to be performed by thirty-six actors. How I wish that before rehearsals begin, the numbers would jump to fourteen playwrights and thirty-eight actors.

I just tried to call Matthew to say good-bye since we leave tomorrow for England. Dad is going to begin taking the new English drug and will need the summer to get adjusted to it, so we are staying in London until Brooke has to go back to school.

I do wish the Van Scoyks were coming with us, but Matthew

has enrolled in a summer program at Georgetown University in Washington D.C. —The High School Juniors' Program to Trick You into Going to College.

Sometimes it seems as if my whole life is crumbling before me. Leona said Matthew would call the minute he got out of the shower. By my count, he has now been in the shower eight and a half hours. I don't know why I am suddenly laughing. Sometimes a person just gets so miserable there is no other choice.

I am on the verge of a nervous breakdown and am running back to Rome. I feel such a spiritual attachment to the women there—they were all constantly being betrayed by the men in their lives.

Matthew called. He told me he fell asleep soon after stepping out of the shower and dreamed about the Haileys. So once more I feel centuries removed from the women of Rome. But I cannot wait until he mistreats me again because while I was waiting for him to call I began writing a play. About the women of Rome.

Perhaps the ancients were so wise because they believed in the power of signs, yet they knew that we make our own. Beginning this play is my sign to leave Rome, but also an assurance that I'll make a return. The research it would take to write a full-length play about all those betrayed women is lovely to contemplate.

I do feel, though, that when it comes to the ancients, I have cracked their shell. There are still worlds more to read and discover and learn, but I would know who most of them were if I met them on the street, and I have formed a great many attachments.

And I think it must be a sign that the ancients approve of my next educational step, since a play showed me it was time to leave Rome and to start reading plays so that maybe I can learn enough to write one of my own.

Dear Julie,
Summer is almost here. So, most important when speaking of

college life and your progress thus far, how's sex coming? Brooke
says she's going to shoot herself if she's still a virgin at eighteen.
My nineteenth birthday is only months away, so she's getting the
pistol ready for me.

> With respect,
> Kendall

Dear Kendall,
Sex, did you say? DID SOMEONE SAY S-E-X?!?! As you can
probably tell, no, I haven't had sex. Tell Brooke to add an extra
bullet for me.

> With respect for now,
> Julie

WHAT I DID:

Found another view from my room.

INTERMISSION IN ENGLAND

WHAT I HOPE TO DO:

Write a bar play if it takes getting drunk to do it.

I am sitting on the plane, a little nervous because I just reached into my carry-on bag and at my fingertips was my favorite pen. As Dad says when he gets a good parking space, I hate to waste luck on little things. Especially when I'm thirty-seven-thousand feet in the air.

I write tonight from the living room of our flat in London because Brooke is a total and absolute tyrant about anyone keeping a light on in the bedroom when she is trying to sleep.

As I slammed the door to our communal sleeping quarters, I told her I preferred being at home in separate bedrooms, to which she replied, "God, how could anything be more boring than your life at home?"

Sharing a bedroom destroys a relationship. I hate to be attacked on such a vulnerable point, i.e., the way I am spending my life. Luckily, after leaving Brooke, I headed straight for two of my favorite people, Mr. and Mrs. Clarence Day. They were captured first by their son Clarence and then by Howard Lindsay and Russell Crouse in their plays *Life with Father* and *Life with Mother.*

Life with Father is still the most successful play in the history of the American stage, having run for seven and a half years on Broadway with Howard Lindsay and his wife, the actress Dorothy Stickney, playing Mr. and Mrs. Day for the first five.

I was most interested to discover this (in a wonderful book, *Life with Lindsay and Crouse,* by Cornelia Otis Skinner), for if I ever do write a bar play, I have a secret ambition to be in it. I don't write about people my own age just for the heck of it.

Reading about Lindsay and Crouse also made me feel much better about how long I have spent trying to write my bar play.

They spent two years discussing and planning *Life with Father* and seventeen days writing it.

Life with Mother, a companion piece and sequel to *Life with Father,* shocked New York by running only eight months. No one could explain it, except perhaps that the titles were so alike people didn't realize it was a new play.

Its short run must have been incomprehensible to Lindsay and Crouse. But, really, they both sound too sweet to get upset that a play as great as (I think even funnier than) *Life with Father* did not get equal attention. As Lindsay said, "The only person who thinks he knows anything about the theatre is a playwright after his first success."

All I know is after reading those plays, I had to spend most of the evening dancing through the flat. I don't suppose there could be a less graceful way of expressing admiration for such beautiful work. And Lindsay and Crouse are both noncollegiates. Well, Lindsay went to Harvard for a year. I'll forgive Father Day a year.

Today we took Mom to her first day of school. This woman is taking a class to learn how to write short stories. Her last creative writing class left her with scars it took twenty years to heal, and now she's taking another one.

I will admit, she did not set out looking for a short story course. She read that one of her favorite modern novelists, Margaret Drabble, was going to be lecturing to this class this summer and so, like the good mother of an autodidact, Mom wrote and asked if she could hear the lecture without taking the class. The answer was no, so she's taking the class. She even asked me if I wanted to take it too.

I wouldn't get near a creative writing class if I were Tolstoy. I'd still be afraid it would destroy my confidence. And I certainly can't afford to get near one while just being me.

Uncle Thomas just pointed out a tennis player in Wimbledon who bears the most amazing resemblance to Matthew. I hope he keeps winning, so I can keep watching.

Boris Becker continues to win . . . and now a report from his Georgetown look-alike on his precollege test of college:

Dear Kendall,
We arrived to a humid Washington and Georgetown. I have discovered, however, that heat does not impair my mother's desire or ability to shop. While I went to inspect the Georgetown campus, she ventured off into the town center and doled out the cash. She has acquired a lovely necklace, pants, two blouses, and three pairs of shoes. This was in a space of forty-five minutes. The merchants have declared a holiday and the Government Office of Budget and Management has asked her to be their trickle-down theory poster girl.
Later, we went on the Metrosubway (the district, to residents), and I was struck terrified and sentimental at the same time. The last time I believe I rode underground was with you all in London; so I kept hearing voices: "Don't lose your ticket! Where's your raincoat!? Ticket! Raincoat!" I was moments from a breakdown, my *dear* Haileys. What have you done to me?
I ask that you write often, for it will be very impressive to pick up a lot of mail at the school's office. Make the envelopes look important. The postcards can be as embarrassing as you wish. Do try to control Brooke, however—the school is a Jesuit organization. I do believe that I am the only Jew within a twenty-mile radius, my dear.
Love,
Matthew

I've been nineteen years old for two hours so far. Rang in my new year with one hundred ten lines of my novel. If I could do that every day of my nineteenth year, being nineteen would not seem so bad. I do just seem to get older and older. I know the twenties will be traumatic, but I think I'll adjust very well to the thirties and forties. I'm rather designed to be middle-aged.

I saw a dog that looked like Puli today and it broke my heart and I thought I'll never let my children have a dog. And then I thought about Nanny. What am I going to do if something happens to her? And can I deny my children a grandmother too?

I am afraid of loss. I feel so close to so many so long gone, but I am still afraid.

In the middle of that sentence I realized how I could use all this in my novel. Thank God. I sometimes think the only reason I want emotions (except for love, of course) is so I can put them in novels.

Mom is a wreck about the short story she has just completed and is supposed to read in front of her class tomorrow.

When all the students were introducing themselves to the class, Mom just said her name was Elizabeth Hailey and that she'd taken a creative writing course in college, nearly flunked, and wanted to try again. She said she'd written novels, but was fascinated by the short story form.

How many other writers would be willing to shed the protective shell of their success and appear as a supposedly unpublished novelist who failed the only creative writing course she ever took?

And now that I think about it, little wonder she is nervous about this short story. For it is only on this that she will be judged. I do respect that woman. She has taken her talent out of the armor of her reputation and had the courage to let it fend for itself again.

It is becoming increasingly difficult to see a wonderful play and watch a wonderful performance every day in London, and read a wonderful one from theatre past and imagine the performances that must have been every night without wanting to try and join in.

I feel so strange about this acting ambition because I have always wanted to be a writer. Even when I wanted to be a ranch foreman, I still wanted to be a writer on the side. To be an actress is such a new goal. I always thought true goals were the ones you had from earliest career planning . . . it just feels so odd finding a second one at this late date.

Perhaps it's like the difference between loving the people you were born loving and loving those that it takes a little more of life to introduce you to, and one love is no more valid than the other (no matter what my father may say).

Dear Kendall,

Here's a day in the life of Matthew at Georgipolis Collegius, per your request.

12:30 P.M.–1:00 P.M. Awake to loud rock music and a lacrosse ball being thrown against my door.

2:00 P.M. Make my way to my personal shower stall across the hall. Note that by this time, the barbarians (i.e., my classmates) have gone out to kill a cow for lunch.

2:15 P.M. Tiptoe across the hall to my room.

2:30 P.M. Eat lunch in my room. The food at the grand university is beyond inedible. Yesterday's treat: *Clam* Burgers.

3:00 P.M. Sit down to the boring author I happen to be reading for my class. The last few days have been particularly dull, for I have had to lock myself in my green room and read the *Politics of Aristotle,* a charming selection of nonsequential ravings and mumblings from one of the world's great thinkers! All it seems to be is: "Sparta *this!* Athens *that!* Oh my! Sparta, Sparta, Sparta!!! I *love* Sparta!" Now this is a class about the elements of political theory. This means you study everything but good old practical political theory. The 1984 Democratic Convention, for instance, will never come up.

5:50 P.M. I leave for class.

5:59 P.M. Arrive class.

6:00–7:30 P.M. Classtime.

The evening is then spent stopping in various clothing stores and looking at fall clothes, eating dinner in my room or going out to

dinner (tonight I did go out since I had not eaten a vegetable since
my arrival and thus was lacking in the essential nutrients they
provide, those very nutrients that Nanny and Thomas have never
digested), and, of course, reading the boring author while watching
TV.

I was very glad to hear in your letter of today that my true love,
Mama Betsy, is thought to be dumb in her writing class. Although
I am progressing fine academically, it always thrills me to think
that the famed novelist is thought to be retarded.

Love,
Matthew

P.S. I saw a news segment on Boris Becker today that featured
people saying that he was "like, soooo cute!" Now, you could have
fooled me, but I suppose my visage is in vogue.

Love to my Betsy et al,
Matt

Today we visited Chartwell, the country home of Sir
Winston Churchill, filled with his paintings and surrounded by an
English garden. I would have given anything to have kicked out
the National Trust people and set up residence.

In honor of Sir Winston, I have been reading plays
that use World War II as a background. It is almost painful to
think how much great work came out of that destruction.

I read *Flight to the West* first. I had never heard of it or, I
confess, its author, Elmer Rice, though I should be reprimanded,
for I now know he is one of our great American playwrights.

The play takes place on a plane getting out of Europe after the
fall of France—the passengers represent the citizens of the world.
If that isn't a basis for drama, then Elmer Rice doesn't know
drama. And I didn't even know who he was.

There is something very frightening about ignorance. I think it
is almost worse than death because after death there's always
Heaven, which I see as a large cocktail party with hot hors
d'oeuvres, but after ignorance, there is only nothingness.

I literally fell off the couch with laughter reading *Over 21* by

Ruth Gordon all by myself, but what I would have given to see her perform it. Ruth Gordon has given me one heck of a push to write a good bar play. I'm beginning to suspect it's hard not to write a great role when you're planning to cast yourself in it.

I ended my reading with the most romantic play of World War II—*The Voice of the Turtle* by John Van Druten. It's about a soldier's weekend leave, and so sweet and lovely, but maddening trying to imagine what the famous performance of Margaret Sullavan must have been like. The battle between me and my ignorance is constant, but at least without casualties.

I told Dad my dilemma and he found me a copy of *Haywire,* Brooke Hayward's book about her parents, Leland Hayward, the agent and producer, and Margaret Sullavan. I have just finished it. It is such a moving and compassionate biography.

One passage in particular haunts me. When Margaret Sullavan came to London for six months to do *The Voice of the Turtle,* her main contact with her young children was through letters. Brooke Hayward quoted a letter she wrote to her mother which, after having informed her of the family news, ended with the sentence, "I must admit I have forgotten what you look like."

I can't imagine the thrill of acting in even so charming a play as *The Voice of the Turtle* night after night would come anywhere near the devastation of receiving that letter. I think I have underestimated what it takes to be an actress.

Dear Kendall,

Today I had to get up at the ungodly hour of 9:00 A.M. to prepare for an aborted trek into the District to protest South African racial policy at the South African Embassy. It turns out that the protest is tomorrow, so I shall have to rise early once more. Now, the protest is sponsored by the law school, so I think I'll be safe if I'm arrested. I imagine that two hundred law students would drive the police so mad that they would be obliged to release us to retain their sanity. Now, I don't think I'll be arrested, but if I am, I hear it is a misdemeanor and the charges are usually dropped. In addition, Amy Carter demonstrated at the very same place a year ago and had Jimmy's blessing to get arrested! I'll tell you how it goes tomorrow.

The good professor was in chipper spirits today and introduced us to Rousseau, who I find to be one of the more noble but tedious writers of the earth's entire history. He is out to do *nothing* but confuse you. Do ask Mama Betsy (if she's in a high faluting mood) for her opinion of Jean Jacques.

Je vou'embrasse (Right?
Most likely not. Well,
Mama Betsy will
understand.)
Matthew

Dear Kendall,
Regarding the protest at the South African Embassy. Well, I am embarrassed to say I got lost and missed the protest. I fear that I will have to turn in my liberal credentials because of this blunder. I don't foresee it being lived down for quite a while yet—don't tell Mama Betsy, let her think I've been arrested.

I have heard through the grapevine that some young lads and lasses are attempting to kill themselves in another part of the campus. They are going to jump off a building that I have a lovely view of from my window. I personally think it is rather humorous that these kids want to do themselves in, for they are part of a program called "College Prep." Its purpose is to teach you how to get into college. Apparently these kids don't think they are going to make it. There's one argument for being an autodidact—it's safer.

Love to all,
Matthew

Have been off my feed today (that is, in terms of reading—I have never, unfortunately, been off my feed in terms of food). I couldn't decide what play to read next, so I picked up a book of Katherine Mansfield short stories I had brought, and actually heard myself muttering, "When are you going to stop writing about females who can't get a grip on themselves?"

Then I picked up my other prose choice for the trip, a novel of

Evelyn Waugh's, and had to put it right back down. When he started talking about the death of a child in those usually so wonderful, venomous tones, I just couldn't take it. So back to the theatre, which is becoming my life. Whether the feeling will ever be mutual, I don't dare ponder.

Today Mama Betsy stood up and revealed herself to her short story class.

The teacher was attacking one of the students (who was actually a high school English teacher) for writing such a boring story based on her own life experience.

At this point my mother, the writer in shining armor, cleared her throat and rose to her feet. She said she'd just written a novel which was about to be published, based on her life experience, about her marriage. And she'd written two other novels, which were also published, *A Woman of Independent Means* and *Life Sentences* (audible gasps from classmates). She said any life, when examined truthfully, could make a novel. Of course, she'd had to rewrite her story for this class several times to find the total truth. But she ended by saying, "Don't let your faith in yourselves be determined by how you fared in this class."

The autodidact's perfect mother.

I would write now, but my half of the room Brooke and I share is such a mess I feel I must sacrifice the theatre for cleanliness.

Just decided against it.

The truth is I simply can't think in a neat room. I like to be surrounded (i.e., piled on the floor, the chairs, the tables, the bed) by things I am interested in. I feel a very hollow person with everything in its place.

Can you understand that? Mom certainly can't. She says a wave of depression comes over her every time she sets foot in this room. My father says no one would ever marry someone this sloppy, but since he doesn't ever want me to get married, he really doesn't mind. I, of course, love an interesting mess. Plus the fact it irritates Brooke a great deal.

Dear Kendall,
I cannot describe my elation at ten epistles arriving from you today. Count them, ten! I invoked the wrath of everyone in the building—the poor one-letter-a-week slobs from Nantucket.

Some of my classmates' blood pressure is running high, for our kind professor will test us on Plato, Aristotle, and Machiavelli in one hour. He has some kind of voodoo testing format that has the class up in arms. I do hate my classmates. They are the dumbest lot I have ever seen assembled—and as shallow as your swimming pool. This, however, gives me a warm and secure feeling.

Yesterday (this is a story) I arrived at class early (a very rare occurrence) and was privy to some of the talk that goes on every day behind the good professor's back. I tell you, it about made me cry. Two young women of about twenty-three years of age were talking of how boring they think our venerable instructor is, and how they *must* go to the bookstore and purchase the texts before the test, so that they can "cram and memorize all of the facts and spit them out again." It about makes me sick. Moist crackers for brains these people (a loose term) have. Moist crackers! It is my thought that they are the lot organized education caters to. O woe is me.

Tonight:
Make that twelve epistles from you today. I received two more when I returned from my exam. I can't thank you enough for them. They are, without doubt, the highlight of my days.

As I write, my head suffers from pain. I suppose a headache should not be odd for a person whose mother has spent most of her life having them and describing them to friends, relatives, and strangers on the street.

At my suggestion, begging, and plea, most of my floor has gone to see *On the Waterfront*, which is being shown on a pillow case tacked to a wall somewhere on campus. They have never seen Ms. Eva Marie do her stuff, and I assured them there is no sexier sight. So they got their spears and trotted off, leaving me behind to a long-awaited night of solitude and Roger Mudd (with moments of John Locke interspersed).

Today I received confirmation that your letters and postcards are the subject of "office conversation" in the administrative corridors of Georgetown. I think that a Hailey epistle would make a good Jesuit curl up and die.

Love,
Matt

P.S. I got a telephone installed today. I'm up at all hours except the early morning ones (i.e., 4:00 A.M. to 10:00 A.M.), if you dare.

Tonight I am calling Matthew at Georgetown. Dad and I had a horrible fight about it last night.

You would not believe how much one phone call of ten minutes to the man I love (I find there is no reduction for love) costs. But only about half as much as it does to go to any boring play (I find there is no reduction for boredom).

Several friends of ours have also come to London this summer, and as we sit on the terrace of our flat looking out over Redcliffe Square, I feel as if we are almost living here. It feels pretty wonderful, and I love being with our friends and going to the theatre with them. Yet, surrounded as I am by the dearest of people, I cannot help but feel a little alone. Such an odd way to feel when I know the addition of just one person to what is already quite a large group—one specific person—would make me feel so unalone.

No matter how close you are to your parents, every night they head up the stairs to spend their last moments of conversation with each other. And Nanny and Thomas have gone to bed long before that. I am infinitely close to Brooke, but I can be pretty sure any intimate confidences whispered to her in trusting moments will be shouted aloud for everyone in the family to hear during our next fight.

If only there were someone who would understand my soul at a glance. The awful thing is that there is, only he's in our nation's capital. But I had eleven minutes of him tonight very long distance. It was the most vulnerable I have ever heard Matthew.

He is so miserable, and I realized for the first time tonight that perhaps he might need me.

I want to be with him (even if it means college), but I want to be with my family too. It is not fair what I am doing to them because every day I judge them and I want them to fail so it will be easy to leave home. In a way, I want to hate them, so I won't miss them.

That is really what the pain of adolescence is all about. We find out we are expected to leave some day. It doesn't make sense to leave someone you are devoted to, and so, more than anything to free ourselves, we begin to hate. That may explain why I never really had an adolescence. My father never presented leaving as an option and I never wanted it as one. Until now.

If only on top of talking to Matthew I hadn't read *There's Always Juliet* by John Van Druten tonight. It's so sweet, so romantic, and so full of love, and so . . . so am I. I better head for Zoë Akins's *The Old Maid.*

I couldn't find a copy of *The Old Maid,* so I decided instead to go ahead and just tell Matthew that if he is going to college, I am going with him.

And this is how I did it: I wrote a bar scene, and a character who is pretty much me says that to a character who is pretty much Matthew. But when I read it over, it didn't work. It just didn't make sense that a character like me would go to college. And I doubt that what doesn't make sense in the theatre would make much sense in life.

So I went one step further and made my play a touch better than life. Matthew's character tells my character that she can't go to college with him because he wants to be an autodidact too.

In life, Matthew will never choose to be an autodidact, but in the theatre, it works wonderfully, and that, as one of my father's characters says, is the reason I love the theatre.

Brooke and I have gotten into fight after fight this summer. I'm afraid proximity does great damage to our relationship.

I used to think that her extreme insensitivity combined with a real gift for outright cruelty (she is always calling my love and devotion to movie stars such as Carole Lombard "pitiful"—her favorite comment being, "All your friends are dead") would mean that she would not be a good writer. But I have just been proved wrong.

This evening, after yet another little disagreement, she slammed into the bedroom (as is her habit) and I stayed in the living room (as is mine). But only moments after saying something about never wanting to look at me again, she reappeared holding a notepad.

"Do you want to hear something I wrote this summer?"

"I'd love to hear something you wrote this summer."

"I'll read it to you in the bathroom, so nobody else will hear."

Moments later, we are in the bathroom, Brooke taking the only available seat and me standing at attention.

She opens the notepad and looks at the first page. She opens her mouth, then closes it. She stops looking at the notepad and looks at me.

"I can't read this to you. It's shit."

I have never looked at something I've written and not felt exactly the same way. Suddenly inspiration strikes.

"Brooke, if it's shit, read it to me holding your nose. Doing that will take your mind off what you're reading."

She holds her nose and begins to read. After a page, the nose no longer needs to be held and I am floored with awe for that sister sitting on the toilet.

"When did you have time to write this screenplay?"

"After our first fight this summer, I slammed the bedroom door and then couldn't think of anything else to do. So after our second fight, I began to write."

Who would have thought writing after fighting would lead to such a loving screenplay?

It is about, as Brooke puts it, "those poor lost souls who don't know what they want to do with their lives," referring to all of her friends. She has found and captured her very own lost generation.

Dear Kendall,
Moments have passed since your unexpected phone call, and I need not say that I am jubilant. It was the highpoint of my stay in Cell Block H.

The other gentlemen on my floor are wearing their bed sheets tonight. And while some may extol that kind of behavior, I can only say that to live through a Toga Party is a fate worse than the lions (No, Miss Brooke, I did not, will not and have never worn a TOGA). I occasionally hear the dull thump of a body being thrown up against my closed (and bolted) door. Cries of "DUDE!" can also be heard from down the corridor. A charming aspect of pseudocollegiate life. Heaven forbid that I conceive what the real thing is like. It *cannot* be pretty. Fine young men have a habit of becoming pond scum when they gather together, hence the formation of the Nazi Party, the Ku Klux Klan, and lodges.

Since I seem to be surrounded by things that I hate (being a civil being among barbarians, a Jew among Jesuits, a nondrinker among alcoholics, and a nontoga wearer among those who do), I will now construct a partial list of things that I like: Mr. John Chancellor, one hundred-watt light bulbs, anything ever said by Adlai Stevenson, anything ever worn by George Will, diet root beer, Prokofiev's First Piano Concerto, looking through other people's wallets, my own shower, and Franklin Delano Roosevelt. And we shall leave it at that.

> I love you all and miss you all,
> Matthew

We are on a train heading out to the English countryside to look at English country homes for future summer vacations. Dad is holding on tight to our four favorite house brochures out of the hundreds we have been sent this summer.

But he keeps asking, "How can we own another house?" He isn't talking about the financial shifting it would involve (and it would involve some). He doesn't feel he deserves the dream that, at last, we can just about afford and that he needs.

Dad has come to see England as the land of a cure. Not just a drug, but perhaps a way of life.

I found out recently that when he was in college, he supported a foster child in a foreign country. My father, who spent his college years living on Saltines topped with Tabasco sauce, or if he was splurging, peanut butter. I've never been hungry in my life, and I've never thought to support a foster child.

And his childhood. The most severe punishment with which he ever threatened me was that he was going to tell me a story about his childhood. I don't remember what I did, but it must have been heinous to have been told this one: During World War II, his father Jack was trying to make a little extra money on the black market and at midnight one night he had to pick up a dozen slaughtered hogs. He loaded them in his pickup truck and told Dad to climb on top of them and lie spread-eagle because they might fall off and Jack couldn't afford to lose a hog.

I think a man who's gone through that deserves anything he wants, but he never will.

But even if he doesn't think he deserves a house in England, he does want it. He is so excited. The rest of us are scared stiff. If we find a house, we have to keep the news from Nanny, since any big expenditure of money sends her to the brink—once when Mom and Dad bought a couch, she burst into tears. Thomas's main stumbling block is stairs. If there are any, we have to keep the purchase a secret from him, too—at least until we figure out how to ramp them. And Mom, Brooke, and I really prefer cities to villages. Brooke is the most leery of country purchases and the attendant speed of country living and has been mumbling that Dad would love seeing her stranded in a "sea of senility."

The sun is setting in the English countryside and we are heading back to London. I will now report what Nanny and Thomas can't yet know.

Little did we know what magicians those photographers are who take the pictures of houses used in brochures. As we looked from the brochure to the real thing, a Georgian mansion turned into a tract house. And to get through the door of a charming Tudor house, you had to drink one of Alice in Wonderland's shrinking potions. As four Haileys and one real estate agent in succession all bumped their heads on a beam, the agent was heard to mutter, "It's going to take someone very small to buy this house."

By teatime, Mom, Brooke, and I thought there was very little chance we'd be settling in the country. But while we had tea, Dad paced. One last brochure had arrived in this morning's mail, describing a house that had just gone on the market yesterday.

The real estate agent called the owners, who were at home and free to show the house. It lies on the main street in a small village, right across from the pub and church. It was built in 1585. There were rosebushes lining the flagstone walk to the front door. As we came in, there was a dining room and a fireplace with an inglenook (big enough to roll Thomas into if he gets on our nerves) on one side and a living room with two fireplaces, one at either end, on the other.

There are four bedrooms upstairs and one down. A modern kitchen and a garden with a greenhouse, circa *Domesday* outhouse, fruit trees, a croquet lawn, and a rose-covered pergola.

But we can't tell Nanny and Thomas any of this. Yet.

Now it is Sunday and two days since we've seen our house. I become possessive pretty fast, a dangerous thing to do before we've even made a bid. Before Dad's last play opened on Broadway, we had decided to buy a house in the Berkshires. But after the play closed—the same night it opened—we couldn't imagine ever traveling to that part of the country for pleasure. I still remember how beautiful it was, but I think, even with houses, it is better to have loved and lost.

Today we went to visit the English actor Barry Foster and his wife Judith, friends we met through Judith Burnley, Mom's English editor on *A Woman of Independent Means* and now one of our closest friends. The Fosters have recently moved to a house in the country and were anxious to see the one we wanted. Dad was not anxious to show it to them however. He was very anxious about appearing overanxious. He had told the real estate agent on Friday he wanted the house and would call him on Monday. The agent said four other possible buyers already had appointments for Saturday. Dad said again that he wanted the house and left it at that.

But I think we all wanted another peek and soon Barry, Judith, Judith, and four Haileys were heading across West Sussex toward the house.

Dad said all we would do was creep around the garden because we couldn't disturb the owners, who had already been so courteous about letting us see it. But we had no sooner peeped over the garden wall than the owner opened the door and invited us to come show our friends the inside. Dad, who has a tendency to be suspicious of pure kindness, whispered, "Ah, this means nobody who saw it on Saturday liked it."

Dad was so enamored of his brief fling with playing it slightly cool that he decided this morning he would wait till Tuesday to put in a bid on the house. An hour before we were due to leave for the theatre the agent called and said, "Mr. Hailey, I thought you were going to call today."

"I am, I am," Dad said, losing all his stored-up cool.

"Ah. Well, two of the people who saw the house over the weekend have already made offers."

"Oh," said Dad.

"Would you care to make an offer, Mr. Hailey?"

"Can you tell me how close to the asking price the other two offers are?" Dad asked.

"The other two parties offered the full price."

"Oh. I see. Well, then, that's what I'm offering. I guess."

"I was wondering, Mr. Hailey, if you would like to offer more than the asking price."

"I will not start a bidding war, no. But if someone else does, be sure to tell me. And please assure the present owners they can stay in the house as long as they like. We won't be back till December."

"I will, indeed, Mr. Hailey. I'll be back to you in a minute."

Minutes pass. At least the problem of what to bid has been solved. Why didn't it ever occur to us? Full price.

The phone rings.

"Mr. Hailey, how would you feel about making a blind bid? That is, all the parties will make one bid without knowing how much the others have offered, and the highest blind bid will buy the house."

"I have tickets for the theatre tonight. I want to enjoy the play, but you are ruining it for me already. No, I will not make a blind bid. I have thus far behaved like a gentleman. You set a price for this house and I offered to pay it . . . but if anyone else makes a blind bid, let me know."

"I will indeed, Mr. Hailey."

As soon as Dad hangs up, we start plotting what our blind bid will be. Just as we have decided to go up a chunk of money plus an extra twenty-five pounds to get the house in case another of the parties decides to go up the same chunk of money, Nanny walks in. The refrigerator in her flat is being defrosted and she has brought all her perishables up to store in Mom and Dad's refrigerator. She, of course, has no idea what we are doing. On her way out, she just misses tripping on the phone cord. To be tripped by a phone cord connected to a phone which is being used to buy a house she does not know exists and would cause her to break into tears if she thought we were going to purchase is not a pretty way to go.

The phone rings again.

"Mr. Hailey, the house is yours."

We talked later to Judith Burnley to inform her of our triumph. She said Dad's master stroke was when he said he had behaved like a gentleman. No Englishman is willing to be outgentlemaned by an American.

We figure that the cost of the house will be almost exactly that of two college educations. I hasten to add that Brooke has no interest in going to college either—though if she changes her mind, we are going to look pretty funny living in half a house.

Our last day in London, and I saw a modern Mrs. Miniver on the subway. She was wearing blue jeans, but she was the only woman I have ever seen, with the sole exception of Greer Garson, to have Greer Garson's smile.

We think the famous are the only people who are looked at, but I look at everyone I see. And the joy people take in their own lives brings joy to mine. I have never seen a woman delight in her own children as much as that modern Mrs. Miniver. It was clear they were the people she most wanted to be with in the world.

There is nothing that turns my stomach more than seeing children mistreated. To me, the height of barbarism in our society is the idea that hitting children teaches them the difference between right and wrong. Of course, all I've ever done to stop it from happening is give rude stares and make remarks in a voice I secretly hope the parents won't hear because I'm afraid of getting punched in the nose.

I wish I could be like Lila Garrett, a writer we know. She was on a plane and saw a parent hitting a child. She approached the woman, talked to her, got her to stop, and was given an ovation by the rest of the plane when she returned to her seat.

I think the most important thing the Prince and Princess of Wales have done is to make so clear that they do not hit their children. It is up to our generation to do all we can for children because they have been ignored throughout history.

I say "our generation," yet George Bernard Shaw said, "If you strike a child, take care that you strike it in anger, even at the risk of maiming it for life. A blow in cold blood neither can nor should be forgiven."

He is a man who has protected every generation.

En route to Los Angeles. Dad has a migraine headache that he doesn't think will leave him until he flies back to England. Little wonder he wants to get back to his new home.

This English drug has made miracles a reality for us again. We've gone to a play almost every day. And the financial dealings with the house, which were frantic enough to have given most a major disease, Dad has weathered perfectly.

Dad is the wisest man I know, but I think he's getting even wiser. To know what you need is the most precious knowledge. And then to get it, the most necessary bravery.

Home. I've already talked to Matthew. His life is so real and mine so imaginary.

He is beginning his senior year of high school as president of his class and editor of the newspaper, while I have spent the summer playing leading parts in plays produced forty years ago.

I suppose any life is a combination of the real and the imaginary, and I don't suppose there is any better practice for the real than the imagined.

After all, it was reading those plays that made me want to write my own, and surely all those imagined performances can do nothing but help what might be my first real one.

WHAT I DID:

What I had hoped to do.

REHEARSAL FOR
REAL LIFE

WHAT I HOPE TO DO:
Prove I can play the real thing.

STEPS TO BE TAKEN
TO MAKE MY LIFE
REAL:

STEP ONE: Give Bill Cort my bar play to read. As director, his approval is essential.

If He Doesn't Like It:	If He Likes It:
My bar play will never be part of the evening. This will lead to despair and no chance that my life will ever be real.	My bar play might become a part of *The Bar off Melrose,* but first it must be read in front of an audience and I must find someone to play the part of Matthew.

STEP TWO: See if Matthew can act.

If He Can't:
My bar play will be a disaster in front of an audience because no one can play the role of Matthew like Matthew.

If He Can:
My bar play might have a chance in front of an objective audience.

STEP THREE: Read the play in front of an objective audience.

If They Hate My Bar Play:
My life will never be real and I'll probably die young for lack of anything better to do.

If They Love My Bar Play:
Matthew and I might very well be cast in the parts, we will do the play before objective audience after objective audience, and my life will be so real I'll have trouble recognizing it.

=================

Step One is in progress. As I write, Bill Cort is reading my bar play. He came over to talk to Dad about the shape *The Bar off Melrose* is taking. After they had discussed the way the evening would be structured, Dad handed him my play to read and then left the room because he couldn't take the tension.

I keep trying to pretend that the shape of my life does not depend on the opinion of this man, whom I liked so much before he started judging my work.

I still like him. And I hope I would have had the good character to continue liking him, even if he were not the first nonrelative to like my play.

Step One accomplished.

Now on to Matthew.

Step Two. I have irrevocably changed Matthew's life. I hope. I asked Mom, after I had already irrevocably done it, if she thought it was right for one person to change another person's life. She said that if a person's life was changed, it was because of something inside of him that wanted to change. Ha! I have changed Matthew's and I know (for the simple reason he has said so time and time again) that he does not want it to be changed.

At a quarter of five today, I tied him to a chair and made him read the play with me. And it turns out that the fellow with whom I have dreamed of playing *Life with Father* and *Life with Mother* can act.

He is going to be an actor. He doesn't know it yet, and he hasn't really consented, but his performance and the entire family's honest and excellent reaction (when my father says so, it's simply true) was just the proof I needed to confirm what I already knew —Matthew can act without even wanting to.

And yet as I write, an awful thought has come to me. Maybe it was not just Matthew's life that was changed today. Maybe it was also mine. How much will I love Matthew if he is a journalist? And how much will I love him if he is an actor and a writer? (You see, I'm already making him be a writer too). I suppose the real question is will those amounts be different?

Both my parents are writers and it's not as if they're always sitting in each other's laps writing. I remember Mom telling me that when they were first married, Dad could not stop asking her if she would love him if he were a plumber. Finally I understand what he meant. Love must be more all-encompassing than the mere issue of what we choose to do with our lives.

And mine will be. But to heck with that now because Step Two is complete. Step Three has already been scheduled at the theatre, but the date is several weeks away, so reality must wait a little longer.

I have a confession to make. It's not too illicit, as it involves Roman literature, but when it comes to education it's shocking, I assure you.

In reading a great deal of what's left of Rome, I somehow managed to miss the *Aeneid*. It was, I confess, a calculated oversight, but a summer immersed in the theatre has given me renewed educational strength. Therefore, I am not only going to read the *Aeneid*, I am ordering myself to lead up to it with *Beowulf* and *The Song of Roland*.

In my education so far, I have read by age, but since the *Aeneid* got left out in my reading of its age, I think I'll try an educational variation and read by genre for a while. I'll never get over my giddiness at the freedom of educating myself. A switch this morning from chronology to form, with no one's permission but my own.

Besides being among the greatest epics ever composed, the

three I've chosen also all happen to be attributed to noncollegiates. Actually, Virgil was sent to Rome to study rhetoric and physical sciences, but he gave it up and came back to the farm to be an autodidact in Greek philosophy and poetry. The authors of *Beowulf* and *The Song of Roland* are, in fact, unknown, but I'll give them credit for not going to college.

I came upon Nanny sitting depressed because she is getting a hearing aid. I thought maybe my mystery novel, finished long ago but kept hidden for the proper moment, might cheer her up. She yawned throughout and when I, instead of killing her, asked if she didn't think it was a little bit funny, she replied, "You know me. Even if something is funny, I don't laugh."

After eight hundred thirty-six lines of *Beowulf,* I'm about to throw up. It is the most disgusting piece of work I have ever read—eight hundred thirty-six lines of violence, blood and gore, and very little beauty.

I will never forget how I felt reading the *Iliad.* Moments of unparalled beauty and feeling . . . and I even read it in school (though I admit I was taught it by a great teacher—one whose comments always illuminated rather than infuriated).

But *Beowulf!* There is something wrong with a society that attacks modern movies for their violence, yet still calls *Beowulf* a classic. I don't think we have read what we are talking about.

"God gives guidance to those who can find it from no one else" (said Beowulf).

Isn't that a beautiful thought? I finally reconciled myself to the violence of *Beowulf,* and I found the thoughtfulness. Yet I do wonder how much beauty to attribute to the unknown author and how much to this lovely translation by Burton Raffel.

In another edition, this line is translated as "God gives aid to the friendless," which could be comforting, but I admire the meaning of Raffel's line.

How lucky that unknown author is. To be read so many different ways.

Ruth Gordon died. Dad said, "I never thought Ruth Gordon would die." She was eighty-nine, but I felt exactly the same way. If Ruth Gordon could die, then so much less seems possible. She was the one person who I thought was stronger than life.

Some might think her strength has been diffused among the inhabitants of the universe, but I know she has taken it all to Heaven with her. It was a brave decision of God's to create a Ruth Gordon in the first place. I wonder if He regrets it now that He has her up there for eternity to advise him.

All we can be sure of is if there is any improvement in the general condition of the world between now and eternity, it's probably due to the intervention of Ruth Gordon. And if there isn't, then she's busy writing another play.

In Dallas with *A Woman of Independent Means.* Standing ovations, but we have heard Dallas critics like to model themselves after New York ones, so we don't know what kind of reviews to expect.

On the lighter side, today we almost killed our grandmother. We were driving to my grandparents' house with Granny Jan and Grandaddy Earl and our darling Brooke all seated in the backseat.

The basic conversation centered around the fact that Granny Jan was perfectly ready to die and planned to do it on the highway with Grandaddy Earl at the wheel. The fact that neither Grandaddy Earl nor most of the other innocent drivers on the Interstate were eager to croak was some cause for disagreement in the backseat. However, Granny Jan held firm that she was ready to leave this world and seemed determined to have an automobile involved.

Well, all I can say is someone up above is looking out for Granny Jan because just as she was proclaiming loudly that she was ready to go and saw tire tracks in her future, we rounded a curve and the door on her side of the car flew open. Had her ankles not been safely wedged under the front seat, she would no doubt have been flung from the car and gotten her wish. However, as the wedged ankles testify, Granny Jan does indeed have a powerful will to live.

I love the life that revolves around my grandparents' house. I walk into their living room and feel as if nothing could ever hurt me. The sanity of their lives seems to have permeated the place where they live them. Whereas our house is no doubt moaning and wheezing even as I write, on the verge of a nervous breakdown, waiting for the reviews from Dallas.

The play is the hit it deserves to be, but I'm sure our house has found something else to worry about.

One of Brooke's favorite things to do is to summon me to her side, look into the mirror (Brooke is usually standing in front of a mirror), and caption what she knows will one day be a photograph in *Life* with the words "Brooke Hailey, star, takes a moment to pose with sister Kendall, poet." And the title "poet" is no compliment. It is simply the profession she considers least threatening to that of star.

I pride myself on taking pride in Brooke. I thought I would die of pride last spring when she appeared on stage for the first time doing a scene from the old play *One Sunday Afternoon* for the Oakwood Arts Festival (coincidentally, the very same scene I was going to do for the Arts Festival in ninth grade, but decided not to when I realized how many afterschool rehearsals there would be —I never did like to stay at school longer than was absolutely necessary).

I could just as easily have watched her with envy, since that was the time I was so desperate to be an actress and no one knew it. But it was sheer pride—a pride I know will carry over to all her accomplishments, no matter to what degree they outstrip mine.

I used to worry that I would be racked with insane jealousy if she got to be a star and I only a poet. But I no longer think I would (and I'm not even sure Brooke would, should the situation by some strange happening be reversed). This great improvement in our characters is due totally to Ramona Hennesy, the sister of Barbara Rush. Ramona is not a poet, and yet she is in a way. A poet of life, which is a lot more important in the end than words. And to see Ramona and Barbara together is to realize it doesn't matter (not to them and not to anyone else) which of the sisters is the star and which the poet.

*B*eowulf does not live up to its reputation. Or, considering *Beowulf*'s reputation, maybe it does. I loved when Beowulf killed Grendel the monster, when Beowulf killed Grendel's mother, and when the dragon killed Beowulf (I don't even mind giving away the plot of something so boring). The parts of extreme violence were the only places where *Beowulf* seemed to have the nobility of an epic.

The rest seemed to be touched by the mundane, and when a hero's life starts sounding mundane, you know why the author chose to remain unknown (don't give me any fake stories about his identity being lost—I've read the thing).

*T*alked to Matthew tonight. He called *To Be or Not to Be* our movie as it is the only movie we've seen all by ourselves together. It thrilled me so when he said it. My plan is to have as many shared references as possible, so even if he doesn't marry me, he'll think of me whenever they come up, and, glancing over at what he has married, be miserable.

I have begun *The Song of Roland* and I already like it so much more than *Beowulf.* I prefer when men fight men rather than monsters. I think it is why I preferred the *Iliad* to the *Odyssey*—just Trojans versus Greeks, and none of them had five heads.

It is interesting the course the epics take. In *Beowulf,* man battles monster. *Song of Roland,* man and man. And *The Divine Comedy,* man and himself—a fiercer opponent than Grendel any day.

If you are looking for solace from violence, don't look to the Church. At least not the Church as it's presented in Roland's *Chanson.* When it comes to war, the Archbishop pictured here puts Patton to shame. For a practitioner of forgiveness and understanding of all men, he is very fond of saying to the enemy, "God send the worst to thee!"

He does finally meet his Maker (I would have liked to have heard that little conversation), but due to his own exhaustion rather than a blow delivered by an infidel.

The most amazing thing is that he is the religious leader of the men who were fighting to spread Christianity. I don't think the Archbishop had gotten to the part about the meek inheriting the earth.

Today we went to see one of my father's plays. If he is called about a production, he is very nice about going to see it . . . no matter how many weeks it depresses him afterward.

Mom and I went too, and as I walked into the theatre—it wasn't really a theatre, it was a barn with a stage—I wondered what our lives had come to. But the play *(For the Use of the Hall)* turned that barn into a theatre.

After it was over, Mom said that if she didn't already know Oliver Hailey, she'd just have to find him. (I feel the same way—unfortunately, she got to him first.)

When I was reading all those plays this summer, I know if I had come across one of his, I would have been sure I had found my soulmate for life. Sometimes I think it's a shame we are so intimately acquainted because if there are two people you forget to appreciate, it is those parents.

Can that man who lies on my bed, watching some awful *film noir,* which he is enjoying thoroughly, and crumbling the most disgusting food, really be the author of the play I saw today? If I had written that play, I think I would just lie back and drink virgin piña coladas the rest of my life—I would have done enough. But there he is, upstairs, crumbling something disgusting in his own bed, thinking about the beginning of his next play.

Roland has just croaked, speaking his last words to his sword. Not a thought for Alude, his fiancée, who drops dead herself on hearing of Roland's demise, but then considering how little space the poet gives to Alude, I tend to prefer Durendal, the sword, myself.

I have just been lying on the floor contemplating the extreme mediocrity of my novel. I made the mistake of reading over what I had written rather than writing new stuff, and, to put it bluntly, I am appalled.

I don't know whether to give it all up and start something else or just go through with it. I know the two hundred pages already written stink, but I do feel strangely optimistic about the two hundred to come. If only I could get somebody else to write them.

Step Three on the road to *The Bar off Melrose.* Tonight Matthew and I read my play (which I am calling "Confessions of an Autodidact") in front of an invited audience, most of whom I didn't know, and it went well. It actually worked. So many drafts that now seem unreal and unimportant. This is a new beginning. And what we read tonight—which I considered a carefully honed, finished play when I came in—is once again raw stuff that will change and grow.

Playing opposite me, Matthew was everything in the world I had hoped for (and you know how much I hope) and more. More. More. More. More. He was so charming and dear and innocent . . . well, I thought men like that were only born before 1910.

And it was our third kiss. There is a kiss in the play. Smart structuring, don't you think? I told him the kiss was to be just like the kind he gives Nanny—if possible, less passionate. Because as Dad said later tonight, "You know, Kendall, the shorter the kiss, the bigger the laugh." Well, Dad was the only one who thought it went on too long.

At the start of the evening (there were a lot of actors reading a lot of bar scenes), a young actress said to Bill Cort, "When you talk about Kendall's play, do you mean the one about the autodidact because I'd like to read that one. I think that's a terrific play." And I could not keep myself from yelling out, "Oh, thank you." I mean whatever she had said, not knowing I was sitting right behind her, would have been my first review in the theatre. I've got one rave to my credit. I have a feeling I may need it.

Though I'm not going to worry about good reviews. After the way critics have treated my family, I think a good review would be an insult. And why worry about praise from those people when I already feel like Lynn Fontanne?

Of course, I still have to wait a little longer before I'm a full-fledged Lynn Fontanne (plus I have to convince Matthew that he's my Alfred Lunt). Rehearsals for the play don't begin till after Christmas. And before rehearsals begin, there still must be one more reading of *The Bar off Melrose* as a whole to make sure all the scenes that have worked individually will work together.

So if my scene does not work well with the others, there is still the lingering chance that my life will never be real. But I won't think about that tonight. I'll think about that tomorrow.

I am about to begin the *Aeneid.* To take my mind off all the ordeals that await me when I make my writing and acting début, I am going to see if I can get through all the ordeals that awaited Aeneas after he lost the Trojan War. His adventures far outweigh in length those of Beowulf and Roland, which is why I have saved him for last.

I confess now that I have always had a sneaking suspicion that had there not been quizzes on them, I, as a sane member of the twentieth century, never would have made it through the *Iliad* or the *Odyssey*. Even as I was reading them during that last year of formal education, I had to pause and wonder if I'd ever have the courage to get through the *Aeneid* on my own.

And here I am. I have at least made it to the starting gate.

One fourth of the way through the *Aeneid* with no signs of giving up yet. How Virgil could have been embarrassed about this work meeting public eyes is something I have a hard time understanding.

My favorite part so far is the appearance of Andromache, Hector's widow whom I first met in the *Iliad*. I find it so inexplicably moving when a character met in an earlier work makes a reappearance in a later one. When a character is brought back to life, it always seems to me that he or she really must exist.

I suppose in ancient times Andromache really did exist, yet I find it equally moving when the characters from Nancy Mitford's earlier novels come to the tea parties given by the characters in her later ones. It is as if the characters are saying, "Ha! And you thought we were just fiction."

I had assumed the *Aeneid*'s Queen Dido was a tramp, but turns out no. Helen of Troy remains the only true tramp in ancient times.

After all, Dido does not fall in love with Aeneas of her own free will. His overprotective mother, Venus, sent Desire to her to make her fall in love with him.

But when Dido falls there's quite a thump. After hearing Aeneas go on for two books about the fall of Troy, the next night she asks: "to hear once more/In her wild need the throes of Ilium,/And once more hung on the narrator's words."

I, too, loved the first two books in the *Aeneid*, but wanting to hear the whole tale two nights in a row is a wish only true love could inspire.

Amazing that Virgil had time for such a powerful love story in the midst of the founding of Rome. I suspect love had once treated him as it did Dido. Before her death, "She prayed then to

whatever power may care/In comprehending justice for the grief/
Of lovers bound unequally by love."

In a world where every power was so carefully assigned, no god
wanted responsibility for unequal love.

Brooke and I spent this evening discussing sex. However, our views on the subject are beginning to diverge, and what
does it say about me that Nanny is staunchly on my side?

To put it quite frankly, Brooke is still planning to shoot herself
if she experiences being nineteen before she experiences something
else.

Actually, since there is nothing Brooke likes better than to hear
Nanny and me shriek each time our morals are offended, I think
most of her talk is just that.

But practically everything that's said in this country about sex
(except what's said in my favorite films) tends to upset me. At one
point in our conversation, Brooke yelled at me, "Will you please
stop using the phrase 'the many-splendored thing'?" I, of course,
refused because I happen to believe in it.

It's just . . . well, goodness, I would like sex to change my
life. I suppose that's asking a lot of sex, but I want it to be the
culmination of a relationship. A sign of trust, and not just the
most popular physical activity in the world. I hope it leads to a
deep desire not to hurt each other, and I think it can only when
you truly love someone.

Brooke agreed with me on this point, but then informed me
that she was planning to fall truly in love at least twenty times. I
said I didn't think you could preplan the number of times you
knew "the many-splendored thing." She agreed with me here, too,
but I can still see she is going to be disappointed if she doesn't
meet her goals of age and variety.

Sometimes I feel so alone in my beliefs. I wonder if even God
believes in "the many-splendored thing." After all, the sexual urge
is implanted in us at an awfully young age. But I think that was to
give us all the time possible to keep our species going when people
lived much shorter lives and the survival rate at birth was very

low. Would any of us be here today if cavemen had waited for "the many-splendored thing"?

Yet we have the luxury of doing so. Just as I now have the luxury of reading the *Aeneid* at my own pace and not because of quizzes, I want luxury in an area reportedly as much fun as literature. And I don't mind if that means that morally I have to agree with Nanny (who does, however, think literature is a lot more fun than the other).

I'm having *Aeneid* problems.

Just at the moment I was becoming deeply involved in the story, the founder of Rome and his people decide to take a little time out to play some games. And Virgil feels the need not only to tell the reader who won every contest but also the names of everyone who didn't. My respect for Virgil has grown so great I must believe his dying words were "trim Book Five."

I am finding it increasingly pitiful the way I spend my Halloween nights.

Brooke is at a party. Matthew is "out to dinner," so said Leona, who was probably just trying to spare my feelings by not telling me he was at a party. Even depressed Michele Arian is at a party.

I don't really want to go to a party. I like Halloween at home. I am just beginning to feel increasingly pitiful.

Do you remember that first Halloween? I sat in the living room reading Will Durant and was fulfilled. The second Halloween? Sat in the living room writing my mystery and was fulfilled. And tonight? I'm sitting in the living room eating Tootsie Rolls.

Virgil more than made up for those games with Aeneas' visit to his father in the underworld. He also happens to run into Queen Dido, who is not exactly thrilled to see him. It makes me think that life after death could be a complicated business for a lot of people.

Christianity tends to view Heaven as so much more fun than

life, but listen to what Virgil says of the inhabitants of the "Blessed Groves": "All joy they took, alive, in cars and weapons,/ As in the care and pasturing of horses,/Remained with them when they were laid in earth." As if Heaven is not a new, unknown type of joy, but rather the joy we took in life. I must say, I think this is a more sensible view. To prepare for Heaven by taking joy in life is to come out ahead even if there happens to be no Heaven.

"Everybody in this family is a goomba. I'm getting out of here," said Brooke as she set out on a fierce post-family-fight walk.

I ran to the door to follow her, explaining to our relatives, "Brooke's running away from home. I'm just walking her to the end of the street."

All the way up the street, Brooke spilled forth brutally honest facts about the faults of everyone in this family. I was in a deep depression by the time we reached the end of the street, wishing I were running away from this group, too. But reciting all the faults seemed to calm her down and she decided—at least for now—to turn around. By the time we reached home we were laughing about those same family faults that had propelled us up the street in anger.

And that is the basic dilemma of family life. There are two ways to look at it—laughingly or honestly. And I'm not sure which is the more accurate.

Yes, every morning Thomas brushes his teeth and washes his face and combs his hair and, while doing so, carries on an impassioned argument with his mirror. He yells about philosophical matters, politics, and, more often than not, family members who have upset him. But when a visitor enters the room, his conversation always makes an abrupt change from "Now listen, Oliver [or, occasionally, "Reagan"]" to "Hi, darlin'." Now, Uncle Thomas can either be viewed as a man on the brink of insanity or as quite a little eccentric, who will be put to perfect use in a family play.

In every day there are so many times when I think how much I love every one of the people I am related to. And, of course, there are so many other times filled with the hatred and disgust only real relatives can inspire.

But to love them and to know you love them is to realize the gift of family life while still part of a family. Of course, I will hate them all and love them all tomorrow and I wish more than anything people were perfect, but if they were, we would not need each other.

I finally understand the importance of who won what game in all those contests of the *Aeneid,* of the Catalogue of Ships from the *Iliad,* and all those other ancient passages the modern reader is so tempted to skim.

Before describing a battle, Virgil says this of the Muses: "For you remember, you can bring to life/That time, immortal ones, while to ourselves/Faint wraiths of history barely transpire."

I love Virgil because he is my soulmate. He wrote the *Aeneid* to keep the faint wraiths of history alive. There is no nobler motive, and I must be worthy of it when reading him.

It is important to remember who won which race for it is a small way of keeping the victor alive, and I think the intensity of how alive we ourselves are is measured by how many live on within us.

I just had my first midlife crisis. I was lying on the floor and suddenly it came to me that I'm going to be twenty in a few months (nine, actually). Of course, I never thought I'd really be nineteen. When I was little, I thought you should be out of the house by twelve. I'm way behind schedule.

I feel I am kind of poised—waiting for *life* to begin. But what if this has been life all along? What if it never gets any realer? I keep attributing this feeling to youth, but what if I go through my whole life without ever feeling it really began?

I suppose the ugly truth is that life begins the moment you're born. And it is asking too much of it to request that it always live up to its reputation of being real.

Helping Mom unpack groceries, I thought of how in the *Aeneid,* the daily grind of getting food and shelter is referred to as the "arts of life." The genius of Virgil as translated through the genius of Robert Fitzgerald makes even an outing to the grocery store poetic.

I have spent the best years of my life cleaning up my closet. I decided to move what was in the bottom of my closet to a drawer, to move what was in the drawer to another room, and to move what was in the other room to the bottom of my closet. Why I am convinced this new arrangement will make me into a happier, more well-adjusted person I do not know.

All I know for certain is that I do not want to give up. And I am not just talking about straightening up my room (I always give up on that). If you want the truth of the matter, I have been straightening my closet to avoid writing my novel. Though I am less afraid of finishing my novel than I am of straightening another inch of my closet. So, to the disappointment of my shoes, I will continue writing.

My father was down here a moment ago. He has not given up on writing, but he has given up on optimism in a way. Of course, he has every right to. He has been beaten to death by critics and gotten so many bad breaks.

Yet I think of all the serious and gifted playwrights we know whose plays will never see Broadway as Dad's have, never be performed all over the country as Dad's have. I remember the first time I realized how much he has accomplished (which is hard to do, since Dad hates to be called anything but a failure). We were in a bookstore and he picked up the new theatre annual and I saw that that year he was the 16th most produced playwright in America, ranking below Shakespeare and Shaw, but above Arthur Miller and Thornton Wilder.

And tonight we were watching *After the Thin Man,* written by Frances Goodrich and Albert Hackett, and he told me he had once gotten a fan letter from them about his play "Who's Happy

Now?" Imagine. I would hope that, no matter what else happened to me, if I got a fan letter from Frances Goodrich and Albert Hackett, I would not give up on optimism.

One of my worst fears is of what I will be in the future. Not really of what will happen to me, but of what it will turn me into. If none of my dreams comes true, will I be embarrassed to keep dreaming? It takes courage to fulfill dreams, but I think even more if we can't.

The world is much too random a place for any of us ever to end up with exactly what we want, but then very few of us are bright enough to know exactly what we want. I just hope that if I go through life without getting what I think I want, it will not change me. Is there a way to want a great deal out of life and yet not be disappointed if I don't get it?

Let us not forget who said, after yet another disastrous experience in the theatre, "Never will I write these plays or try to produce them, not if I live to be seven hundred years old." Chekhov.

Let me be like posterity and not bother with immediate success or failure.

The *Aeneid* is like a classical version of *Upstairs Downstairs* with the gods as the Bellamys and we mortals as the servants.

The gods provide such a refreshing calmness to the fervor of man. We gave up a lot when we gave up paganism. It's not like the gods were anything special to look up to (in fact, it would be hard to find a group with looser morals), but I love thinking the universe is being run by people who, though immortal, are as human as we.

Tomorrow we leave for England for Christmas, but tonight was the last step needed to make life real. Matthew and I read my play again in a run-through of *The Bar off Melrose,* and it worked again and flowed with the other scenes. It will be part of the evening.

Matthew worried that another reading would ruin his journalistic credibility, but when I told him Mike Wallace had once been in a play on Broadway, he felt much better.

After the reading, we stayed in the lobby of the theatre talking, and he said there was just no way he could actually be in the play. Not because of journalistic credibility, but that thing called high school.

It was the first time he'd told me anything I didn't want to hear. Reality invading us. But then I said, "I guess you know this means I'm going to have to kiss a creep." And he said, "That's exactly what I'm worried about."

As you know, the extent of our physical contact is on the minimal side (though an extra kiss tonight, thanks to my genius as a playwright). After the reading, the four Haileys and Matthew and another playwright were all walking together to our cars. Of course, Matthew is embarrassed to kiss anyone in front of furniture, let alone people. He'd hugged Brooke and Mom and then we all kind of stepped back and I thought, "I've missed out yet again."

Everyone was in the car and it was only the playwright and me and Matthew, and I thought I'll be lucky to be waved to. And then he hugged me and he kissed me and then I thought it was all over because who could ask for anything more and then he hugged me again.

I tell you, life just gets better and better and better.

WHAT I DID:

Auditioned for the part I wrote for myself in my own play and got it. Anything wrong with that?

LIFE
(at last and again)

WHAT I HOPE TO DO:

Live up to It.

On his first walk through our new English house, Dad found an abandoned butcher's cleaver at the bottom of the garden. It turns out that in long-ago village days, our house belonged to the butcher. Being the son of a butcher himself, Dad feels as if his life has come full circle. As he hung the cleaver on a wall, I heard him remark, "It's just like the one my dad used to chase me with."

Strange things happen to a house that is no longer filled with furniture. It is a scientific fact that it shrinks in size. Of course from a small age I have been the holder of original scientific theories.

The thing that baffled me most throughout my younger years was the fact that when we would go out for dinner, certain buildings would be on my right as we drove to dinner and on my left coming home.

My only explanation for this phenomenon was that while we were eating dinner, all the streets were lifted up and turned around. It did bother me that this was an awful lot of trouble to go to just so certain buildings could be on my right going one way and on my left going the other, but I could never think up a more logical explanation.

And so perhaps our sixteenth-century house did not shrink scientifically, but something very strange did happen to it. Dad decided the remedy was to knock out a wall. A false one that hid a door. But having no wall-knocking-down equipment, Dad and I first walked to the hardware store, one of the three shops in the village, to get some.

Dad asked the proprietress if she had a hammer, since there

was none in sight. She replied that she had had one once, but someone had bought it. Over the years people had also bought the screwdriver and the saw. Luckily for us, no one had ever wanted the ax.

So Dad is hacking away with it, restoring a little more of the sixteenth century. I am sitting in the inglenook by the fireplace. To think people have been sitting here from the death of Queen Elizabeth I to the birth of Prince William.

This is England. I have been looking for the complete Herodotus ever since I got to know the Greeks. Today I found it in the bookshop at Victoria Station. Nothing against my countrymen, but can you imagine a bookshop owner in a United States train station having enough faith in our collective intelligence to stock Herodotus' *Histories*? There were two copies, so it is nice to think that at some time in the future an English commuter will also be reading Herodotus.

The inhabitants of the villages of England are breathing testimonies to the fact that Dickens did not write larger-than-life characters.

In a nearby town lies our favorite antique store, with prices almost as low as their beams. It was opened by a couple in the 1920's, then their daughter and two sons took over, and now their grandchildren are learning the family craft. On our first visit, we were met by one of the younger members of the family. Brooke asked if he had anything old and strange, to which he replied, "Well, I could introduce you to my father."

Thanks to them, we have practically furnished the entire house —with the exception of a twentieth-century couch, which we ordered from a store in Guildford, one of the largest cities south of London and close to our village. However, due to a Hailey-type mix-up, the couch had been brought to the house when we were out, and so was taken back to the warehouse. The next possible delivery date was not until after our return to California.

We tried to hire a truck. However, due to the season, none

could be found. Dad decided the only solution was to call our friends at the antique store. He did the deciding, but made Mom (who tried unsuccessfully to convince him that their business was selling antiques, not delivering new stuff) do the calling.

She explained the situation to one of the older generation, who replied, "Indeed, Mrs. Hailey, this is not customary, but it is Christmas, isn't it?"

I am almost to the end of my novel. Why didn't anyone tell me emotional, climactic endings were hard to write? I think you should be given that information at about age five so you can look into other career opportunities.

As I near the end of my novel, I keep changing my mind about how to end it. And if I don't stop going out to look at the garden and start writing, I'll never finish. But then I think the definition of happiness is having too little time for all you want to do.

Feeling hopelessly inferior.

Did you know Jane Austen wrote *Pride and Prejudice, Sense and Sensibility,* and *Northanger Abbey* before the age of twenty-three? Brooke, who just finished reading *Northanger Abbey* for school and detested it, told me that. Brooke says she thinks the main problem is Jane Austen was a virgin, and she hates virgin authors. We'll have to lie when the time comes and tell her the Brontë girls got around.

Christmas Eve. Dad just came back from the village hardware store. During our stay, he has made dozens of trips and never yet come back with what he needed. Today, when the proprietress was yet again out of what he wanted (and has so far shown no interest in reordering), she called to him as he was leaving, "I'll be closed Christmas Day, luv."

Christmas Day. A time, of course, to share and so, fittingly, everyone in the village saw what we all got.

Not valuing privacy to any great extent, we have been rather lax about getting curtains for the dining room, which looks directly onto the street. Our house is also right on the way to the village church.

Understandably, it's difficult for any good churchgoer not to peek in. By the afternoon service, we were holding up our favorite presents for the passersby to admire.

We have to say good-bye to our house for the first time tomorrow. As we were rolling up the carpets tonight, Dad suddenly said, "We wouldn't have this house if it weren't for Mama Thomas." I asked why and he explained his grandmother, Mama Thomas, had wanted her daughters to be able to support themselves, so it was because of her that Nanny had a teacher's certificate. A certificate she used many years later to support herself and Thomas, giving Dad the freedom to go to Yale and become a playwright.

I thought as I got into bed that we have added a little more history to this house with so much.

"I sing of warfare and a man at war." So begins Robert Fitzgerald's translation of the *Aeneid*, which I have just this moment finished. It's books like that which make me believe in some kind of greatness. I have always thought the most powerful argument for the divinity of Christ is Handel's *Messiah*. It is hard to believe beauty like that could be inspired by a mortal.

My favorite piece of poetry from the *Aeneid* is the description of Jupiter as "the author of men." What a gift Robert Fitzgerald gave the world when he shared his poetry with Virgil.

I saved the last book of the *Aeneid* for the plane trip home, and I've finished it with eight hours in the air still to go. I hope Divine

Providence strikes me with my next educational step pretty quickly.

I read somewhere that the *Aeneid* is considered unfinished. I knew it was considered unpolished, but I don't think it is unfinished. It ends as Aeneas kills the last man who stands in the way of the founding of Rome. We do not really need to be told that Aeneas went on to found Rome. We know that. Virgil's work ends when the good plot runs out.

Frankly, I suspect that had Margaret Mitchell written in ancient times and *Gone with the Wind* been unearthed, people would have thought it was unfinished. But she and Virgil both knew the trick of leaving the last leg of the story to the imagination. Just as I think Aeneas and Rome end up together, I believe the same about Scarlett and Rhett.

Which brings me to Nanny. She spent 1936 reading what most of America was reading—*Gone with the Wind.* Actually, she didn't come anywhere close to spending the whole year reading it. She read it in three days. She couldn't afford to buy it, and she had borrowed it from a friend who had borrowed it from another friend who needed it back so she could lend it to another friend.

The point is, Nanny could read *Gone with the Wind* in three days, but never the *Aeneid.* What sometimes frustrates me about Nanny is that she has read fast and furiously all her life and if she'd ever given a thought to being intellectual, she could have easily read all the great books. But Nanny reads what interests her and, sadly for literature, is without literary pretensions. Or even the ambition to pick up a few.

After I loved *Anna Karenina,* I told her how much she would and she read it and did, telling me, "Kendall, it was as good as *Dora Thorne.*" I was stunned to think anything could compete with *Dora Thorne,* the Victorian romance that remains her favorite novel.

I so admire her total lack of pretension accompanied by an equal abundance of curiosity. We are sitting together on the plane and the minute I laid the *Aeneid* down, she picked it up. When I asked her how she liked it, she said, "It's interestin'. I may have to read it."

And that is the reason a real intellectual does begin the *Aeneid.*

I began it because it was called the *Aeneid,* but I finished it because it was interestin'.

Home. Matthew picked us up at the airport. He said
it had always been a fantasy of his. Well, of course, it's always
been a fantasy of mine—we must start getting together more often
on these things.

He stayed all day long, even through the mandatory grocery
store outing (which he loved, confiding that household errands are
always great fun when they are not your own) till I nearly fell
asleep talking. The only ill effect of this heavenly day was that
Matthew has just about shamed me into reading *Moby Dick.* Every time we talk about books, he brings it up. Of course, one
should never discuss literature when suffering jet lag.

Over jet lag and about to start *Moby Dick.* It is my
first sacrifice for love.

Today we had our first huge gathering of everyone
involved in *The Bar off Melrose.* I think the number of people
sitting in the theatre we practically filled was equaled only by the
level of excitement. Excitement that seemed at an equal level in
everyone—no matter how much experience was behind them.

The thirty-eight actors range in experience from Marie Wind-
sor, the movie star (who plays a movie star having a few stiff
drinks in the bar off Melrose before making her stage début in an
Equity-waiver production down the street), to a young actress
with no experience on stage or screen, namely me. And the fourteen playwrights range in experience from Dad to a young playwright never produced before, and that also happens to be me.

But how I love the theatre on very first glance. And do I have
casting news. Turns out Matthew does not have a monopoly on
playing Matthew. The actor who'll be playing him is so handsome
and charming, to say nothing of talented, that I suspect the real
Matthew will have a long overdue attack of jealousy on seeing

Dean and me do the play (Dean Howell is the new Matthew's name and he's as close to James Dean as our generation is going to get).

I wonder if the theatre is always like this. Dad keeps telling me that, in his entire career, this is his best experience, and assuring me all else will be strictly downhill. But the top of the hill is so grand I plan to enjoy the slide down, too.

Little wonder they call it the theatre. At least I turned on it before it got a chance to turn on me.

I had my first rehearsal today and I just hated it. It was so dull. I couldn't believe that here I was getting to be a real actress, and here I was bored. Hating it so much has messed up a great many of my life plans.

I adore Dean, but the play has changed without Matthew. Before, the two characters were equal, and now she seems to be taking him by the hand and leading (in fact, almost tugging) him down the road of life.

But maybe Dean has helped me find the truth of the play. I told Matthew I really wrote it for Jean Arthur and James Stewart, but they refused to do Equity waiver. And in both *You Can't Take It with You* and *Mr. Smith Goes to Washington*, it is she who guides him.

But the way it is now, I certainly don't feel like Jean Arthur. Something strange has happened to my whole character now that I'm not playing opposite Matthew anymore. Perhaps I do sound rather arrogant and pretentious and self-absorbed when I'm not talking to Matthew, who sounds just like me.

However, I've got to learn the difference between life and art. After all, Myrna Loy found William Powell on the screen, but in real life she was married four times. I'd rather save Matthew for real life. In the meantime, I have a little work ahead of me as a playwright and as an actress, but I think I'll be able to muddle through kissing Dean.

Nanny, by popular demand, got a hearing aid early last fall, yet still remained oblivious to most spoken conversation. A state which is convenient on occasion, but irritating on the whole.

Yesterday we took her back to the ear doctor and found out that for four months she thought the "on" button was the "off" button and the "off" button was the "on" button. For four months, she had been turning the hearing aid off and putting it in her ear. Then, when she took it out at night, she turned it on to save the battery.

We all thought this discovery would make her life much happier, but after twenty-four hours, she announced she could hear better the other way.

Just called Matthew to tell him I really could have done without those whale quotes at the beginning of Melville's masterpiece. He tells me they're terribly symbolic, but then anything you don't quite see the point of usually is.

However, I promised to persevere. And it was a lovely conversation. So beautifully orchestrated. To me, our talks are an art. I might even miss them a little if we get married.

Today, for the very first time in my life to date, I enjoyed acting as much as writing.

I was due at the theatre for a second rehearsal, and for hours before leaving I went over my script, mulling over each line, and suddenly it hit me why I had not enjoyed the first rehearsal. The play had gone so well when Matthew and I read it in front of an audience that I thought my performance must be perfect.

It's because I have writers for parents instead of actors. I know writers are never supposed to stop writing. We are now rehearsing what is close to the twentieth version of my five-page play (though I do hope longer plays require fewer versions).

It is only thanks to Uta Hagen and her book, *Respect for Act-*

ing, that I have realized actors keep acting. Though I have always worshipped actors, I never quite understood how hard it is possible for them to work. But I know now every part of life is of use to an actor. And when you can learn something from every part of life, there's very little excuse for being bored.

I woke up so happy about my scene I could not wait to get out of bed because the sooner I lived Tuesday, the sooner it would be Wednesday and we could rehearse again.

I wonder how many of us wish we had never lived this Tuesday. I know there were children born today and that is wonderful, but today the space shuttle exploded and six astronauts and the teacher who seemed to represent the rest of us were all killed.

Isaac Singer said something very right about tragedies. When asked how there could be a God when there is so much that is terrible in the world, he said, "Maybe He's a little God."

We will go on, but those seven did not die in vain. When all of humanity stops to care about the same thing at the same time, there is something good in that. When all our separate pains are brought together as one, there is some kind of beauty in that.

Though they did not live to carry out their mission, those men and women extended the boundaries of the human spirit today. I have seen the footage again and again and again, yet every time I see it I seem to block how it will end, and I cannot help but feel joy and pride in those first few moments as the space shuttle soared. And the best that is life rarely lasts longer than a moment.

As the President said, " 'They slipped the surly bonds of earth to touch the face of God.' " And they know what we are trying to understand.

Parkinson's disease and miracles do not mix. At least not for very long. The English miracle drug is now beginning to wear off. Nothing works for too long, and the best advice there is for treating Parkinson's we heard too late: Go for as long as you can with as little medication as you can.

Dad was given so much medication in the beginning that he did have almost three miracle years, barely feeling the effects of the disease, but he is paying for them now. He is taking so much medication, but it isn't helping his tremors and he is losing his energy.

He sometimes lies down at the back of the theatre during *Bar off Melrose* rehearsals. When things aren't working, I sense Bill Cort wanting to join him there. But other times I get so worried.

Bill said to me at today's rehearsal, "I'm trusting you to know when he's tired and make him go home." As he said it, for a moment I felt so responsible and in charge, finally living up to the Antigone my father wanted me to be. But then I felt so sad.

Dad has always taken responsibility for everything, and I feel as though I'm taking something away from him when I do. But maybe this is the little bit of good this disease has brought us. Dad has finally given up trying to think of a reason why he needs to go everywhere I need to go, and as I climbed in the car yesterday to drive to a rehearsal by myself, I heard him say, "I know why I got this disease. It was the only way God could think up to get me to let go of my daughters."

Julie Reich is home for a semester break. I call her up every night and, without waiting for hello, say, "Tell me everything you've done the past twenty-four hours." It is a crash course in having a certified peer near again. Someone with whom to compare one's progress in a day. Which is something I have missed a little bit.

However, I'm beginning to think college kills ambition. This is her sophomore year. The cold world is just two years away. I should think it would be nice to have a career warming up before being handed a college diploma. So I have devised a plan to encourage her.

All Julie's short stories revolve around the same character, despite the fact the character has a different name in every story. She just has to realize she has been doing the thing all writers must do, writing about herself. If she gives the character the same name throughout, then she's got a collection of short stories.

We spent tonight reading her stories while feasting on hot chocolate (diet hot chocolate, of course) and Cheez-Its (there is no such thing as diet Cheez-Its). Julie isn't quite ready to believe her stories make a book, and I have to remember it isn't my place to order her to believe it. But when it comes to making writers believe in what they write, I have been trained by masters, named Mom and Dad.

Today Mom finally got her hands back on our family album of photographs. After I saw the photographs of John Swope, I took her camera and never gave it back. As she turned the pages of our album, she wailed, "This album used to be a history of our family—where are we for the last year? There are only pictures of clouds in here." I apologized for discontinuing our headless history of family photographs, but explained that though I liked painting people, I preferred photographing clouds. People can always use the little bit of transforming a paintbrush can give them, but clouds are perfect as they are.

I think lack of college kills ambition, too. Michele Arian showed me some of her photographs today. She can do clouds and people. Her work is stunning, so stunning she should never leave her room without her camera around her neck. But she does.

And yet I sort of enjoy telling her she mustn't because we are on equal footing. We have made the same choice, so no one's on the defensive.

With collegiates (except for Julie, since we share an equal footing in our choice of careers, and that is our main concern these days), depending on my mood, I either feel very much on the defensive or, if I am full of confidence, think that they should be.

But Michele and I both faced the beginning of life without school. Early and together. I wonder if Thoreau had a good friend living on a neighboring pond. I hope he did, because I sure needed mine.

I have been practically ordered not to call Matthew until he calls me. Everyone from my father, who I thought was wise, to Brooke, who is out to get me, seems to be urging me to play hard to get. Suppose he does call me? There'll still be the same conversations to make work, the same lives to make work.

And what if he is too certain that I adore him? I hardly think that's dangerous. We will all have to look back on our lives some day, and I don't want to look back and think I could have loved him more. It takes a lot of courage to do anything, even love a slightly freckled seventeen-year-old.

My friends the gods must have seen I was on the edge, for Matthew called today.

As the line I cut from my play goes, "I only feel like who I am when I'm with you." Better it was cut from the play, but I'm glad it was in when I did it with Matthew. I'm glad I said it to him.

At the exact time of his call, I was with a friend, Amy Turner. She wants to be a film director, so we were having a double feature of *Double Indemnity* and *Born Yesterday* (I certainly don't think anyone should be a film director without having watched them). We were in the middle of *Double Indemnity* when his call was announced, and I thought it would be rude to leave Amy alone with Barbara Stanwyck in the murdering mood, so Brooke took the call and a more wonderful thing could not have happened.

I have stated my principle of not consciously trying to make jealous or unhappy someone I love. However, I am happy to report that that is definitely not one of Brooke's principles. The entire time Barbara Stanwyck was tormenting Fred MacMurray, Brooke was doing the same to Matthew.

After *Double Indemnity,* Amy had to go to the bathroom, as all future film directors do after seeing a great film, and I got on the phone for a moment.

The first words out of his mouth were an indignant: "Now who is this Dean?" I winked at Brooke and will be forever grateful I got her in the draw for sisters.

Now that Matthew's called, I can start reading *Moby Dick* again. I can't read it without thinking of him. If this were a novel, and not my life, imagine the symbolism of not being able to read *Moby Dick* without thinking of your true love? Or maybe I shouldn't imagine it.

Today I finished the reason (other than romance) I have been reading *Moby Dick* so slowly. *Act One* by Moss Hart. Since my first play opens in a week, I wanted to start reading about the lives of playwrights. I began with Moss Hart's *Act One* because it's about his life leading up to his first Broadway hit, *Once in a Lifetime.* It is also considered one of the best autobiographies written by a playwright, and like the *Aeneid,* lives up to its reputation.

The most important thing I learned from it is this: that *Once in a Lifetime* was Moss Hart's seventh play. His first Broadway production and his first hit, but the seventh one he wrote. So thanks to him, I can write six not-so-good ones before I begin to get nervous.

Little wonder so many actresses are absolutely round the bend. I had the most glorious rehearsal today, and then I came home and nothing could match it.

I finally decided to dust (I also see why a great many are obsessed with cleanliness). But if I am going to live life to its fullest, I must do more than act and dust.

Yet I have been haunted by my father telling me that when Teresa Wright was doing his play "Who's Happy Now?" he asked her how she had such incredible stage energy, and she told him she stayed in bed all day to save her energy for the play. So any time I have the slightest inclination to do anything, I think, no, I'd better save my energy. Pretty soon I am going to have to face the fact that while she had the lead in a three-act play, I am one of thirty-eight characters in a two-act play, and my time on stage, if we keep the pacing right, should be under ten minutes.

And since I cannot rehearse all day (though there is nothing I would like better), I have got to get back to work. Or what I call work. Writing my novel.

Dean has to go to real work. To make money. I feel awfully guilty at having what everyone wants. Time to do my own work. Now the least I can do is do it.

I talked with Matthew tonight about *Moby Dick.* He told me about all the sexual symbolism I had missed. Apparently, the ocean is teeming with it.

Tomorrow is the opening night of my first play. And at the last preview tonight, before making his entrance, Tom Troupe, the most distinguished theatre actor in the cast, gave me the good luck charm that he has carried throughout his career. He said an older actor had given it to him at the beginning of his career in the theatre, and now he wanted to give it to me.

It is a little wooden Buddha, arms stretched up to the heavens, wearing a look of total joy. And every night, before making my entrance, I am supposed to rub his stomach three times.

Tom makes his entrance just before I do, so we stand backstage together every night. We have the same ritual. First he goes backstage. I pace for energy for a few more moments and then I step backstage. He squeezes my hand and then we both begin preparing for our entrances.

And I have to tell you the time I feel most like a real actress is not onstage but standing backstage with Tom, waiting to go on.

All afternoon I sang, "Another Opening, Another Show," and then tonight (my first opening night performance) I absolutely and totally lacked concentration of any kind. I was awful. I think it's all Tom Troupe's fault. I was so touched by his gift I got carried away before going onstage tonight and rubbed the Buddha's stomach thirty-three times.

I have already begun reading *Respect for Acting* again. But if I am going to continue this awful business of acting, I simply can't take every performance that goes poorly as badly as I am taking this one. I was ready to burst into tears from the time I came offstage. And still am.

The wonderful thing about writing is that even when it's just awful, it never makes me want to cry.

Another performance and I'm back in love with the theatre. It's just like accepting the outrageous faults of a person who can also be outrageously wonderful. And I am as enchanted by the theatre as I have ever been by anybody. The feeling after a good performance is like none on this earth—even the intense agony after a bad one is kind of bracing. I find any emotion that takes the time to be intense worth the time it takes.

Brooke told me when she got home from school to-day that a girl at Oakwood was hit and killed last night by a drunk driver, with two previous convictions for drunk driving.

What was her name? All I remember now is Alexandra. And that she was going to be an actress.

So standing in the wings tonight, waiting to go on, I was thinking about her. Then an actor came up and offered to kill a critic for me, thereby giving away the caliber of my first review. Suddenly I didn't know why I was there, why I put myself through it when no one really liked me or cared, anyway.

It is just so awful to try your best and then be torn down by people who've never tried. But then I thought of Alexandra, who didn't get the chance to try. She didn't get the chance to hear she'd gotten a terrible review and then go out and give the best performance she'd given yet. So I did it for both of us.

I meant all of the above and I cried writing it, but it has not solved the pain I still feel. How do I confess the guilt of this next sentence? Not pain at the death, but pain at the bad review.

Is nothing in my life going to turn out as well as I want it to? Perhaps I'll never succeed. How can I face life if I don't? I always thought I'd be able to.

Little wonder J. D. Salinger stopped publishing. I'm not even published and I think I'm going to stop. Public exposure is just about the most awful thing ever invented.

I think I'll just stay in my room and write. I don't ever want to go near the stage again. And I go on tomorrow night.

Who would you trust? A critic or the actress you thought of the first time you stepped on a stage? I'll trust Nancy Walker. She and her husband David Craig, the renowned vocal coach, are legendary for being the toughest critics around. When Dad told me last week they had tickets for the show, I nearly fainted and told him never to tell me information like that again.

After the performance tonight, Mom was waiting in the lobby for me (and I think trying to duck them for fear of hearing something awful) when Nancy came over to her and said, "I was going to write you a letter about your daughter, but now I can tell you . . ." And she and David went on to say such things that all I'll have to do is remember them after I hear about any bad review I ever get.

And then after the play (in which I gave my best performance yet again), I went straight to a party for Uta Hagen (yes, Uta Hagen, do you believe it?), at which she said of critics that no one who knew nothing of painting would dare to criticize one, but anyone thinks he can judge an actress.

She is absolutely magnificent. As like Joan of Arc as anyone could be. Heaven knows, I would fight for all she believes in.

It seems so unreal that after idolizing her in print, I got to sit next to her in the flesh. And be introduced to her as an actress. It was all because of the host, Charles Nelson Reilly, who, I believe, is God's gift to the human race. (I suspect on the day he was born, the human race was just kind of depressed and God looked down and decided to give us a Charles Nelson Reilly—He had obviously been saving him for a day like that.)

I cannot help but feel I have compensated for that bad review with my life. Nancy Walker said I was wonderful, and Uta Hagen treated me as if I were her equal. And that's a life beyond criticism.

Dad has just ordered me to read *The Ordeal of Richard Feverel* by George Meredith. My education at the moment seems to be organized by suggestions from men I respect. I am losing a bit of control, but if I like Herman and George as much as Matthew and Oliver, then nothing will have been lost.

I am a little weary of nonexistent whales (when does Moby Dick come into this thing?), and so I have moved on to Richard Feverel for a little while. I adore it as I do George Meredith. "Largely self-educated" and a wonderful fellow.

George says the sweetest thing about distinguishing comedy from satire: "You may estimate your capacity for comic perception by being able to detect the ridicule of them you love, without loving them less."

I also must read a bit of his poetry because it is for that he most longed to be remembered. When I was little, I used to be passionate about poetry, but ever since all the analysis of school, I have had a nagging feeling that I must be missing at least one level whenever I read a poem. But I will plunge in, keeping in the forefront of my mind that everything was originally written for people—even what we least suspect to have been when reading it.

Tonight, before leaving for the theatre to perform my short play, I got to see Brooke perform her short play, *Apricot*

Chutney, at the Oakwood Arts Festival. She wrote it over Christmas in England—after our fights, as is her habit.

Watching the Arts Festival before Brooke came on, I began to understand how nervous Brooke says she is watching *The Bar off Melrose* before I come on. Watching a sister make her entrance is much more terrifying than making your own. Because all the terror is there, but you are completely powerless to do anything about it. Except try to will the audience into being responsive. But Brooke's audience needed no willing from me.

In every play I read I mentally assign one female part to me and one to Brooke (and try to divide the leads equally). Much as I fight with Brooke, I would give anything if I could spend every night of every day of my life (plus matinées) sharing a stage with her. Because sharing a stage will be the best fight we'll ever have.

Thanks to the play, I have now kissed Dean tons more times than I've ever kissed Matthew. I see them both tomorrow. That means two kisses with Dean (we always rehearse it once before we go on), while I doubt if Matthew will even touch my arm (his usual passionate greeting).

Yet even when I'm not in love with him, I want to be. Or do I? Well, tomorrow is Mom's book party to celebrate the publication of *Joanna's Husband and David's Wife,* the novel in which the character based on me runs away with her childhood sweetheart. Fiction has such advantages over life.

I am worried about Matthew. My anxiety has to do with that nasty seven-letter word, *college.* But you'll never guess what's upsetting me. I, who would have given my soul for him not to go to college, am now worried that he won't get into the colleges of his choice.

The problem is this: He is a brilliant and original student, plus being simply riddled with extracurricular activities, but SAT's are another story. I am writing about education and this is the first time I have mentioned the SAT's, which shows you exactly how much I think they have to do with education. However, they have too much to do with what college Matthew and the rest of those poor souls get into. My only advice about taking the SAT's is not to care, which I didn't and I did rather well—but I certainly haven't told Matthew that (surely you've heard Rosalind Russell sing "A Hundred Easy Ways to Lose a Man").

Matthew, unfortunately, does care. He has already taken them for a second time because he said Leona got the vapors when she saw his math scores. That, specifically, is where the problem lies. For a man possessed of the wit of Dickens and the vision of Tolstoy, his grasp of Algebra II is frightening.

Brooke, who shares his weakness in the numbers area, said recently, "Anyone who's good at math will not be good in bed," which is a comforting thought, despite the fact that she said it to me and she knows I'm good at math.

But what I worry about is not his grasp of Algebra II (heaven knows, I have yet to encounter it in the real world—it takes nothing more than addition, subtraction, and a gift for deceit to balance a checkbook), but what effect possible rejection by these so-called institutions of learning might have upon him.

He seemed so lost at the book party today. Even his bow tie was crooked. But at least I finally got to introduce him to Norman Lloyd (one of his few non-news idols). Norman took one look at Matthew and said, "You're me, except with hair." At that moment Matthew's bow tie straightened magically. How much more important is the Norman Lloyd test than the SAT test.

I don't quite know how to break this news, but I am now famous. Thanks to *The Bar off Melrose,* I have been asked for my autograph once and recognized in the grocery store twice. I don't know why celebrities complain about celebrity. I adore it.

I even got a good review (one bad review, one good review—and when you come out even in the theatre, you've come out ahead). The same review praised Dad's play for the evening, so I must be on the right track as a playwright.

And tonight, because of the play, something else extraordinary happened. The mother of a collegiate friend of mine came to see it and after it was over, she told me that I should do my scene for all the parents of college-bound children every year. She said her daughter hadn't really wanted to go to college, but as a parent, she had never felt there was any other choice. Watching my scene was the first time she had realized people might turn out all right if they didn't go to college.

That's all I've ever wanted to say. And tonight, someone heard it.

I spent most of today scrubbing, sweeping, and dusting. I wake up every morning to Mom embarked on another housecleaning project, and so I feel compelled to join in . . . but if she doesn't start a fourth novel soon and stop cleaning the house, I'll lose my mind.

Hanging around Mom too much can make you lose all ambition to be a successful novelist and force on you the knowledge of how much more important it is to be a successful person. It is nearly impossible for my mother to do anything the care of a house demands without humming.

The mystery of her life is that she hummed while living in an apartment in Greenwich Village with the bathtub in the kitchen, and she hums now with three best-selling novels. Having a bathtub in the kitchen did not stop her from humming (she said she liked having company while she cooked), and having had great success is not what makes her hum now.

It is more than *joie de vivre*. It is *joie de* cooking a dinner she's cooked a hundred times before, *joie de* cooking it for the same five people yet again, *joie de* getting up, *joie de* going to sleep, *joie de* licking stamps, *joie de* taking out garbage, *joie de* climbing stairs, *joie de* writing books, *joie de* writing letters, probably *joie de* breathing. It is not just joy in living, it is joy in living all that is life.

Matthew called with college news. His opening words were, "Should I give four years of my life to Columbia or Wesleyan?" He got in everywhere he wanted, despite not being able to multiply.

I have just been looking through my mother's secret writing notebook—it is frightening and fascinating. She keeps writing down schedules of her days.

I was a little shocked to discover how much Mom questions the way she is spending her life. Maybe she's not as happy dusting as I thought.

It takes very little to change our lives and our views of them. Appearing on stage for ten minutes, four nights a week has absolutely changed mine. If I wake up on a Thursday, Friday, Saturday, or Sunday, I think I am going to do the play tonight (being a hit, we have added a Thursday night performance, which has helped my week considerably). If it is Monday, Tuesday, or Wednesday, I count how many days until I'm onstage again. Since we began rehearsals, I have never awakened wondering what the point of life is. Which is a question I have occasionally asked in the past.

And I confess there is nothing I love as much as getting ready for the theatre, driving to the theatre, being at the theatre, running through the scene, waiting backstage to go on, going on, coming off, jumping up and down at the result or planning to do it differently tomorrow night, taking the curtain call, walking through the lobby, and coming home.

I still have a lot of work to do on the rest of my life, but I have solved the hours from seven to ten-thirty-five.

As a portrait painter, my nerves have been pretty much shattered. Only two portraits to my credit and both models still in a pout. Actually, I was recently able to cheer Nanny up by "fixing" her portrait—now nobody can see her face, and that's the way everybody likes it.

So tonight I tried to create the least tense surroundings for my most tense art. I suggested to Brooke that instead of spending the evening discussing sex, I paint her picture and she paint mine. To my surprise, she agreed.

I did her face in a very few brushstrokes, figuring the fewer brushstrokes, the less tension. As a background, I surrounded her face with the best copy I could manage of the painting she was doing of me. So it is a nice merging of souls, even if no one but me can quite recognize whose souls they are.

Last night I wanted to punch the audience after I came off. Tonight I decided to punch them before I went on, and it worked wonders.

Another dead audience (as Joan Roberts, one of the cast, says of a bad audience, "The comedy interpreter was in a bus accident on his way here tonight").

I always stand backstage from the top of the second act, listening to the two scenes that come before mine. And tonight I just started punching the air.

"And here's for not laughing at that." *Pow!* "Here's for a mild chuckle—not an adequate response." *Pow!* "Here's for no exit applause." Break a jaw!

And I gave a stunning performance. I galvanized that audience. Energy is amazingly important. And I think the great enemy of energy is fear. But when you have already beaten your audience to a pulp, there's nothing to be afraid of.

Julie Reich got home for the summer in time to see *The Bar off Melrose.* She told me that driving home after the play her father said to her, "Kendall's in that play and has really started to live. Don't you wish you were doing something like that?"

My poor friends. The tables have turned on them. We are halfway down the path, I guess it is their turn to be on the defensive. With four years of college ahead of them, they were all so confident of the paths their lives would take. Now, two years of the path are behind them and the rest is going to run out pretty quickly. And whatever path they choose next, I doubt any will be as well worn as the one that led to college.

Today was a day I have been anxiously awaiting/dreading as I suppose we do all important days in our life.

Today was the day Matthew was coming to see me in the play. I am making such progress with each new performance and always feel so embarrassed about those I have given previously that I didn't want him to come any sooner.

Of course, as I always do, I had imagined everything that could happen with the evening. What I did not imagine was that when I pulled up at 8:01 (I like to arrive after the audience is seated and can, since I'm in the second act), he would be standing outside the theatre.

In a typical Matthew gesture, he had brought the headmaster of his school to see my play about the joy of being an autodidact, and they arrived just before 8:00, by which point their tickets had already been sold to standbys hoping to get in.

Matthew was mortified and extremely apologetic, but I couldn't have been happier—being so suddenly freed of all my nervousness at performing for him.

We talked for a little and then I walked them to their car and as they were getting in, Matthew and I decided it must be fate. Then in front of God and his headmaster, he put his arms around me and he kissed me—kissed me as if to say, I'm sorry, and you're a swell kid, and, perhaps even, I love you. And if that is fate, how I adore it.

Yet fate does not end there. After the performance (my best yet —I lost my concentration only once, in the middle when it was going so well I did wish Matthew had been there), I called him, and we talked for a lovely, long time. And then, at the end, he apologized again, and said, "You know I love you very dearly."

And I was without words. How easily "I love you" comes to my lips now. But on the phone, all I could say was, "Ohhhhhh" in a rather lilting and, I hope, loving-sounding way.

And then he said he hoped we'd talk again soon. And I said I doubted if I could keep from calling tomorrow night and we said good-bye.

Do you think I should tell him tomorrow night that I love him very dearly?

I never actually thought it was a dilemma until I started writing about it. I don't know if I like fate so much now. Perhaps fate not only gives but asks something of you, too.

I am suddenly terrified. My whole life could change. I've come so close to reconciling myself to Matthew being at college. And now. What if I do tell him how dearly I love him . . . well, I could end up at college.

What if I didn't hear him right? What if my sense of hearing is as bad as my sense of smell (which is deplorable)? What if he said I love you *nearly*? Or *wearily*? Or *merely*?

I do know one thing. Doing the play and being so happy has shown me for certain that we are fools to think a life is a long time. It goes faster than any of us has been led to believe. It's funny, life has been going on for centuries yet I feel as if I am the first ever to have such a dilemma.

I can hear Nanny putting away the dishes from last night's dishwasher load, and I wonder if I should ask her advice. Despite the fact that she had the worst marriage in the history of West Texas (where there are a lot of duststorms and competition), I feel I ought to.

Her advice: "Just keep bein' your own friendly, sweet self and let him be the progressor—I can't even think of the word . . . *pursuer.* He's discovered you're far and away above the girls he goes to school with, and they're probably the only other girls he knows."

I have never had more fun with Nanny. She laughed so hard at Matthew being turned away from the theatre, you would have thought he'd fallen down a flight of stairs (Nanny thinks household accidents are among life's most amusing moments).

I have calmed down a great deal. It was so reassuring, talking to Nanny. The permeating odor of her buttered toast and the early morning sunshine almost convinced me I was back in school

with only P.E. to worry about (though I suspect in the end I will
have worried more about P.E. than I ever do about marriage).
And perhaps she does have the key. After all, my whole scene
in *The Bar off Melrose* is about how dearly I love him, so it's his
turn to be the "progressor." But as Nanny says, "If he tells you he
loves you again, you can tell him you like him a lot."

Tonight, I finished *The Ordeal of Richard Feverel.*
Whatever we have to say of the world, thank God chivalry is no
more. Chivalry, social rules, and most polite behavior, as far as
I'm concerned, only get in the way of the joy of life.

Of course, I am not ruled by chivalry and yet how many single
solitary moments in a day do I spend reflecting on the heaven of
life? We should be dancing up and down every moment for the
chance to lose and love and everything else and yet we don't. But
perhaps I will a little more for having read about Richard Feverel.

Actually, I'm not sure if that is really the point of *The Ordeal.*
But whenever you come away from a book wanting to celebrate
life, how can the misinterpreted author be too angry with you? I
often think the feelings we get from a book—even when they have
only a slight connection to what we are reading—are almost as
important as the book itself.

Still, I would love to talk to George Meredith about it all. Who
will I look for first in Heaven—him or Carole Lombard? Whoever, I'm going to have to wait a while, I hope, and that novel was
so affecting that I will never get to sleep without a little Jean
Harlow, who is third I would like to meet in Heaven, followed
very closely by Tolstoy.

Ever since I read that George Meredith really wanted
to be thought of as a poet rather than a novelist, I have been
worried that we never end up being what we dream of being.

I have dreamed all my life of being a writer, but now I am so
loving getting to be an actress. Better hours for me have never
existed than those spent talking to the actors backstage or actually

being in the play onstage. And when I am not in the theatre, I like nothing better than to come home and read about it.

Tonight, I finished *Acting: The First Six Lessons* by Richard Boleslavsky.

The autodidact in me loved this thought of Boleslavsky's:

> Notice everything around you—watch yourself cheerfully. Collect and save in your soul all the riches of life and the fullness of it. Keep those memories in order. You can never tell when you will need them, but they are your only friends and teachers in your craft.

I suppose, in Heaven right now, George Meredith thinks he is a poet. And I suppose some part of me will always think first and foremost I'm a writer, but I do continue to wonder if that is all I want to be. Every day the world gets wider. Every day I see something else I want to learn and something else I want to do. Sitting in my own little room, I have watched my horizons broaden so much.

I had the most wonderful time with George Bernard Shaw and Ellen Terry last night.

I wonder if reading the letters written to someone adored isn't the best way to find out the truth about anyone. Certainly, they have revealed to me the truth about Shaw. Turns out he was as sweet as he was opinionated.

How wonderful Ellen Terry was, too, but how heartbreaking that her letters and her autobiography are all that really survive her. Her name will always live in the theatre, but her artistry is gone without a trace—except what it left in the audiences who saw her.

It's hard to be an atheist when you love the theatre so much. Lack of permanence terrifies me. I have to believe one day I'll get to see Ellen Terry perform. I have to think that up in Heaven right now, when she is not doing Shaw, Shaw's begging her to do Ibsen, and Henry Irving (who was frightened of Shaw and Ibsen and who I think I could very happily avoid seeing on the stage through all eternity) is having a hissy fit.

It is odd, sitting here in the hazy California sun, how overwhelmed I am by all the history that surrounds me. Whenever I drive to the Melrose, I always go by Grauman's Chinese Theatre and I think of all the famous footprints outside and I remember that Myrna Loy's first job in Hollywood was as a dancer in the chorus there (called Grauman's Egyptian Theatre then).

Yet last summer in London we saw a play in the Lyceum Theatre, where Henry Irving and Ellen Terry had their company, and it didn't seem like history at all. Perhaps that is where the theatre has my beloved keepers of permanence, the movies, beat.

Whenever I drive through Hollywood, I just have to imagine what was once here. But when I walked into the Lyceum, it seemed that all its history, though not on view that very moment, was still lurking backstage, ready to leap out and do a little Shaw if the modern play was not working out.

I began *The Sun Also Rises* last night (I tend to use Hemingway as a kind of literary cleanser after any writer who likes a long sentence) and, after a few pages, I thought, "If he was under thirty when he wrote this, I'll kill myself." He was twenty-four . . . but I'm still here.

Slightly calmer now. I have been looking up novelists' vital statistics. The next novel I will read is going to be by Stendahl. He didn't write his first novel till he was forty-four and didn't have any success till he was forty-seven. My kind of fellow.

Miserable, it being 8:33 P.M. and a Monday—so no performance in sight for three days. How useless are the hours from 7:00 to 11:00 without an audience. So I have spent my time discovering the only autodidact I don't want to claim.

Rainer Maria Rilke. (Perhaps I would like him better if I could figure out how to pronounce his last name.)

His book, *Letters to a Young Poet,* was a present from Karen Weiss, an actress/playwright of *The Bar off Melrose,* whom I've adopted as a role model—in writing, acting, and life. She said she swings from thinking Rilke's book is the most wonderful ever written to thinking it's the most pretentious.

I am voting for the most pretentious.

Mom told me she believed it was Rilke who thought attendance at his daughter's wedding would interfere with his pure poetic life. And my mother told me this as she was mopping the kitchen floor. I decided the least I could do for her pure novelistic life was to finish the floor.

Finished *The Sun Also Rises.* I wish I could live and write like that.

Hemingway does use the phrase, "It was good" about almost everything, but that's the way he makes you feel when you read him.

It feels rather useless to talk about Hemingway when practically everyone in the world has an opinion about him (the poor man). But I have rarely—if ever—seen anyone create such a world of his own. Everyone else takes a little bit of the world we all know and writes about it, but Hemingway creates his own. With its own pace, logic, values, beauty, and ugliness.

Of the writers I've read, the others who seem to create their own world are Dickens, Dostoevsky, and Evelyn Waugh.

Tolstoy seems to me to stick with this world. As does Jane Austen. I would say the Brontës stick to this world—granted, it's what's happening on the moors of this world.

Proust can't even be talked about here. He's totally in his own world . . . and usually in his own bed.

I straightened out my school shelves today. Brooke informed me last night that my old school papers occupied three shelves, leaving hers only one, and since she will be a junior next year, it was time we got equal space.

While sorting through all my papers (I decided the best way to clean up was to throw away all those with grades below "A"), I came across the summer reading list that made me shudder so almost four years ago.

I had long since forgotten the books on that list, so I had to chuckle when I saw *The Sun Also Rises*. If I'd been in the mood to read that book four years ago, I might be completing my sophomore year of college today. Where would I be and where wouldn't I be?

Coming home from the theatre tonight we were talking about books, trying to convince Brooke she really might like them if she got to know them. We mentioned some book and Dad said, "I never read that," as if his reading years had passed and it was a book he had simply missed.

I swear my reading years will never pass. I came home tonight and hopped right into the Middle Ages. I even went ahead and peeked into *The Divine Comedy*. At last I've found someone as crazy about Virgil as I am. First thing Dante does in the underworld is meet him and ask him to please be the one to show him around. My plan exactly, the minute I get there.

I think my life is actually working out. How nice it is, too, to keep track of a life, so that the progress is clearly marked.

Here I am in a play, for heaven's sake. Part of which I wrote, for heaven's sake. Sometimes my lucky stars are so many I can barely see the sky. Tonight, it is especially hard to see because tonight Matthew really did see me in the play.

I have always had the sneaking suspicion (make that galloping) that no one would ever go on about me as my parents do. To have that kind of unceasing, more than devoted, creating kind of love that does make you believe you can do anything was something I never assumed could happen more than once in a lifetime. But it has.

I was so happy when tonight's performance was over. I knew Matthew was watching and I knew I'd given my very best performance yet. But when I took a peek at the audience to watch

Matthew watch the rest of the play, I could have sworn I saw him with a floozy leaning on his shoulder—which I did think was a little low.

After the curtain call, I waited a few seconds, trying to think of something appropriate to say to the floozy, and finally, finding nothing appropriate, I took my chances and walked out.

Matthew rushed right over and kissed me and I forgot all about the floozy who never was. Then he began talking about the play and my performance. I've never heard Matthew more passionate about anything (John Chancellor included). He, frankly, couldn't stop talking about it.

He called me a "lightning rod" and the writing "as intricate as a mosaic" and said his only regret was that he could not rush from the theatre the moment I walked offstage because he could have gone on in even better detail.

The curse of being blessed with parents as wonderful as mine is that you may not expect life to give you that kind of love a second time, but you will demand it.

And not only because they love me so (though Dad always says the reason he is so nice to me is to ruin my judgment when it comes to men), but because they love each other so. They respect, admire, delight in, and adore everything the other does (except when they think it should be cut).

Little did I suspect that by my careful observance, I was being trapped into not settling for less. In its own sweet way, tonight is a glorious trap too. I know enough of the world (and, at nineteen, I really feel I do) to know that you never let go of that person who can talk about your performance for longer than it took you to give it.

We ended the evening with the best kiss of our lives so far. (Two kisses in one evening—you see what I mean about the progress of lives?) It was as we were all saying good night. Brooke had just ordered Matthew to kiss her, which he started to do (Brooke said he was maturing greatly), but didn't quite finish because Brooke decided to lick him instead, which did make him shriek.

Then he and I kissed. And after the kiss, for the slightest moment we just looked at each other, and it was as if we were both saying, "Oh, my!" (I think I may have actually said it).

I am beginning to wish *The Bar off Melrose* had been filled with more of the theatre's legendary temperament. I'm going to work only with the unpleasant from now on—it doesn't break your heart to take leave of a louse.

We set out hoping to play four weeks, and at closing we will have played four months. Four months that have changed my life forever. And in another way, they may have allowed my life not to change. They have shown me (as one hopes they would have) what it is like to be an actress.

And before deciding what you must do in life or what you could bear to miss, you have to know what you're talking about. I didn't before, but now I do. At least a little bit.

I now know the terror of the time between reading a play aloud for the first time and making it work, and making it work on opening night. The first time was just luck and instinct, and the second was luck and learned instinct.

And now I know what it's like to do a play again and again and again. In four months, not once have I been bored. I can easily imagine doing this five-minute play for a decade and still not discovering all the ways possible to do it a little bit better.

I know what it's like to come offstage and jump up and down (which Dean and I frequently did), and I know what it's like to come offstage and think the whole world is as lousy as you just were.

I have known a camaraderie that I suspect only war or the theatre permits. And now I know what it is like to take your leave, not knowing if we'll ever share the same stage again.

But I can't bear to talk about my farewell to the theatre yet. I have one performance left. And one performance contains within it all the possibilities the theatre ever had.

I leave for the theatre in less than an hour to make my last entrance into that bar I love so much. And I have just finished packing for England. We leave tomorrow.

Dad said today that if he had not already bought the house, he would never have had the strength to buy one.

But fate, though possessed of a cruel streak, has been kind to us. We were able to buy what we hope will make the years ahead easier for him, just as the disease is making every day harder for him.

Dad is so happy in England I think that it might finally be the place I can leave him to grow up (the "grow up" refers to us both).

I am so glad for his sake I lived the beginning of my life a little fast. Thank God I graduated early. And thank heavens I did not go to college. What a terrible waste of life it would have been. Of so many lives.

I feel I have lived through so much in the past four years, but then I have always had a desire to feel that way. I remember when I was six or seven, deciding that everyone had to live through a certain number of tragedies (I think I decided three should be maximum) and trying to count up how many I had lived through. I somehow managed to fill my quota and breathed a sigh of relief, knowing all grief was behind me.

It is only living through more than our quota of tragedy that makes us see that the best measure of grief is the strength taken from it.

I am so thankful the mind is so dumb. As my father loses his energy and has a harder time walking and eating and speaking, I cannot easily remember the way he was before. And so I miss it less.

I was awfully depressed being an autodidact before I started the novel I have almost finished rewriting. I always thought it was beginning this novel that made me see such a great point to life. And when I finished the first draft of the novel, I thought it was being in the play that had kept me so happy.

I realize now that it has been seeing my father hold on to the life in him and grasp and tug to keep it that has made me grasp and tug just as hard for the joy lurking beneath life.

I am home from the final performance of the play, sitting in my costume, which I seriously doubt now I will ever take off.

Tonight, before making what I kept remembering was my last entrance—though I did keep reminding myself that if I let a little truth enter my performance, I should realize that this was the first time I was entering that bar to look for Matthew—I said to myself a line from my father's play *For the Use of the Hall:* "Thanks for the use of the hall. That you were there at all. That you got the chance to try."

Then after the play I walked into the lobby and saw the man who had said those lines in the television version of the play produced for PBS by Norman Lloyd. George Furth. The same George Furth who wrote me a letter telling me what I least wanted to hear now took me in his arms and told me what I most wanted to hear.

He said, "I always wondered why some of my friends never had the big careers they should have because I thought they were so talented. And then one day I realized that they were just imitations of Carole Lombard and Norma Shearer. But you were an original tonight, Kendall, and yet you represented all those women. Intelligent, pretty without knowing they're pretty, giving, kind. You represented them all."

But I now leave my Cetological System standing thus unfinished, even as the great Cathedral of Cologne was left, with the crane still standing upon the top of the uncompleted tower. For small erections may be finished by their first architects; grand ones, true ones, ever leave the copestone to posterity. God keep me from ever completing anything. This whole book is but a draught—nay, but the draught of a draught. Oh, Time, Strength, Cash, and Patience!

My favorite thought yet from the novel that makes me think of Matthew. Therefore, I plan to take as long reading it as Melville did writing it, which Matthew says is a most proper idea anyway.

I saw him today for what may be the last time for a long time. He came to the house to see us off for England. He leaves for college before we get back in September.

He promised to write every day and on the way to the airport I quoted to Brooke the line from *A Woman of Independent Means* with which Bess urges her husband to write often: "Release me with words until I am back again in your arms," which Brooke rephrased to fit Matthew and me: "Release me with words until I am back again on the phone with you." Why doesn't Brooke's rephrasing sound any less romantic to me?

Perhaps because I finally understand that phrase "the fabric of life." As we were driving to the airport, we were discussing Matthew's college vacations and how our time together would coincide when Brooke turned to me in her sly way and said, "Wouldn't it be funny if you didn't see Matthew for a whole year?"

It was at that moment I realized Brooke is part of the fabric of my life. Polyester, definitely, but part of it.

As I write, I am sitting on the plane headed for England and summer and life and have taken another Melville break by beginning Thoreau's *Walden*.

I have always known I would love Thoreau. Being born on the same day, I knew we would think alike. He is, though, more argumentative than I had expected. I suspect living on a pond for so long tends to make you a little cranky.

Symbolism, which I so detested in the eleventh grade (I will insist to my dying day that the river in *Huckleberry Finn* represents not a cleansing effect but simply a faster mode of transportation when combined with a raft than dry land), I am finding I rather like in life. And so as we fly to meet the morning (how nice to have the world awake with me at 3:00 A.M.), I know I have left what was at least my first Walden Pond forever.

I suspect the four years Matthew is in college will be four of the most exciting I shall ever spend (though I also suspect life just keeps getting more exciting). Happiness is like everything else. The more experience you have, the better you get at it.